FUNDAMENTALS OF GENEALOGICAL RESEARCH

Laureen R. Jaussi
Gloria D. Chaston

929. 1

Published by
Deseret Book Company
Salt Lake City, Utah
1977

To Our Husbands—

August W. Jaussi

A. Norton Chaston

Who have encouraged us in this writing and who were
our first genealogical instructors

Brief Table of Contents

VI

Table of Contents

X

Preface

This is the third edition of *Fundamentals of Genealogical Research,* a genealogical reference book that emphasizes the first four generations of ancestry and lays a foundation for extending the pedigree. This reference provides the beginning genealogist with instructions on how to perform his own genealogical research, provides the experienced genealogist with a convenient ready-reference, and provides the genealogical teacher with well-organized source materials and corresponding lesson assignments.

This edition includes current information on genealogical records and services and is more comprehensive than previous editions. The first edition included information on basic research and Utah records. The second edition included only information on basic research, and the information on Utah records was incorporated into an additional reference, *Genealogical Records of Utah* (Salt Lake City, Utah: Deseret Book Company, 1974). This third edition contains the same information on basic research as did the second edition and has been expanded to include the following:

1. "Tax-Exempt Organizations," Chapter 12.

2. "Genealogical Society Temple Processing Records," Chapter 17.

3. "The Name Tabulation Program," Chapter 19, which has been expanded to include nine different entry programs.

4. "The Computer File Index," Chapter 20.

5. "Lesson Assignments for Fundamentals of Genealogical Research," Section IV, which includes suggestions for home study and for continuing workshops. The lesson assignments are also available as a separate publication.

SECTION I

GENEALOGICAL RESEARCH TERMINOLOGY

1
Introduction

Genealogy is the study of the recorded events in the lives of individuals and their ancestors. Genealogical research is the method used to identify individuals from the recorded events and to establish their relationships in families. *Fundamentals of Genealogical Research* introduces the theory applied in searching the recorded events. To learn the theory and memorize the details does not make one a genealogical research specialist. Both theory and practice are involved in genealogical research; readings, lectures, and study complement the practical application.

GENEALOGICAL THEORY

The most desirable records for establishing correct identity are birth records, marriage records, and death records. When the researcher does not have the correct information or enough pertinent information to obtain a birth, marriage, and/or death record, he searches other records for clues that will lead to these records. When birth, marriage, and/or death records are not available, he searches other records for information to be used as a substitute for birth, marriage, and/or death records.

In addition to establishing correct identity, members of The Church of Jesus Christ of Latter-day Saints who desire to have a complete and accurate family group record should determine and verify the complete date (day, month, and year) of each LDS baptism, endowment, and sealing.

In genealogical research, one bases his research upon information that has been proven to be correct. When new information is found, it should substantiate and add to previously proven information.

In genealogical research, one's goal is quality rather than quantity. Quality pertains to the accuracy of the research and can be judged by the sources searched and not by the quantity of information obtained.

In genealogical research, one proceeds in an orderly step-by-step approach by acquiring a practical knowledge of the following:

1. Genealogical research terminology (see Section I)
2. Genealogical research tools (see Section II)
3. Basic genealogical records (see Section III)
4. Lesson assignments (see Section IV)

Genealogical Research Terminology

A knowledge of genealogical research terms is necessary to properly evaluate, interpret, and communicate genealogical information.

1. Elements of identity (names, places, dates, and relationships) are important because one searches a particular record, for a particular name, in a particular locality, for a particular period of time, and establishes relationships of one individual to another.

2. The origin and classification of records helps one to understand which records are most beneficial in genealogical research.

3. The analysis and evaluation of information helps one to determine which records to search and to evaluate the record sources.

Genealogical Research Tools

Genealogical research tools are aids to the genealogical research method and save the researcher time and money.

1. The Book of Remembrance is used to organize pedigree charts and family group records.

2. A note-keeping system based upon file cards is essential for quick recall of records searched and of information found or not found.

3. Correspondence is a means of obtaining information without making a personal search or incurring travel expense.

4. Libraries are repositories for genealogical source material.

5. Reference books provide technical information.

6. Family organizations are helpful in combining research time and money and distributing genealogical information pertaining to the family.

7. Tax-exempt organizations provide an incentive to individuals to contribute financially to genealogical research.

8. Research services are helpful for obtaining specialized information.

Basic Genealogical Records

Basic genealogical records are applicable to all genealogical research. They verify names, places, dates, and relationships, and provide clues to further research. These records lay a foundation for research in geographic areas, but do not require a special knowledge of a foreign language, early handwriting, or advanced reference books. In this text, the basic records are introduced in the suggested order of search:

1. Home records (provide clues to birth, marriage, and death records and to temple processing records)

2. Biographical records (provide clues to birth, marriage, and death records and to temple processing records)

3. Vital records (verify birth, marriage, and death places and dates)

4. Temple Records Index Bureau (verifies endowment dates, and provides clues to baptism and sealing dates and to birth, marriage, and death records)

5. The Name Tabulation Program and Computer File Index (verify baptism, endowment, and sealing dates, and provide clues to earlier temple ordinance dates and to birth, marriage, and death records)

6. Family group records and pedigree charts (verify LDS baptism, endowment, and sealing dates, and provide clues to earlier temple ordinance dates and vital records)

7. Temple recorders records (verify baptism, endowment, and sealing dates, and provide clues to birth, marriage, and death records)

Lesson Assignments

Lesson assignments (see Section IV) provide exact instructions and an orderly research method. Each assignment provides information for the next assignment, and the researcher learns an organized approach to genealogy.

Lesson 1. Begin a pedigree chart and a corresponding first four-generation family group record.

Lesson 2. Organize a Book of Remembrance.

Lesson 3. Assemble a card file for note keeping.

Lesson 4. Use gazetteers and maps to establish correct place names.

Lesson 5. Obtain names and addresses of unknown relatives and begin an address file.

Lesson 6. Obtain genealogical information from biographies, family histories, and locality histories.

Lesson 7. Obtain genealogical information from newspaper obituaries.

Lesson 8. Obtain government and church vital records.

Lesson 9. Search the Temple Records Index Bureau.

Lesson 10. Search the Computer File Index.

Lesson 11. Search Genealogical Society family group records and pedigree charts.

Lesson 12. Search temple recorders records.

GENEALOGICAL APPLICATION

Since genealogical research requires that one work from the known to the unknown, and since the researcher is best acquainted with himself, the first step is to place his own name on a pedigree chart on line #1, his father's on #2, his mother's on #3, father's father on #4, father's mother on #5, mother's father on #6, mother's mother on #7, great-grandparents on #8 to #15, and second-great-grandparents on lines #16 to #31, and record other identifying information as indicated.

The pedigree chart published by the Genealogical Society is recommended for this beginning step. (See Figure 1.) The pedigree chart is a guide to direct-line family relationships and provides an overview of the research program.

After the known information is recorded on a pedigree chart, the researcher begins a family group record for each married couple on the pedigree chart by recording identifying information on a family group record published by the Genealogical Society. (See Figure 2.) For suggested standards of recording information on pedigree charts and family group records, see Figure 3.

The researcher completes the research assignments using the family group record, not the pedigree chart, as his guide. Research assignments are completed for all children on the family group record as well as the husband and wife.

In a basic research course the researcher begins the assignments with his first-generation family group record (if married) and completes all assignments in the research course using this family group record as the objective family group record.

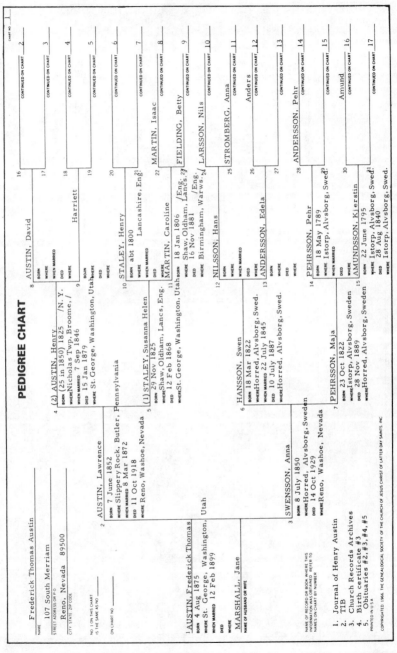

PEDIGREE CHART

NAME
Frederick Thomas Austin

STREET ADDRESS OR P.O.
107 South Merriam

CITY, STATE, ZIP CODE
Reno, Nevada   89500

NO. 1 ON THIS CHART
IS THE SAME AS NO. _____
ON CHART NO _____

2 AUSTIN, Lawrence
BORN 7 June 1852
WHEN MARRIED 8 Mar 1872
WHERE Slippery Rock, Butler, Pennsylvania
DIED 11 Oct 1918
WHERE Reno, Washoe, Nevada

1 AUSTIN, Frederick Thomas
BORN 4 Aug 1875
WHERE St. George, Washington, Utah
WHEN MARRIED 12 Feb 1899
DIED
WHERE

NAME OF HUSBAND OR WIFE
MARSHALL, Jane

3 SWENSSON, Anna
BORN 8 July 1850
WHERE Horred, Alvsborg, Sweden
DIED 14 Oct 1929
WHERE Reno, Washoe, Nevada

4 (2) AUSTIN, Henry   (25 in 1850) 1825   /N.Y./
WHERE Nicholas Twp, Broome,
WHEN MARRIED 7 Sep 1846
DIED 15 Jan 1879
WHERE St. George, Washington, Utah

5 (1) STALEY, Susanna Helen
BORN 29 Nov 1825
WHERE Shaw, Oldham, Lancs, Eng.
DIED 12 Feb 1868
WHERE St. George, Washington, Utah

6 HANSSON, Swen
BORN 18 Mar 1822
WHERE Horred, Alvsborg, Swed.
WHEN MARRIED 22 July 1845
DIED 10 July 1887
WHERE Horred, Alvsborg, Swed.

7 PEHRSSON, Maja
BORN 23 Oct 1822
WHERE Istorp, Alvsborg, Sweden
DIED 28 Nov 1889
WHERE Horred, Alvsborg, Sweden

8 AUSTIN, David
BORN
WHERE
WHEN MARRIED
DIED
WHERE

9 Harriett

10 STALEY, Henry
WHERE abt 1800
WHEN MARRIED
WHERE Lancashire, Eng.[1]
DIED
WHERE

11 MARTIN, Caroline
BORN 18 Jan 1806
WHERE Shaw, Oldham, Lancs.[27] /Eng.
DIED 16 Nov 1881   /Eng.
WHERE Birmingham, Warws.[24]

12 NILSSON, Hans
BORN
WHERE
WHEN MARRIED
DIED
WHERE

13 ANDERSSON, Edela
BORN
WHERE
DIED
WHERE

14 PEHRSSON, Pehr
BORN 18 May 1789
WHERE Istorp, Alvsborg, Swed.[2]
WHEN MARRIED
DIED
WHERE

15 AMUNDSSON, Kierstin
BORN 22 June 1795
WHERE Istorp, Alvsborg, Swed.[31]
DIED 28 Aug 1840
WHERE Istorp, Alvsborg, Swed.

16 _____
CONTINUED ON CHART 2

17 AUSTIN, David
CONTINUED ON CHART 3

18 _____
CONTINUED ON CHART 4

19 _____
CONTINUED ON CHART 5

20 _____
CONTINUED ON CHART 6

21 STALEY, Henry
CONTINUED ON CHART 7

22 MARTIN, Isaac
CONTINUED ON CHART 8

23 FIELDING, Betty
CONTINUED ON CHART 9

24 LARSSON, Nils
CONTINUED ON CHART 10

25 STROMBERG, Anna
CONTINUED ON CHART 11

26 Anders
CONTINUED ON CHART 12

27 _____
CONTINUED ON CHART 13

28 ANDERSSON, Pehr
CONTINUED ON CHART 14

29 _____
CONTINUED ON CHART 15

30 Amund
CONTINUED ON CHART 16

31 _____
CONTINUED ON CHART 17

NAME OF RECORD OR BOOK WHERE THIS
INFORMATION WAS OBTAINED. REFER TO
NAMES ON CHART BY NUMBER

1. Journal of Henry Austin
2. TIB
3. Church Records Archives
4. Birth certificate #3
5. Obituaries #2, #3, #4, #5

PRINTED IN U.S.A.

COPYRIGHTED 1966. THE GENEALOGICAL SOCIETY OF THE CHURCH OF JESUS CHRIST OF LATTER DAY SAINTS. INC.

Figure 1.   Pedigree chart.

HUSBAND (2) AUSTIN, Henry (cabinet maker)

Born	7 Sep 1846	Place Slippery Rock, Butler, Pennsylvania
Chr.		Place
Marr.	15 Jan 1879	Place St. George, Washington, Utah
Died	19 Jan 1879	Place St. George, Washington, Utah
Bur.		Place

(25 in 1850) 1825 Place Nicholas Twp, Broome, New York

HUSBAND'S FATHER AUSTIN, David HUSBAND'S MOTHER , Harriet

HUSBAND'S OTHER WIVES (2) 8 Oct 1871, HANSSON, Maria (sld 23 Mar 1880 SG)

WIFE (1) STALEY, Susanna Helen

Born	29 Nov 1825	Place Shaw, Oldham, Lancashire, England
Chr.	28 Dec 1825	Place St. Mary's, Oldham, Lancashire, England
Died	12 Feb 1868	Place St. George, Washington, Utah
Bur.	16 Feb 1868	Place St. George, Washington, Utah

WIFE'S FATHER STALEY, Henry WIFE'S MOTHER MARTIN, Caroline

WIFE'S OTHER HUSBANDS (1) 10 June 1844, STEPHENS, Oscar

SEX	CHILDREN Given Names SURNAME (CAPITALIZED)	WHEN BORN DAY MONTH YEAR	WHERE BORN TOWN	COUNTY	STATE or COUNTRY	DATE OF FIRST MARRIAGE TO WHOM	WHEN DIED DAY MONTH YEAR
M 1	AUSTIN, Henry Allan	b 1 Sep 1847 chr 7 Sep 1847	Slippery Rock	Butler	Penn	12 Dec 1879 POTTER, Ruth Ann	7 May 1885
M 2	AUSTIN, John Staley	18 Nov 1850	"	"	"		bur 22 July 1856
M 3 X	AUSTIN, Lawrence	7 June 1852	"	"	"	8 Mar 1872 SWENSSON, Anna	11 Oct 1918
M 4	AUSTIN, Frank (twin)	25 May 1855	"	"	"		18 Mar 1865
F 5	AUSTIN, Freda (twin)	25 May 1855	"	"	"	10 Apr 1873 (div) BENTLY, George (1)	29 Jan 1929
? 6	AUSTIN, stillborn	abt 1857	Salt Lake City	Salt Lake	Utah		stillborn
F 7	AUSTIN, Helen	24 July 1859	Salt Lake City			7 Oct 1880 SMITH, Marvin	21 Aug 1867
M 8	AUSTIN, Norman Oliver	16 Aug 1864	St. George	Wash-ington		unmarried	6 Apr 1938
9							
10							
11							

SOURCES:
1. Journal of Henry Austin, in possession of Frederick T. Austin.
2. Temple Records Index Bureau (TIB).

SOURCES OF INFORMATION
3. St. George Sealings of Children to Parents (GS F 170,583).
4. 1850 Census, Butler Co., Penn (GS F 020,610).
5. Obituaries for husband, wife, children #5 and #8.
6. Christening record of wife, rec'd by correspondence.
7. Membership records Salt Lake City 4th Ward (GS F 026,654).
8. Membership records St. George 1st Ward (GS F 027,334).

OTHER MARRIAGES
Child #5, Freda, md (2) 18 Aug 1896, CARLTON, Mark.

Husband (2) AUSTIN, Henry 1825

Wife (1) STALEY, Susanna Helen

NAME & ADDRESS OF PERSON SUBMITTING RECORD
Frederick T. Austin
107 South Merriam
Reno, Nevada 89500

26 May 1972

FAMILY REPRESENTATIVE
AUSTIN, Frederick Thomas

RELATION OF F.R. TO HUSBAND g son RELATION OF F.R. TO WIFE g son

TEMPLE ORDINANCE DATA

	BAPTIZED (DATE)	ENDOWED (DATE)	SEALED (DATE — to Temple) WIFE TO HUSBAND
HUSBAND	10 Aug 1849 EH	27 Aug 1858 EH	27 Aug 1858
WIFE	14 July 1848 EH	27 Aug 1858 EH	
1	19 May 1856 SG	12 Dec 1870 EH	6 May 1880 SG
2	child	child	6 May 1880 SG
3	7 June 1860 EH	4 Feb 1872 SG	6 May 1880 SG
4	10 June 1863 SG	4 May 1880 SG	6 May 1880 SG
5	10 June 1863 SL	8 Apr 1935 SL	8 Apr 1935
6	stillborn	stillborn	DO NOT SEAL
7	21 Aug 1867 MA	16 Oct 1970 LG	BIC
8	14 July 1867 LG	July 1940	BIC

Husband 1. Ward 2.
Examiners 1. 2.
Stake or Mission

© 1964 The Genealogical Society
of The Church of Jesus Christ of Latter-day Saints, Inc.

NECESSARY EXPLANATIONS

FAMILY GROUP RECORD

To indicate that a child is an ancestor of the family representative, place an "X" behind the number pertaining to that child.

Figure 2.　Family group record.

SUGGESTED STANDARD FOR RECORDING
INFORMATION ON PEDIGREE CHARTS
AND FAMILY GROUP RECORDS

NAMES

1. Record the surname in capital letters:

AUSTIN, Henry or Henry AUSTIN

2. Record the name of a woman by her maiden surname.
(If the maiden surname is the same as the married surname, underline the surname to show it has been recorded correctly.)

3. The patronymic "dotter" may be changed to "son:"

Anna Swensdotter to Anna Swensson

DATES

1. Record dates in the order of day, month, year:

4 June 1852

2. A christening date is a baptism or christening date in a
church other than The Church of Jesus Christ of Latter-day Saints.
When a christening date is given for a child, prefix the christening
date with "chr," and the birth date with a "b."

3. Write the months in full or abbreviate:

Jan	Apr	July	Oct
Feb	May	Aug	Nov
Mar	June	Sep	Dec

4. If two dates appear to be in conflict, and they have been
recorded correctly, underline the dates.

5. If the date of burial of a child on the family group
record is used in place of a death date, prefix with "bur:"

bur 18 July 1865

6. If the date of banns or license is used in place of the
marriage date, prefix as follows:

banns 21 Nov 1798 lic 18 Aug 1870

7. If an age at a dated event is known, calculate the year
of birth:

1842 (age 60 in 1902)

Figure 3. Suggested standards for pedigree charts and family group records.
(Continued on next page)

SUGGESTED STANDARD FOR RECORDING
INFORMATION ON PEDIGREE CHARTS
AND FAMILY GROUP RECORDS

DATES (cont.)

8. Above the endowment or sealing date record the initials of the place or temple where the endowment and sealing were performed:

EH		MT	
14 Sept 1858		8 June 1884	
AL	Alberta (Cardston)	NV	Nauvoo
AZ	Arizona (Mesa)	NZ	New Zealand
EH	Endowment House	OG	Ogden
HA	Hawaii	OK	Oakland
HO	Historian's Office	PO	President's Office
IF	Idaho Falls	PV	Provo
LA	Los Angeles	SG	St. George
LD	London	SL	Salt Lake
LG	Logan	SW	Swiss
MT	Manti	WA	Washington

9. If a child was born after a temple sealing of parents, record BIC for "born in the covenant" in place of the sealing to parents date.

10. If a child died under the age of eight, record "child" in the column for baptism and endowment.

11. If a child was stillborn, record "stillborn" in the column for baptism and endowment, and record "do not seal" in the column for sealing to parents date.

PLACES

1. Place names are recorded with the modern spelling with the smallest division first (additional examples are in Chapter 10):

Wattenwil, Bern, Switzerland
(town)   (county) (country)

McIndoe Falls, Barnet Twp, Caledonia, Vermont
(village)   (township)   (county)   (state)

Sandfallet, Baggetorp, Kvistbro, Örebro, Sweden
(farm)   (village)   (parish)   (county) (country)

Shaw, Oldham, Lancashire, England
(town) (parish)   (county)   (country)

St. Mary, Warwick, Warwickshire, England
(parish)   (city)   (county)   (country)

Figure 3. Suggested standards for pedigree charts and family group records.
           (Continued on next page)

SUGGESTED STANDARD FOR RECORDING
INFORMATION ON PEDIGREE CHARTS
AND FAMILY GROUP RECORDS

PLACES (Cont.)

St. Nicholas, Warwick, Warwickshire, England
(parish)   *(city)*   *(county)*   *(country)*

2. Names of towns, townships, and parishes should be written completely. Names of counties and countries may be abbreviated:

Salt Lake City, S.L., Utah
Shaw, Oldham, Lancs., Eng.

3. Names of places are recorded with the modern spelling.

4. Places which have changed names are recorded with the modern name followed by the former name in parentheses:

Danvers (formerly Salem Village), Essex, Massachusetts

5. The place of marriage is a geographic locality and not the name of a temple.

MISCELLANEOUS

1. Record the name and the birth year of the husband and the name of the wife in the upper right-hand corner of the family group record for ease in alphabetizing and locating the family group records.

2. Record the date the family group record was prepared in the upper right-hand corner under "name & address of person submitting record."

3. Record sources in detail, including the Genealogical Society call numbers when applicable. When additional space is needed for recording sources, use the unused space provided for children rather than the back of the family group record.

4. Information of value not recorded elsewhere, may be listed under "necessary explanations."

5. When an ancestor marries more than once, make a separate family group record for each marriage. Prefix the name with the number of the marriage:

(2) HALE, Donald

6. If there are more than eleven children, use a second family group record, and change the numbers of the children to correspond to their number in the family.

Figure 3. Suggested standards for pedigree charts and family group records.
(Continued on next page)

**SUGGESTED STANDARD FOR RECORDING
INFORMATION ON PEDIGREE CHARTS
AND FAMILY GROUP RECORDS**

MISCELLANEOUS (cont.)

7. Place an "x" in the sex column for the child that is your direct ancestor.

8. When a marriage ends in divorce, indicate after the marriage date.

18 Sep 1898 (div)

Figure 3. Suggested standards for pedigree charts and family group records. (Concluded)

When the assignments are completed on the first-generation family group record, the researcher selects the second-generation family group record as the objective family group record and again completes all the research assignments. This procedure is repeated with each of the first four-generation family group records. (See Figure 4.) Research beyond the fourth generation should not be attempted until all eight of the four-generation family group records have been completed and verified, which may include additional research in particular geographic areas.

If the genealogical researcher will limit his research to the first four-generation family group records, learn the research terminology, and apply the research tools by searching the basic records in the order suggested in the text and the lesson assignments, he will have learned the basic genealogical research techniques which apply to all geographic areas. With this experience, the researcher is prepared to continue his research in the records of the specific locality which requires a detailed understanding of the records, procedures, and techniques peculiar to each geographic area and can be learned by studying a more detailed textbook on genealogical records of the specific locality.

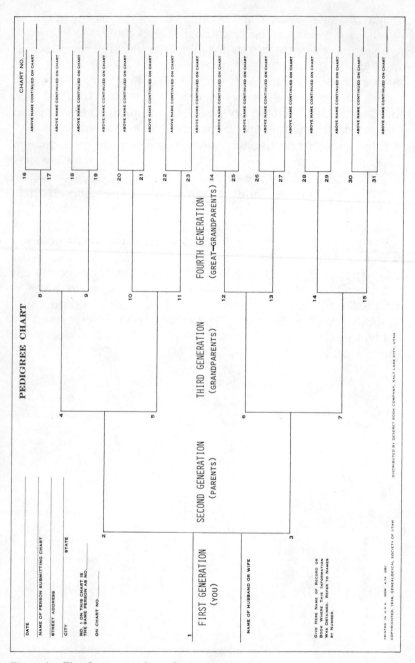

Figure 4.   First four generations of ancestry.

2
Elements of Identity

There are six elements of identity:
1. Names (names of individuals)
2. Places (names of places where events occurred)
3. Dates (dates of events)
4. Relationships (blood relationships between individuals)
5. Occupations (occupations of individuals)
6. Sex (sex of individuals)

The elements of identity are used to identify, or distinguish, one individual from another. Two persons in the same community may have the same name and may have been born about the same time; in which case, relationships are necessary to distinguish one individual from another. The occupation of an individual may further identify him, particularly when more than one person with the same name resides in the same locality at the same time, and it is not possible to determine relationships. The sex of an individual may also further identify him; it is not always possible to determine the sex of an individual by his name only, as certain names are used by both males and females.

The researcher searches records of the same locality and time period as listed on the objective family group record and eliminates records where the locality and time period differ from the family group record.

The researcher would not search a family history of the Egbert family in the locality of Oregon for the time period 1890-1900 if his particular Egbert family resided in the locality of New York in 1890-1900.

In order to find the name of an individual in a particular record, the locality and time period in which the individual resided and the locality and time period of the record must be the same:

Name of Individual		Genealogical Record
Locality	=	Locality
Time period	=	Time period

NAMES

Two different methods are used when searching for names of individuals:

1. Specific name search—searching in a record for the name of one particular individual; for example, Robert Harrison Barker.

2. General surname search—searching in a record for the names of all individuals with the same surname; for example, Barker.

The lesson assignments (see Section IV) require a specific name search for each individual on the objective family group record. General surname searches are used in genealogical research in certain geographic areas, but are usually not applicable to the first four generations of ancestry.

Origin

A study of the origin of surnames indicates that persons with the same surnames are not necessarily blood relatives, and members of the same family may have different surnames. Surnames originated from the following:

1. Places   4. Personal characteristics
2. Occupations   5. Masters and landowners
3. Ancestry

1. *Place surnames* often originated from a man's place of residence or geographic location such as a hill or brook. A man may originally have been called "John of the Hill" or "John by the Water" or "John by the Brook." Later the name may have been shortened or changed to John Hill, John Bywater, or John Brooks. At the time surnames originated, most persons could not read or write, and residences, inns, and shops displayed signs denoting the name of the establishment; usually the signs showed an object (bell), animal (fox), or bird (swan). Individuals who lived or worked at these places often acquired their names from the objects: "John of the Bell," "Henry at the Fox," and "William Swan."

2. *Occupational surnames* have been acquired as a result of an individual's vocation or occupation and include such names as Baker, Taylor, Carpenter, Cook, and Smith.

3. *Ancestral or Patronymic surnames* originated from the name of an ancestor, usually the given name of the father. The suffix "son" or "dotter" was added. (See Figure 5.)

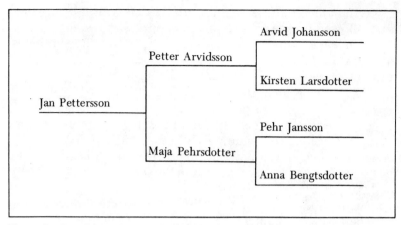

Figure 5.   Swedish pedigree illustrating patronymics.

For examples of other names with a prefix or suffix indicating "son" or "son of," see Figure 6.

Nationality	Prefix or Suffix	Example of Name
English	s, son	Richards, Richardson
Gaelic	Mac	MacDonald
German	sohn, son	Mendelssohn
Hebrew	ben	Solomon ben David
Irish	O'	O'Neil
Norman	Fitz	Fitzgerald
Russian	ov, ovich, ovitch	Ivanov, Ivanovich
Saxon	ing	Harding
Scandinavian	sen, son	Jensen, Johansson
Welsh	ap, P	ap Rice, Price

Figure 6.   Prefix and suffix of patronymic surnames.

4. *Personal characteristic surnames* have been acquired as a result of an individual's physical appearance or personal title and include names such as Little, Armstrong, Knight, and Noble.

5. *The surnames of masters and landowners* have often been adopted by slaves and domestic help.

Customs and Traditions

1. In some countries, names are written with given name first, followed by a middle name and/or surname: John Thomas Grange.

2. In some countries names are written with the surname first, followed by one or more given names: Sun Huang Ti.

3. In some countries individuals have compound surnames in which the surname of the child has been derived from the surname of parents, grandparents, or other relatives:

Leon Gomez Alonso   Henry Barton-Lloyd

(*surname*)   (*surname*)

4. In some countries and among some religious groups, there are customs for naming children, and children's given names may be clues in determining correct identification. Note the following example of a custom in some families of Scotland:

The first boy is named after the paternal grandfather.
The first girl is named after the maternal grandmother.
The second boy is named after the maternal grandfather.
The second girl is named after the paternal grandmother.
The third boy is named after his father.
The third girl is named after her mother.

Subsequent children may be named after aunts, uncles, cousins, etc.

Variations in Spelling and Recording Names

There is no particular standard for spelling and recording names, and the same name may be written more than one way in a single document. When searching indexes or alphabetized lists of names, variations should be considered or a particular name may be overlooked.

A person who cannot read or write cannot give the correct spelling of his name or check to see if his name is being written accurately by a recorder. A recorder does not always know if he is writing a name correctly, and even the informant who can read and write is not always aware of how his name is being recorded. Because there is no standard for spelling names of individuals, names are usually spelled the way they sound. This is called phonetic spelling, and many spelling variations result. The following are reasons, with examples, for variations in spelling names and recording names:

1. Vowels have similar sounds and are often interchanged: a, e, i, o, u, y.

2. Some consonants have similar sounds: c and k; g and j; t and d.

3. Some double and single letters sound the same: l and ll; t and tt; e and ee.

4. Different combinations of letters have similar sounds: sh and sch; ch and j; ee, ie, and y; cks and x.

5. Some letters are silent: K in Knight.

6. An additional letter is added because of a local dialect: r in Hallebone—Hallerbone.

7. Pronunciation of a name may be altered because of the accent of a different language, and a recorded version may be much different from the usual spelling. A name spoken with a Swedish accent and recorded in English by a person from Scotland may be spelled much differently than the Swedish person would spell it. For example, Johnsen for Jansson.

8. Translation of a name from one language to another may change the name: Stina Maja to Christina Maria; Schmidt to Smith.

9. Misinterpretation of handwriting or copy errors may occur: David for Daniel.

10. Initials may be recorded instead of given and/or middle names: Albert E. Long, A. Edward Long, or A. E. Long.

11. Names may be abbreviated and some abbreviations refer to more than one name: Ed. for Edmond or Edward; Jn. for John or Jonathan; Jos. for Joseph or Josiah.

12. A given or middle name may be omitted: Albert Long or Edward Long instead of Albert Edward Long.

13. Given and middle names may be interchanged: Edward Albert Long instead of Albert Edward Long.

14. A woman may be recorded by her maiden name or married name(s).

15. Nicknames may be recorded: Bill for William; Polly for Mary.

16. Synonymous names may be recorded: Robertson or Robinson; Per, Pehr, Peder, Peter, or Petter.

17. An alias may be recorded.

18. A name may be changed because of adoption or other personal reasons.

19. When the correct name is known, an incorrect name may be given intentionally because of illegitimacy or desire to lose identity.

20. An incorrect name may be given unintentionally because of lapse of memory of the informant.

21. An incorrect name may be given unintentionally because of lack of knowledge of patronymic names: Peder Larsson son of Lars Andersson may be Peder Andersson.

Figures 7, 8, and 9 illustrate various ways of spelling and recording particular names.

ALLIBONE

    Alebone
    Allebone
    Allerbone
    Alibone
    Allibone
    Ellerbone
    Halebone
    Hallebone

Figure 7.   Variations of the surname of Allibone.

DUNN, Helen
    md. James Malcolm

    Dun, Ellen
    Dun, Helen
    Dunn, Ellen
    Dunn, Helen
    Malcolm, Ellen
    Malcolm, Helen
    Malcolm, Helen D.
    Malcom, Ellen Dunn
    Malcom, Helen Dunn
    Malkom, Ellen Dunn

Figure 8.   Variations of the name of Helen Dunn Malcolm.

```
LARSSON, Peder Christian
(son of Lars Andersson)

Andersen, Peter Larson
Anderson, Peter
Anderson, Peter Chris
Anderson, Peter Christian Larson
Andersson, Peder Christian
Larsen, Peter
Larson, Peter C.
Larsson, P. C.
Larsson, Pehr Christ.
Larsson, Peder Chris
Larsson, Petter Christian
Larsson, Christian Peter
Larsson, C. Pehr
```

Figure 9. Variations of the name of Peder Christian Larsson.

PLACES

Genealogical research involves searching for particular names of individuals in the records of particular places where the individuals resided. Many genealogical problems are unsolved because searches are made in records of places where the individuals did not reside. The genealogical researcher should establish the correct place name for each event on the family group record; this can be accomplished through the use of gazetteers and maps. (See Chapter 10.) Incorrect place names may result for the same reasons as incorrect names of individuals:

1. Phonetics
2. Incorrect spelling
3. Misinterpretation of handwriting
4. Copying errors
5. Foreign accents
6. Anglicization
7. Lack of knowledge

In addition, there are situations peculiar to place names that could result in incorrect conclusions and searching the records of the wrong locality.

1. There may be an ancient and modern spelling:
   Ancient—Qvistbro, Örebro, Sweden
   Modern—Kvistbro, Örebro, Sweden
   Ancient—Styvechale, Warwickshire, England
   Modern—Stivichall, Warwickshire, England

2. There may be an incorrect combination of town, parish, and/or county; for example, Istorp, Värmland County, Sweden instead of Istorp, Alvsborg County, Sweden.

3. Names of actual places are given, but the ancestor did not reside there. The name of a nearby large city may be mentioned rather than the name of a small town; the event may have occurred in a locality other than the usual residence; or a port of embarkation may have been mentioned as a place of residence.

4. Boundary changes may occur. For example, Butler County, Pennsylvania was formed from Allegheny County in 1800.

5. Place name changes may occur: Commerce, Illinois, to Nauvoo, Illinois; Romsey, Southampton, to Romsey, Hampshire.

6. Two or more places may have the same name: Winterton, Lincolnshire, England; Winterton, Norfolk, England; Winterton, Durham, England.

7. The place name is mispronounced and/or misspelled because of an odd spelling: Woostasher instead of Worcestershire; Toowilla instead of Tooele.

DATES

Genealogical research involves searching for a particular name of an individual, in a particular place, at a particular period of time. The period of time to search in a record can be determined by the researcher:

1. When an exact date is known, one should search at least five years prior to and five years after the date.

2. When a date is calculated from an age at a dated event, one should search at least five years prior to and five years after the calculated date.

3. When a period of time is approximated from other clues, one searches the approximated period of time.

Dates may not always be written clearly. January, when abbreviated to Jan., may be confused with June, and Mar. with May. Numbers that may be easily mistaken for one another are 7 and 2, 7 and 9, 4 and 7, 1 and 7, 6 and 4, 5 and 8, 5 and 3, and 8 and 3.

When numerals are used to indicate months, the day and the month may be misinterpreted for numerals below 12. A date written 6-7-1850 could be interpreted as June 7, 1850, or 6 July 1850. A date recorded 28-7-1850 is correctly interpreted as 28 July 1850, because the number of a month is never higher than twelve.

RELATIONSHIPS

Relationships must be combined with names, places, and dates in order to correctly identify an individual. When more than one individual with the same name is residing in the same community at the same period of time, lives to maturity, and has children, establishing correct relationships may be the only way to identify the individuals. Problems that may occur in establishing correct relationships are often a result of misinterpretation and miscalculation, incorrect use of terminology, assuming nonexistent relationships, belief in traditions that cannot be proven, and desire to be related to famous persons.

The goal in genealogical research is to compile and complete an accurate pedigree, with a corresponding family group record for every ancestral couple on the pedigree. When one thinks of the requirement of a family group record for each ancestral couple, the task of genealogical research is not so overwhelming as when gathering information about other relatives or people who happen to have the same surnames as one's ancestors.

Each line of ancestry is important. A person may by choice prefer to do research on one particular line over another, or may change his research from one line to another as genealogical information becomes more easily available, but this does not change the goal of completing a family group record for each ancestral couple on the pedigree.

For members of The Church of Jesus Christ of Latter-day Saints, a sealing line may be different from the blood line, in which case one should consult the Genealogical Society for instructions concerning the pedigree line of first responsibility.

To identify each individual in his proper place on family group records and pedigree charts, correct relationships must be established:
1. Direct-line relationships
2. Brother-sister relationships
3. Uncle/aunt—nephew/niece relationships
4. Cousin relationships
5. Half, step, and in-law relationships

Direct-Line Relationships

A direct-line relationship is a relationship between individuals in the same line of descent from a common ancestor;
for example, father to son, grandfather to grandson. Relationships to direct-line ancestry are indicated on a standard
pedigree chart. (See Figure 10.)

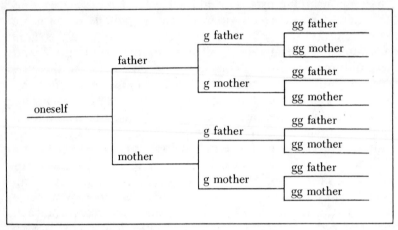

Figure 10.   Relationships of direct-line ancestors to oneself.

Figure 11 illustrates direct-line relationships and indicates
the relationships of oneself to his ancestors.

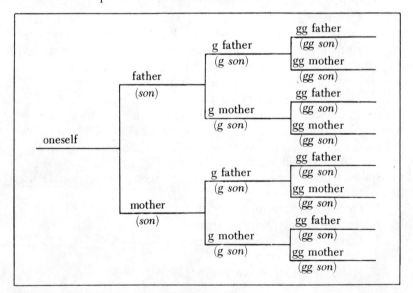

Figure 11.   Relationships of oneself to direct-line ancestors.

Brother-Sister Relationships

A brother-sister relationship is a relationship between two individuals with the same parents. Figures 12, 13, and 14 indicate brother-sister relationships.

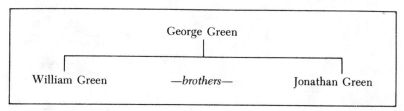

Figure 12.   Brother relationships.

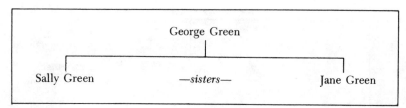

Figure 13.   Sister relationships.

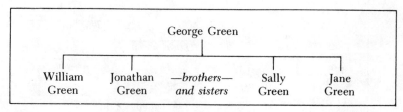

Figure 14.   Brother-sister relationships.

Uncle/Aunt—Nephew/Niece Relationships

An uncle/aunt—nephew/niece relationship is a relationship between an individual and the brothers and/or sisters of his direct-line ancestors. The brothers and sisters of one's grandparents are his granduncles and grandaunts; the brothers and sisters of one's great-grandparents are his great-granduncles and great-grandaunts; and the brothers and sisters of one's second-great-grandparents are his second-great-granduncles and second-great-grandaunts. Figures 15 and 16 indicate the relationships between oneself and the brothers and sisters of his direct-line ancestors.

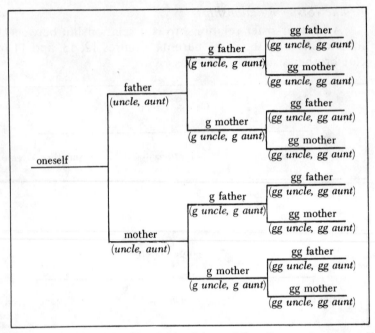

Figure 15.   Relationships of brothers and sisters of direct-line ancestors to oneself.

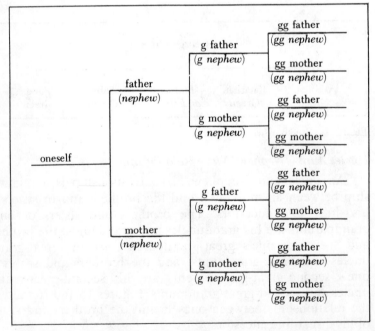

Figure 16.   Relationships of oneself to brothers and sisters of direct-line ancestors.

Cousin Relationships

A cousin relationship is a relationship between two individuals having a common ancestral couple, but the direct line of descent from that common ancestral couple is different. To calculate a cousin relationship, two factors must be known:

1. The nearest common ancestral couple from which both are descended, and

2. The line of descent from the common ancestral couple to each individual.

When the number of generations in each line of descent is equal, there is a full-cousin relationship, as illustrated in Figure 17. When the number of generations in each line of descent is not equal, there is a cousin-removed relationship, as illustrated in Figure 18.

George Green and Martha Brown (common ancestral couple)

William Green	—brothers—	Jonathan Green
David Green	—1st cousins—	Thomas Green
Israel Green	—2nd cousins—	Peter Green
Thomas Green	—3rd cousins—	Archibald Green

Figure 17.   Full-cousin relationships.

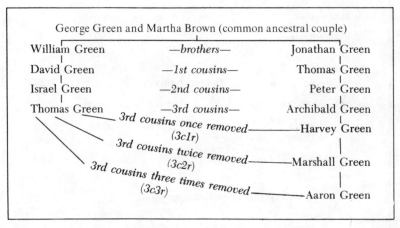

Figure 18.   Full-cousin and cousin-removed relationships.

Half, Step, and In-Law Relationships

1. A half-relationship is a relationship between two individuals having one member of an ancestral couple in common.

2. A step-relationship is a relationship between two individuals having no ancestral couple in common, but one member of the couple is an ancestor of one individual, and the other member of the couple is the ancestor of the other individual.

3. An in-law relationship is a relationship between two individuals in which one individual is a blood relative of a particular family and the other individual marries into that family.

Suggested Standard Abbreviations for Recording Relationships of Oneself to Individuals Listed as Parents on the Family Group Record

self—oneself (The individual appears on a family group record as a parent.)

son—son

dau—daughter

father—father

mother—mother

uncle—uncle

aunt—aunt

neph—nephew

niece—niece

g—grand (g son; g dau; g neph; g niece)

gg—great grand (gg son; gg dau; gg neph; gg niece)

2 gg—second great grand (2 gg son; 2 gg dau; 2 gg neph; 2 gg niece)

c—cousin

r—removed

2c3r—second cousin three times removed

il—in-law

step—step

half—half

Figure 19.   Standard abbreviations of relationships.

3
The Origin and Classification of Records

After the genealogical researcher has selected the objective family group record, he searches specific records to verify and complete the information for each individual on the family group record. The records he searches are those that have been determined through the successful experience of others to contain the best genealogical information. Genealogical records originate in jurisdictions and are classified by record type.

JURISDICTIONS

A jurisdiction is the authority or governing body that initiates the keeping of records. The jurisdictions most frequently used in genealogical research and which initiate the best records for genealogical use are the government (civil) jurisdiction and the church (ecclesiastical) jurisdiction. The subdivisions of the government (civil) jurisdiction are known as city, town, township, state, county, province, shire, etc., varying with each country. The subdivisions of the church (ecclesiastical) jurisdiction are known as parish, ward, archdeaconry, diocese, conference, district, etc., varying with each church. Other jurisdictions that may originate genealogical records are private jurisdictions, such as the home, business, social, etc.

When a new jurisdiction is formed from an existing jurisdiction, the former jurisdiction retains all records, and the new jurisdiction begins with new record books. A new jurisdiction is formed when the following situations occur:

1. When one or more jurisdictions are divided to form one or more new jurisdictions
2. When two or more jurisdictions are combined
3. When boundaries of existing jurisdictions are changed

RECORD TYPES

Similar or like records are grouped together for convenience in studying and discussing the records. These are sometimes referred to as record types or record categories. The following record types are basic to all genealogical problems and can be obtained and understood without a knowledge of a foreign language and early handwriting, and are discussed in detail in this text:

1. Home records
2. Biographical records
3. Vital records
4. Temple ordinance records

The following record types are representative of research in a specific geographic locality. The time period, origin, contents, availability, genealogical application, and genealogical limitations vary with each locality and with each record. Their genealogical value and usage can be properly understood by studying in detail the genealogical records of the particular locality, learning the legal terminology peculiar to each record, and learning the language and handwriting of the locality:

1. Census records
2. Probate records
3. Land records
4. Court records
5. Military records
6. Emigration–immigration records
7. Cemetery records
8. Social and commercial records

Home Records

Home records, such as family Bible records, diaries, journals, photographs, letters, and scrapbooks, give valuable clues to names, places, dates, and relationships and lead to searches in other records. Figure 20 illustrates information from a Bible record.

```
DOUD, Jeremiah Osborne (1817)                    marriage


   Jeremiah O. Doud and Lucy Jane Wilsey were
   married 22 June 1846




Family Bible of Olive Jane Doud Lott in possession of
   Lola Marie Richardson Wendt, Rt. 1, Cathlamet, Wash.
```

Figure 20.   Information from a Bible record.

Biographical Records

Biographical records include individual life stories, family histories, biographies in locality histories, and obituaries. These give valuable clues to names, dates, places, and relationships and lead to searches in the original records from which the printed record may have been compiled. Figures 21 and 22 illustrate information from an obituary and a locality history.

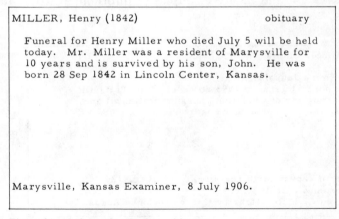

```
MILLER, Henry (1842)                    obituary

   Funeral for Henry Miller who died July 5 will be held
   today.  Mr. Miller was a resident of Marysville for
   10 years and is survived by his son, John.  He was
   born 28 Sep 1842 in Lincoln Center, Kansas.




Marysville, Kansas Examiner, 8 July 1906.
```

Figure 21.   Information from an obituary.

```
DOUD, Ebenezer (1802)                        locality history
                                      Ohio, Crawford, Liberty

  Ebenezer Dowd was the first tailor and purchased the
  lot where the Schaber-Volk Block now stands, and
  here he opened his shop.  He had a brother and sister
  who came with him, and in August 1825, Elihu Dowd
  married Polly Ketchum, and in December of the same
  year Eunice Dowd married James Dorland of Liberty
  township.




History of Crawford County, rec'd by correspondence
from Ohio State Library, Sept. 1971.
```

Figure 22.   Information from a locality history.

Vital Records

Vital records include records of birth, marriage, and death kept by the government (civil) authorities, and records of christening (baptism), marriage, and burial kept by the church (ecclesiastical) authorities. These are the most valuable genealogical records, and if a birth, marriage, and death record were available for each member of each ancestral family, the necessity for searching other records would be greatly reduced. Figures 23, 24, and 25 are examples of information from vital records.

```
JAUSSI, Emma (1893)                                birth

  Emma Jaussi
    born 31 January 1893 at 9 o'clock in Wattenwil
    daughter of Christian Jaussi of Wattenwil and
              Maria Wenger




Certificate in birth register, Book II, p. 130, #6
Wattenwil, Switzerland
From Civil Registrar by Correspondence August 1965
```

Figure 23.   Information from a government birth record.

```
LONG, James                                    marriage

  James Long of Great Yarmouth, bachelor
  Married 17 July 1833, banns
  Mary Ann Westgate of Great Yarmouth, spinster




Great Yarmouth, Norfolk, England, Bishops Transcripts
   rec'd by correspondence with Norfolk & Norwich Record
   Office, Central Library, Norwich, Norfolk, England.
```

Figure 24.   Information from a church marriage record.

```
WALKER, William                               death

  William Walker, male, bachelor
    age 21, no occupation
    died 18 Sep 1920 at 12 Oberon Street
    of general tuberculosis, 6 months duration

  Reg. 20 Sep 1920 by Wm. Walker, father, present
    at death.


Certificate in death register, Belfast Urban No. XI, #126,
   Supt. Reg. Dist. of Belfast, Down, Ireland. Received by
   correspondence from civil registrar.
```

Figure 25.   Information from a government death record.

Temple Ordinance Records

Temple ordinance records result from ordinance work performed in the temples of The Church of Jesus Christ of Latter-day Saints. These records are used to provide, correct, and verify temple ordinance dates on family group records and to provide names, places, dates, and relationships to be used as clues in determining other records to search. Figure 26 is an illustration of information from a temple ordinance record.

```
FORSLING, Johanna Sophia (1842)              sealing
                                             to parents
   Sealed 21 June 1894

   Parents:  Lars Frederick Forsling (dead)
             Magdalena Sunman Forsling (dead)

   Children:
     Johanna Sophia Forsling Elg, b 23 Oct 1842
        Sundsvall, Westmor, Sweden
     Fredericka Magdalena Forsling (dead), b 9 Aug 1851
        Sundsvall, Wesemor, Sweden
        (proxy--Johanna Elg)


S. L. Temple records of sealings of children to parents
GS F 184,652
```

Figure 26. Information from a temple ordinance record.

Census Records

Census records result from the enumeration of residents of
certain areas for the purposes of taxation and economic statistics. Census records often list families together in a group, and
some give relationships, places of birth, and age at the time of
census. Census records provide clues that lead to searches in
other records. Figure 27 illustrates information from a census
record.

```
WALKER, David (1815)                        1851 census

   David Walker marr hd 36 blacksmith, b. Falkirk, Stirling
   Jean     "       "   w 37              b.            Ayr
   Jean     "         dau 12 scholar      b. Glasgow, Lanark
   William  "         son  9    "         b. Maryhill,   "




1851 Census of Maryhill, Lanark, Scotland, Dist. 4, p. 17.
GS F 103,712
```

Figure 27.   Information from a census record.

Probate Records

Probate records result from the settling of an estate and the distribution of the property of a deceased individual. Probate records are valuable for obtaining names of relatives and places of residence, and particularly for establishing pedigree connections. Figure 28 illustrates information from a probate record.

```
ALLIBONE, Elizabeth                              probate

   Elizabeth Abbott of Irchester, died 4 Aug 1850
      Will dated 10 Jan 1850
      Widow of Thomas Abbott

   Bequeath to son John Abbott
               son William Abbott
               dau Ann Palmer, widow
               dau Harriett, wife of William Desborough

   Property left to Elizabeth by will of her late husband.

   Executor--James Cooper
   Witnesses--Robert Burditt, clerk; Caleb Green, servant


Probate in the Archdeaconry Court of Northampton,
England.  GS F 187,844
```

Figure 28.   Information from a probate record.

Land Records

Land records result from the establishment of ownership of land, the transfer of land from one individual to another, or the transfer of land from the government to an individual. These records are valuable for establishing former places of residence, dates of residence, and names of relatives to be used as clues to lead to searches in other records. Figure 29 illustrates information from a land record.

```
RICHARDSON, A. B. (1815)                         land

   Emily F. Richardson, widow of A. B. Richardson, de-
   ceased, and Ella F. Gilham, dau of deceased and F. M.
   Gilham, her husband, and Albert Orson Richardson, son
   of deceased and Gracie C. Richardson, dau of deceased,
   being the widow and all heirs.

   Lots 2 and 1 in Block 27, Astoria, Oregon, Selling these
   lots via land agent in San Francisco, where widow and
   all heirs now reside.

   Selling these lots to John C. Dement and J. F. Hamilton
   of Astoria for $2500.00.  Deed made 15 Nov 1886 and
   recorded 24 Nov 1886.


Deed Book, Clatsop County, Oregon, Book 11, page 491.
Searched in person, June 1961.
```

Figure 29.   Information from a land record.

Court Records

Court records result from the settling of disputes by legal means, or the establishment of decisions that require legal authority. Court records of value in genealogical research are adoptions, guardianships, divorces, property disputes (land records), and distribution of property of a deceased individual (probate records). These records give information on names, dates, places, and relationships that lead to searches in other records. Figure 30 illustrates information from a court record.

```
EDWARDS, John W.                                    orphans ct.

   John W. Edwards, a minor
      Child of Charles Edwards of the County of Chester
      Under the age of 14 on 27 Apr 1846

   Petition for Oliver Alison to be appointed guardian.
   Refused by Oliver Alison, and Charles Lloyd appointed
      guardian.




Pennsylvania Orphans Court Record
GS F 020,895
```

Figure 30.   Information from a court record.

Military Records

Military records are a result of military service, registration for military service, and/or pension requests for military service. These records are valuable for dates, places of residence, and relationships, and provide clues that lead to searches in other records. Figures 31 and 32 illustrate information from military records.

BURCH, Josiah (1847)   military

Josiah Burch was born at Jersey, Channel Islands, St.
Helier's Parish on 18 Aug 1847. On August 1862 he
entered the Royal Navy as a Boy, 2nd class on board
HMS St. Vincent and on 18 Aug 1865--on attaining the
age of 18 he volunteered for continuous service for 10
years. Consent for this engagement was signed by his
father, Josiah Burch. His usual place of residence is
listed at Portsmouth and he was Church of England.

Naval Record obtained via agent, November 1958
Public Records Office, London, England

Figure 31.   Information from a military record.

DOUD, Isaac (1754)   Revolutionary
                                            Pension application

We, Isaac Doud, Ebenezer Doud, Deborah Phillips, late
Deborah Doud of Lenox Township, County of Susquehanna
and state of Pennsylvania, children of Eleanor Doud
(dec'd) widow and children of Isaac Doud (dec'd) who was
a Revolutionary Pensioner of the United States. We appoint our Brother Elihu Doud of Winnebago County and
State of Wisconsin our true and lawful attorney for us
and in our names respectively to receive from any agent
or accounting officer for paying our equal share.

29 January 1853

Revolutionary Pension Application rec'd by correspondence from National Archives, Washington, D.C.

Figure 32.   Information from a pension application.

Emigration-Immigration Records

Emigration-immigration records are a result of an individual's leaving a particular locality (emigrating) and entering a
particular locality (immigrating). These records are used to determine former places of residence, approximate dates of
residence, and give clues that lead to searches in other records.
Figure 33 illustrates information from an emigration record.

```
SCHLUNEGGER, Susanna (1889)              LDS Emigration

   Sailed 4 Oct 1912, S.S. "Tunisian"

   Schlunegger, Anna 52 F Wid. Swiss Swiss-Germ. Miss.
                                          to Montpelier, Idaho
        "    Susanne    23 F S      "            "
        "    Margritha  21 F S      "            "
        "    Elise      19 F S      "            "
        "    Herman     14 M S      "       cancelled
             [did not immigrate to Idaho]




   Emigration Registers of The British Mission
   GS F 025,694 (Lib. No. 3067, p. 559)
```

Figure 33.   Information from an emigration record.

Cemetery Records

Cemetery records include tombstone inscriptions and cemetery sexton records. They are valuable for obtaining dates of birth and death, and are most often used for clues that lead to other records to search. Figures 34 and 35 illustrate information from cemetery records.

```
ELG, Knut August (1843)                      cemetery

   K. A. Elg, b. 3 Nov 1843 Newcoping, Sweden

   Father: Conrad Elg
   Mother: Anna Weger
   was married
   died in Sandy, 15 Feb 1903  of pneumonia
   buried         18 Feb 1903




   Sexton Records of Sandy Cemetery, Salt Lake Co., Utah
   GS F 027,300   entry #447
```

Figure 34.   Information from a cemetery sexton record.

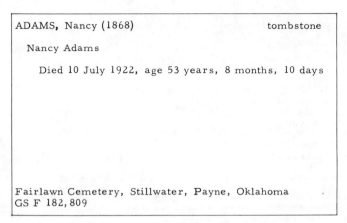

```
ADAMS, Nancy (1868)                                  tombstone

  Nancy Adams

     Died 10 July 1922, age 53 years, 8 months, 10 days






Fairlawn Cemetery, Stillwater, Payne, Oklahoma
GS F 182,809
```

Figure 35.   Information from a tombstone inscription.

Social and Commercial Records

Social and commercial records include records of funeral homes, private schools, professional organizations, insurance companies, hobby groups, and patriotic societies. These records provide names, dates, places, and relationships to be used as clues to other records to search. Figures 36 and 37 illustrate information from social and commercial records.

```
DOUD, Jeremiah Osborne (1817)            funeral home

  Name: Jeremiah O. Doud--widower
  Died:    12-12-98 St. Vincent's Hospital, Portland
  Born:    No exact date given, but 82 years old;
              State of Pennsylvania
  Occupation: Farmer.  Lived in Kansas prior to coming
              to Portland--resident here for about 10 years
  Cause of death: Cancer
  Buried: 12-13-98 in Lone Fir Cemetery, Portland,
              Lot 30, Block 1 in an unmarked grave.



Records of Finley's Funeral Home, S. W. 4th at Montgom-
    ery, Portland, Oregon, rec'd by corres. , 29 Sep 1956
```

Figure 36.   Information from a funeral home record.

```
┌─────────────────────────────────────────────────────────────────────┐
│ DOUD, Isaac (1754)                              DAR Application       │
│                                                                       │
│   Isaac Dowd served as private in Capt. Herrick's Co.,               │
│     1775, and in Capt. Ball's Co., in 1776 under Col.                │
│     Shepard of Mass.                                                  │
│                                                                       │
│   Children of Revolutionary Ancestor:                                │
│     Elizabeth b. abt. 1802)                                          │
│     Ebenezer  b. abt. 1802)  twins                                  │
│     Isaac                                                             │
│     John b. 3-28-1785                                                 │
│     Marilda b. abt. 1789                                              │
│     Sarah b. abt. 1791                                                │
│     Deborah b. abt. 1794          Elihu                              │
│     Esther b. 2-16-1798           Eunice b. abt 1807                 │
│                                                                       │
│ DAR Application and Lineage Paper for Mrs. Maxine P.                  │
│   Hansen, New Haven, Conn., rec'd by correspondence.                 │
└─────────────────────────────────────────────────────────────────────┘
```

Figure 37.   Information from a patriotic society.

4
Analyzing and Evaluating Genealogical Information

The goal of genealogical research is to supply the information requested on the family group record and to obtain this information from the most reliable genealogical sources. The genealogical researcher cannot produce a living, personal witness to verify each genealogical event, so he searches records that contain the desired information. To accomplish this objective, he does the following:

1. Analyzes the information on the objective family group record.

2. Determines the records to search (Chapters 14 to 22)

3. Searches the records (Chapters 14 to 22)

4. Copies the genealogical information onto note cards (Chapter 6)

5. Enters the genealogical information on the objective family group record (Chapter 6)

6. Analyzes the new family group information

7. Evaluates the record sources where there is conflicting information

FAMILY GROUP ANALYSIS

The genealogical researcher should analyze the information recorded on the objective family group record and do the following:

1. Determine the source of each item of information on the family group record.

2. Determine which information is missing or incomplete.

3. Determine possible places of residence from the place names listed on the family group record.

4. Determine possible places where events could have occurred if place names are missing.

5. Determine migration pattern and time period of migration from places and dates listed on the family group record.

6. Determine if the parents and/or children migrated from one country to another.

7. Determine if both parents on the family group record were born in the same country and/or state.

8. Determine if either parent could have changed residence between the date of birth and the date of marriage.

9. Determine if the parents changed residence between the date of marriage and dates of the births of their children.

10. Determine if the parents changed residence from the date of birth of the last child and the date of the death of either parent.

11. Determine the possible time period when events could have occurred if dates are missing.

12. Determine if all children listed on the family group record belong to the parents on the family group by comparing the birth dates of the children with the marriage date and death dates of the parents.

13. Determine if there could be additional children and stillbirths by noting if there are more than three years between the births of any of the children.

14. Determine which parent died first and if any children preceded the parents in death.

15. Determine clues to possible ancestral surnames by noting unusual or surname-type given names for the parents or children.

16. Determine if the given name of the children agrees with the sex marked in the left-hand column.

17. Determine if previous research has been performed by noting name and address of patron and sources searched.

18. Determine the number of the marriage for the husband and the wife (first marriage, second marriage, etc.).

19. Determine if the identifying information for the husband and wife on the family group record is the same as on the family group record where they appear as children.

20. Determine if there is conflicting information.

Individuals who are members of the LDS Church will also want to do the following:

21. Determine from the birth date of the children and the sealing date of the parents if the children were "Born in the Covenant" (BIC) or sealed to parents in life.

22. Determine if ordinances need to be performed by noting missing and incomplete ordinance dates.

23. Determine if any children died under the age of eight and do not need a baptism and endowment performed.

24. Determine which ordinances were performed in life and which by proxy by comparing ordinance dates with death dates.

25. Determine in which temples the ordinances were performed by noting temple initials in the ordinance columns.

26. Determine if there could be a repeat sealing of the couple or of the children to parents by noting if a proxy endowment and proxy sealing were performed in different temples.

27. Determine if there could be a repeat sealing of the couple and of the children to parents by noting if the proxy sealings were performed more than six to ten years after the proxy endowments.

28. Determine if the grandparents on the family group record could have been members of the LDS Church by noting if the parents were baptized near the age of eight.

29. Determine if ordinance dates and/or name of temple could be incorrect by noting the dates and places of the ordinances and comparing with the chart, "Chronology of Temple Ordinances to 1970." (See Chapter 22, Figure 330.)

RECORD SOURCE ANALYSIS

As the genealogical researcher searches the records and analyzes genealogical information, he often finds that information from one record does not agree with that which is in another. If he obtains conflicting information from two or more records, he must evaluate the records as to the following:

1. Source of information
2. Type of information
3. Type of record
4. Type of copy

Records judged to be the most reliable because of their source of information, type of information, type of record, and type of copy could contain errors. If this is the case, it may be necessary to search additional records that give the same information and either accept an item as correct because the majority of evidence is favorable to that conclusion, or withhold judgment until further information is obtained. A more complete evaluation can be made when the researcher understands the origin, history, contents, genealogical application, and genealogical limitations concerning each record.

Source of Information

The most desirable genealogical record is that in which the information was provided by a witness or participant who gave the information at or near the time of the event. All genealogical information has its origin in the memory of those who witnessed or participated in the event. The further removed the individual is from the event, or the longer the time lapse between the event and the time the information is provided, the less reliable the information. The source of the information is classified as either primary or secondary. *Primary source information* is information given by a witness or participant at or near the time of the event. *Secondary source information* is information that is *not* given by a witness or participant and/or *not* given at or near the time of the event.

Type of Information

The most desirable genealogical information is that which answers the problem directly without having to make calculations and assumptions. The type of information is classified as either direct or circumstantial. *Direct information* is that which provides an answer directly without assumptions and calculations. *Circumstantial information* implies or assumes an answer or provides an answer after some calculations.

Type of Record

The most desirable genealogical record is the original or first recording of a particular event or a photocopy of the original record. Each time a handwritten or typed copy is made from another handwritten or typed copy, the possibility of error increases. The type of record is classified as either original or copied. An *original record* is the first recording of a particular event. A *copied record* is a handwritten or typed copy of an original record.

Type of Copy

The most desirable copy of genealogical information is that which has been copied exactly and completely. However, it is not always possible or practical to copy exactly the entire contents of some genealogical records, in which case, only the genealogical information is abstracted. The type of copy is classified as either an extract or an abstract. An *extract* is a complete and exact copy of the information found in the record. An *abstract* is a digest or summary of the genealogical information found in the record.

SECTION II

GENEALOGICAL RESEARCH TOOLS

5
Book of Remembrance

The Book of Remembrance (Family Record Book) is a genealogical research tool used to organize and file both completed and uncompleted genealogical sheets, including:
1. Pedigree charts
2. Family group records
3. Personal record

For the most efficient use of the Book of Remembrance, it should be indexed with plain white guide sheets and plastic index tabs.[1] Three-eighth-inch yellow plastic index tabs are recommended for the pedigree chart guide sheets; ½-inch clear plastic index tabs with letters of the alphabet are recommended for the family group record guide sheets; and a colored plastic index tab is recommended for the personal record guide sheet. (See Figure 38.)

PEDIGREE CHARTS

The recommended pedigree chart published by the Genealogical Society is an 8½″ x 14″ five-generation chart. This chart provides for information about births, marriages, and deaths for four generations of direct ancestry. The fifth generation is listed by name only, and each fifth generation name is repeated as the first generation on the next chart. Space is also provided for the name and address of the compiler and the current date. Each pedigree chart is filed behind the guide sheet with the corresponding yellow plastic index tab.

---

[1] J. Grant Stevenson, *A Genealogy Check List*, 9th ed. (Provo, Utah: Stevenson Supply, 1971), p. 27.

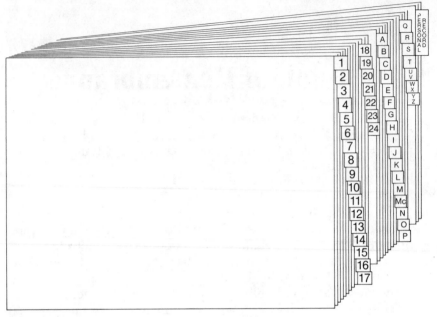

Figure 38.   Book of Remembrance with plastic index tabs.

There are four sets of reference numbers on each pedigree chart that are used for the following purposes (see Figure 39):
1. Numbering individuals (persons)
2. Numbering pedigree charts
3. Extending the pedigree lines
4. Cross-referencing person # 1 on each chart

Numbering Individuals (Persons)

The researcher uses the lines that are prenumbered 1 to 31 to write names of persons in the direct line of ancestry. Person # 1 on any chart can be either male or female. Thereafter, male names (fathers) are recorded on even-numbered lines, and female names (mothers) on odd-numbered lines.

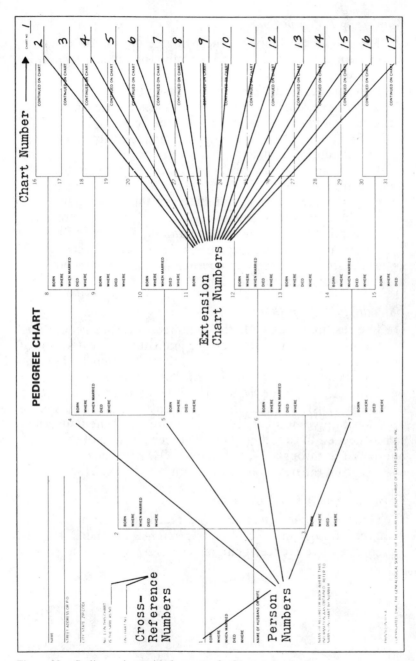

Figure 39. Pedigree chart with four sets of reference numbers.

Numbering Pedigree Charts

The researcher numbers the pedigree charts consecutively rather than using letters of the alphabet or unusual combinations of numbers and letters:

1. Numerical order is easier and faster to use.

2. Pedigree charts with closest ancestry are used most frequently and are filed at the front of the book.

3. The total number of pedigree charts is easily determined by the last numbered chart.

4. Pedigree chart numbers are never any larger than the total number of charts.

Each pedigree chart is numbered in the upper right-hand corner where indicated: "chart no. _____ ." When doing one's own research, the pedigree chart beginning with oneself is chart no. 1. The next 16 pedigree charts are numbered 2 through 17, as in Figure 40. When an additional chart is needed, it is assigned number 18, then 19, 20, 21, etc.

Extending Pedigree Lines

The researcher extends the pedigree to earlier generations by adding extension numbers. He indicates the extension of pedigree chart no. 1 by writing numbers 2 through 17 in the right-hand column where indicated: "above name is continued on chart _____ ." (See Figure 41.) When any chart numbered 2 through 17 is extended, the new extension chart is given the next consecutive number, 18. (See Figure 42.) When an extension is needed for another chart, whether it is one of the charts numbered 2 through 17, or chart no. 18, the new extension chart is given the next consecutive number, 19, 20, 21, etc.

Cross-Referencing Pedigree Charts

The researcher refers to more recent generations on the pedigree through the use of cross-reference numbers. The researcher cross-references pedigree charts by referring to person

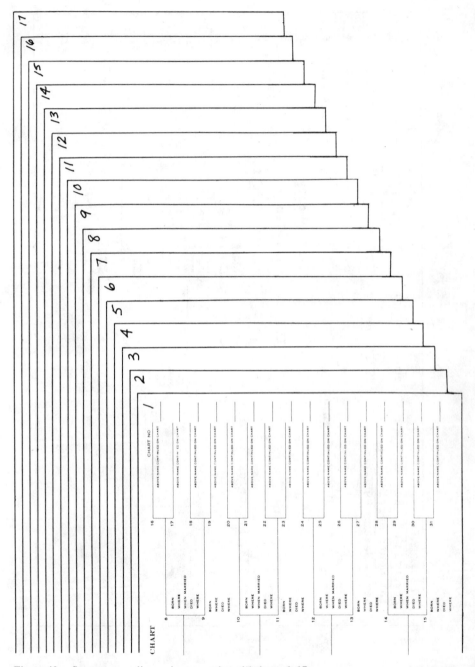

Figure 40.   Seventeen pedigree charts numbered 1 through 17.

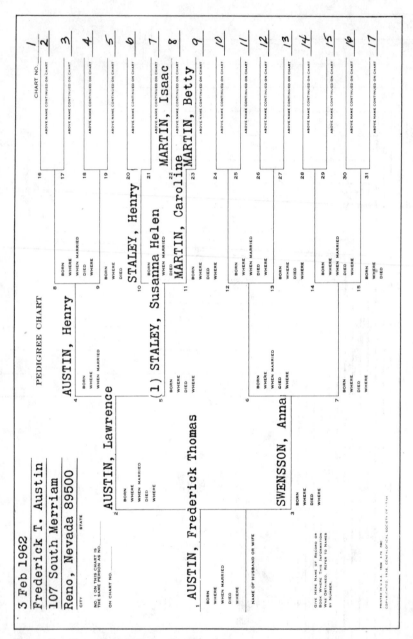

Figure 41.   Extending pedigree chart No. 1.

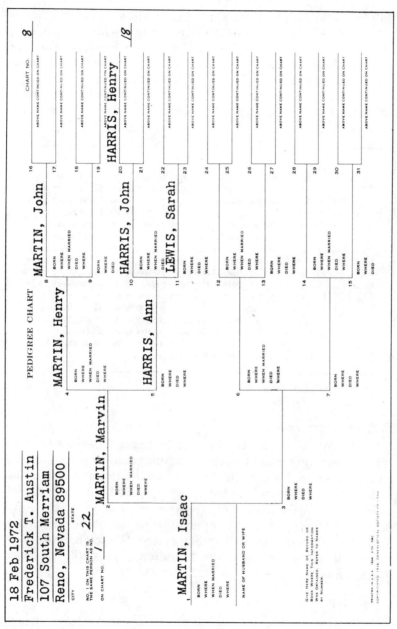

Figure 42.   Extension of pedigree chart No. 1 with cross-reference numbers.

numbers and pedigree chart numbers. When a pedigree line is extended and the fifth-generation name is *repeated* on line # 1 of a new extension chart, the cross-reference information for the new chart is determined and written in the upper left-hand corner where indicated: "no. 1 on this chart is the same person as no. _____ on chart no. _____." (See Figure 42.) The cross-reference numbers for charts numbered 1 through 17 are indicated in Figure 43.

Chart no.   1—not applicable
Chart no.   2—no. 1 on this chart is the same person as no. 16 on chart no. 1.
Chart no.   3—no. 1 on this chart is the same person as no. 17 on chart no. 1.
Chart no.   4—no. 1 on this chart is the same person as no. 18 on chart no. 1.
Chart no.   5—no. 1 on this chart is the same person as no. 19 on chart no. 1.
Chart no.   6—no. 1 on this chart is the same person as no. 20 on chart no. 1.
Chart no.   7—no. 1 on this chart is the same person as no. 21 on chart no. 1.
Chart no.   8—no. 1 on this chart is the same person as no. 22 on chart no. 1.
Chart no.   9—no. 1 on this chart is the same person as no. 23 on chart no. 1.
Chart no. 10—no. 1 on this chart is the same person as no. 24 on chart no. 1.
Chart no. 11—no. 1 on this chart is the same person as no. 25 on chart no. 1.
Chart no. 12—no. 1 on this chart is the same person as no. 26 on chart no. 1.
Chart no. 13—no. 1 on this chart is the same person as no. 27 on chart no. 1.
Chart no. 14—no. 1 on this chart is the same person as no. 28 on chart no. 1.
Chart no. 15—no. 1 on this chart is the same person as no. 29 on chart no. 1.
Chart no. 16—no. 1 on this chart is the same person as no. 30 on chart no. 1.
Chart no. 17—no. 1 on this chart is the same person as no. 31 on chart no. 1.

Figure 43.   Cross-reference for charts 1 through 17.

Pedigree Chart Index

It is impossible to number the pedigree charts so that all charts containing like surnames are numbered consecutively or located together. When the pedigree charts become numerous and it becomes difficult to locate a particular name, a pedigree chart index can be made. This is done by grouping each name or surname in alphabetical order showing the chart number(s) on which the name or surname appears. (See Figure 44.) It is wise to leave space for future additions. The pedigree chart index is filed just before pedigree chart no. 1.

PEDIGREE CHART INDEX

ABERG
  Lena, 1, 11

ABBOTT
  Mary Ann, 1
  Thomas, 8
  William, 1, 8

ALLIBONE
  Charlotte, 1, 9
  Joseph, 9

AIKIN
  Margaret, 22, 40

BARRETT
  Rebecca 3, 30
  Joseph, 30
  Thomas, 30

BELGRAVE
  Thomasin, 28

BELL
  John, 2
  Naomi, 2

BLESSING
  Joanna, 25

BURGESS
  Ruth, 27
  Thomas, 27

CARR
  Ann, 3, 22
  George, 22

CHESHIRE
  Charlotte, 1
  Thomas, 1, 6

DICKEY
  Adam, 2
  John, 2
  Margaret, 2

DOWNS
  Sarah or Mary,
  6,34

DUNCAN
  George, 2, 18
  Gloria, 1
  Homer, 1
  Homer Horace, 1
  John, 1, 2

Figure 44.   Page from a pedigree chart index.

FAMILY GROUP RECORDS

The 8 ½″ x 14″ family group record published by the Genealogical Society provides space for the names of three generations, as the parents of the husband and wife are listed as well as the children of the husband and wife.

The family group records are arranged in alphabetical order by the name of the husband to save time and conform to the filing system used in the Library of the Genealogical Society. (See Chapter 21.) If there is more than one family group record for individuals with the same name, the family group record for the individual with the earliest birth date is filed first. Each family group record is filed behind the guide sheet with the clear plastic tab that has the same letter of the alphabet as the initial of the husband's surname.

PERSONAL RECORD

The 8 ½″ x 14″ personal record published by the Genealogical Society provides space for specific personal information on the left side and space for important personal events on the

PERSONAL RECORD

Field	Date	IMPORTANT EVENTS
		List below and on the reverse side items such as schools attended, vocation and business activities, Church positions, places of residence, special talents and interests, unusual and faith promoting experiences, travel, genealogical and temple work. Church leaders and other outstanding characters you have met, etc.
Name in full: Christopher Lynn Davis		
Father's name: Thomas Edward Davis		
Mother's Maiden name: Mary Ann Coles		
When born (day, month, year): 7 Apr 1926		1926, Apr 7 — Born at LDS Hospital, Salt Lake City, Utah.
Where born (town, county, state): Salt Lake City, Salt Lake, Utah		1926, May 2 — Blessed by Father, First Ward, Liberty Stake.
When blessed (day, month, year): 2 May 1926		1931, Sept — Started Kindergarten Emerson School.
By whom: Thomas Edward Davis		1932, Aug 29 — Mother passed away.
When baptized (day, month, year): 4 Aug 1934		1933, July 22 — Dad married Hazel Atwood.
Where baptized: Salt Lake City, Salt Lake, Utah		1933, Sept — Started 2nd Grade at Hamilton School.
Baptized by: Leonard Erickson		1934, Aug 4 — Baptized by Leonard Erickson.
When confirmed: 5 Aug 1934 By whom: Gerald C. Bloomquist		1934, Aug 5 — Confirmed by Gerald C. Bloomquist.
Priesthood ordinations:		
Office Deacon By whom Walter J. Carr	Date 5 June 1938	1938, June 5 — Ordained a Deacon by Walter J. Carr.
Office Teacher By whom Rufus M. Jackson	Date 20 Apr 1941	1939, Sept — Started as Freshman at Roosevelt Jr. High School.
Office Priest By whom Clayton B. Hales	Date 18 Apr 1943	1940, Sum. — Newspaper carrier for Deseret News.
Office Elder By whom Thomas E. Davis	Date 29 June 1943	1940, Sept — Paid for my bicycle out of my own earnings.
Office Seventy By whom Levi Edgar Young	Date 25 Nov 1946	1940, Sept — Worked as a cashier at Roosevelt for lunch.
Office High Priest By whom John D. Taylor	Date 20 Sep 1964	1941, Apr 20 — Ordained a Teacher by Rufus M. Jackson.
Married to Sharon Lee Woodbury by John A. Widtsoe	Date 12 Sept 1949	1941, Sept — Started as a Junior at South High School.
Where married 12 Sept 1949		1942, Aug — Started work at Cummings Drive-Inn.
Where endowed Salt Lake Temple	Date 3 Sept 1946	1942, Sept — Started as a Senior at West High School.
Where sealed Salt Lake Temple	Date 12 Sept 1949	1942, Fall — Worked for Huntsman Shields making welding shields.
To whom (husband or wife) Sharon Lee Woodbury		1942, Fall — Repairman for Johnson Electric.
Patriarchal blessing by Fred G. Peterson	Date 13 Dec 1942	1943, Apr 18 — Ordained a Priest by Clayton B. Hales.
Departed for mission to Great Britain	Date 25 Nov 1946	1943, May 4 — Enlisted in the United States Naval Reserve.
When returned 25 Dec 1948		1943, June — Graduated from West High School.
Special appointments High Councillor; Bishop		1943, June 29 — Ordained an Elder by Thomas E. Davis.
		1943, July 1 — Active Duty U.S. Navy.
Where died	Date	1944, — Reported for duty at Pre-Midshipman School, Asbury, N.J.
Where buried	Date	1945, — Commissioned Ensign in U.S. Naval Reserve.

Figure 45.   Personal record.

right side. (See Figure 45.) The following list may be helpful for recalling important personal events:

Birth	Illnesses
Description of parents	Accidents
Relatives	Church ordinances
Home training	Religious experiences
Holiday traditions	Church positions
Family entertainment	Mission experiences
Family projects	Military experiences
Childhood memories	Courtship and marriage
Friends	Children
Hobbies	Occupation
School days	Places of residence
Graduations	Community service
Work experiences	Special achievements
Travel	

Before recording personal events on the right side of the personal record, each important one should be recorded on a separate 3" x 5" card.[1] (See Figure 46.)

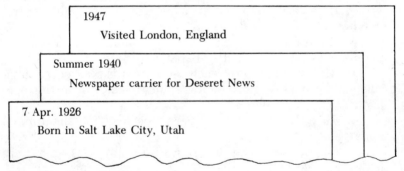

1947

Visited London, England

Summer 1940

Newspaper carrier for Deseret News

7 Apr. 1926

Born in Salt Lake City, Utah

Figure 46.   Note cards for personal events.

The cards are filed in chronological order, and when the notes on the important personal events are complete, the events are recorded on the personal record in chronological order, one event to a line. This sketch of important personal events becomes the outline for a more detailed life story. The personal record and the complete life story are filed behind a guide sheet with a colored plastic tab that has "Personal Record" written on it.

---

[1] J. Grant Stevenson, *A Genealogy Check List*, 9th ed. (Provo, Utah: Stevenson Supply, 1971), p. 19.

6
Note Keeping

A note-keeping system for genealogical research should prevent unnecessary duplication of research and provide easy access to the information on each individual. A system that meets this criteria is based upon 3″ x 5″ file cards and utilizes the following:

1. Card file with guide cards
2. Note cards
3. Research folder

The card system for note keeping also provides the following advantages:

1. It is easily understood by others who may desire to use the information.

2. It is easily adapted to research in any country.

3. It is easily adapted to experienced or beginning researchers.

4. All information on each individual is retrieved immediately as cards are filed alphabetically by surname.

5. All information on each individual is filed chronologically and provides a brief biographical sketch from birth to death.

6. Records searched in each locality are determined easily.

7. Records searched, where no information is found, are determined easily.

8. The information is available exactly as recorded in the record.

9. Information is sorted, analyzed, and refiled easily.

10. All information for each family group is assembled quickly and easily.

11. The genealogical information that provides the proof for each item of information recorded on the family group record is easily available.

12. The source of information is easily determined for compiling references for family group records.

13. New information about family members is easily added to the card file.

14. A separate file can be kept for each country.

15. If a search is made and no information is found, an explanatory note or "nil" is written on the card, and the note card is filed behind the appropriate surname.

16. Notes regarding the condition of the record or other unusual circumstances concerning the record can be recorded on the note cards in brackets [ ].

17. Small newspaper clippings can be trimmed and pasted onto note cards.

18. Information can be photocopied, cut, and pasted onto the note cards.

19. A date stamp can be used to record the date of search.

20. A number stamp can be used to stamp the call number.

21. Relationship can be indicated on the card.

22. It is possible to separate cards for individuals identified as relatives from cards for individuals not yet identified as relatives.

23. Several note cards can be photocopied at the same time.

24. As ideas occur, a note card can be made for each record to search and cards sorted as to library searches and correspondence.

CARD FILE WITH GUIDE CARDS

A card file is divided with guide cards and used to alphabetize and file 3″ x 5″ note cards. It can be a recipe file box, a shoe box, or a commercial file of cardboard or metal. (See Figure 47.)

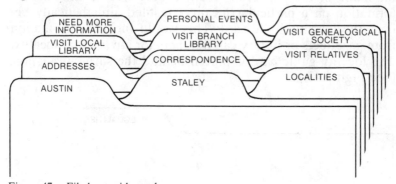

Figure 47.   File box guide cards.

The guide cards represent five main sections:
1. Surname section
2. Locality section
3. Address section
4. Search section
5. Personal event section

Surname Section

The surname of the husband and the maiden surname of the wife are each written on separate guide cards and placed in alphabetical order in the file. (See Figure 48.) Note cards completed as a result of searching genealogical records for specific individuals are filed alphabetically behind the appropriate surname guide card. Note cards for women are filed by their maiden name; their married surname can be added in parentheses.

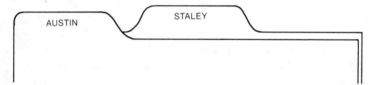

Figure 48.   Surname section guide cards.

Locality Section

The locality section is indicated by one guide card with the word "LOCALITIES" (see Figure 49) or can be subdivided by the name of the particular locality. Note cards containing information on a particular locality are filed alphabetically behind the locality guide card. This would include information from gazetteers or library call numbers for a particular locality. The locality guide card is placed behind the surname section. (See Figure 47.)

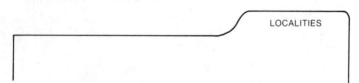

Figure 49.   Locality section guide card.

Address Section

The address section is indicated by one guide card with the word "ADDRESSES" (see Figure 50), or can be subdivided by the type of addresses, such as relatives, agents, research specialists, libraries, etc. The address guide card is placed behind the locality section. (See Figure 47.)

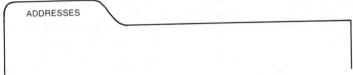

Figure 50.   Address section guide card.

Search Section

The search section is indicated by several guide cards that represent the method of search and/or the location of the records: "CORRESPONDENCE," "VISIT RELATIVES," "VISIT LOCAL LIBRARY," "VISIT BRANCH LIBRARY," "VISIT GENEALOGICAL SOCIETY," and "NEED MORE INFORMATION." (See Figure 51.) Note cards that indicate future searches are filed in this section until the search is made. The search guide cards are placed behind the address section. (See Figure 47.)

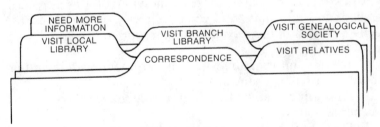

Figure 51.   Search section guide cards.

Personal Event Section

The personal event section is indicated by one guide card with the words "PERSONAL EVENTS." (See Figure 52.) The personal event note cards (see Chapter 5) are filed chronologically in this section. The personal event guide card is placed behind the search section. (See Figure 47.)

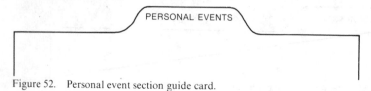

PERSONAL EVENTS

Figure 52.   Personal event section guide card.

NOTE CARDS

Appropriate 3″ x 5″ note cards are made that correspond with the sections in the card file:
1. Surname note cards
2. Locality note cards
3. Address note cards
4. Search note cards
5. Personal event note cards (see Chapter 5)

Surname Note Cards

A separate card is used for each individual for each record searched, and information is copied directly from the record, exactly as found in the record, onto appropriately colored note cards:

1. Yellow—information from a government birth record or a church christening (baptism)

2. Pink—information from a government marriage record or a church marriage

3. Blue—information from a government death record, church burial, or other death record

4. Orange—information from an LDS Church ordinance record

5. White—information from all other records

Space is left in the upper left-hand corner of each card to type or print the name and birth year (complete birth date for a patronymic name) of the individual. A standard spelling of surnames and given names should be established for easier filing and retrieval. The name of the record is written in the upper right-hand corner. The source of information, including the name of the library and library call number, is recorded in the lower left-hand corner.

The surname note cards are filed in alphabetical order behind the appropriate surname guide card in the card file.

The information from a birth record (Figure 53) or christening record (Figure 54) is recorded on a yellow card, which immediately identifies the type of record.

WALKER, Mary Malcolm (1892)   birth

Mary Malcolm Walker, female
    Born: 23 July 1892 at 10 Newcastle Street
    Father: William Walker of 10 Newcastle St., coppersmith
    Mother: Mary Robinson Walker, formerly Malcolm

Informant: William Walker, father
Registered: 25 July 1892

Birth certificate in the District of Castlereagh No. 1,
    Union of Belfast, in the County of Down, Ireland, Cert.
    No. 52.

Figure 53.   Yellow surname note card for a government birth record.

JAUSSI, Peter (1727)   christening

"Pierre, legitimate son of Christophe Jossi and of
Benoite Dousse, his father and mother, Swiss milker,
in this locality, of the Calvanist sect, is born the 30th
June 1727. He was baptized the same day.

Godfather: Pierre Gemeaux
Godmother: Anne-Nicolle Lapiene

Record of Catholic Church, Benestroff, France, rec'd
    from the Minister by correspondence.

Figure 54.   Yellow surname note card for a church christening record.

The information from a marriage record is recorded on a pink card, which immediately identifies the type of record. For direct-line ancestral couples, a card is made for each spouse. (See Figures 55 and 56.)

```
CARLSSON, August (1852)                    marriage

  Carlsson, August, drang, Stora Lunnag, age 24
    married 27 Dec 1876
    Markusdr. Susanna, piga, Kransbro, age 26




  Parish Reg Extracts of Istorp, Alvsborg, Sweden
  GS F 200,780
```

Figure 55.   Pink surname note card for a marriage record.

```
MARKUSDOTTER, Susanna (1850)               marriage

  Carlsson, August, drang, Stora Lunnag, age 24
    married 27 Dec 1876
    Markusdr. Susanna, piga, Kransbro, age 26




  Parish Reg Extracts of Istorp, Alvsborg, Sweden
  GS F 200,780
```

Figure 56.   Pink surname note card for a marriage record.

The information from a death certificate, burial, or other type of death record is recorded on a blue card, which immediately identifies the type of record. (See Figures 57, 58, 59, and 60.)

JAUSSI, Emma (1892)   death

    Emma Jaussi, female;white;single;22 yrs, 1 mo, 24 da
        Died: 23 Mar 1914, LDS Hospital, Salt Lake City, Utah
        Born: 29 Jan 1892, Switzerland
        Father: Christian Jaussi, born Switzerland
        Mother: Mary Wenger, born Switzerland
        Occupation: cook
        Cause of death: A severe burn extending from waist
            to ankles. Also both hands. Burned while cooking
            meal. 33 days duration.
        Undertaker: Jos. Wm. Taylor, City.
        Place of burial: Parris, Idaho
        Date of burial: on arrival, 1914
        Informant: John Jaussi of Parris, Bearlake Co., Idaho
        Date filed: 23 March 1914
Death Cert. No. 432, Utah State Health Department.

Figure 57.   Blue surname note card for a government death record.

JAUSSI, Emma (1892)   obituary

Miss Emma Jaussi died this morning from burns suffered
on February 10 when she was taking fire from the furnace
in the home of Charles C. Crismon, 13 East First North,
where she was employed as a domestic. She was in the
act of putting paper and excelsior from wrapped china into
the fire. There was little hope of her recovery from the
first.

She was born in Switzerland, Jan 29, 1892, and immi-
grated to Idaho in 1901, where her mother and six brothers and sisters live. She came to Salt Lake 10 months
ago. Her body will be prepared here for burial, and will
be taken by her mother to Paris, Idaho where funeral
services will be held.

Deseret News, March 23, 1914, p. 2.

Figure 58.   Blue surname note card for an obituary.

JAUSSI, Emma (1892)   death

    Jansu, Emma, age 22
        b. 29 Jan 1892, Berne, Switzerland
        d. 22 Mar 1914, results of burns

Salt Lake City, Utah 21st Ward, Ensign Stake, LDS
    Church, Form E report of death--GS F 025,748

Figure 59.   Blue surname note card for an LDS Church death record.

```
JAUSSI, Emma (1892)                            tombstone

    Emma Jaussi
       Born 29 Jan 1892
       Died 23 Mar 1914




Cemetery Tombstone in Paris, Idaho
```

Figure 60.   Blue surname note card for a tombstone inscription.

The information from an ordinance record of The Church of Jesus Christ of Latter-day Saints is written on an orange card, which immediately identifies the type of record. (See Figures 61, 62, 63, and 64.)

```
FORSSLING, Lars Fredrik (1803)              baptism

   #10670  Lars Fredrik Forssling born 1803

      Baptized:  19 June 1894
      Proxy:  Knut August Elg--son-in-law




S. L. Temple recs of baptism for the dead
GS F 183, 412
```

Figure 61.   Orange surname note card for an LDS temple baptism record.

```
┌─────────────────────────────────────────────────────────────────────┐
│ FORSSLING, Lars Fredrik (1803)          endowment (TIB)             │
│        PC      TEMPLE      Salt Lake                                  │
│   NO.              NO.  9094      BOOK   B        PAGE   257          │
│                                                                       │
│   NAME  Forsling- Lars Fredric                                        │
│   BORN        10 Aug 1803                                             │
│   WHERE  Sundsvall, Westmanland, Swed.                                │
│   DIED        22 Aug 1862                                             │
│   F.   Lars Forsling (1772)                                           │
│   M.   Marta Stina Roberg                                             │
│   MD.  2 Aug 1836      TO  Magdalena Sundman                          │
│   F.R.  Knut A. Elg                              son il               │
│   BAPT. 19 Jun 1894      PROXY                                        │
│   END.  21 Jun 1894      PROXY                                        │
│   SLD. H.                         TO                                  │
│        W.                         PARENTS                             │
│                                  Corrected from Lars                  │
│                                  Frederick Torsling                   │
└─────────────────────────────────────────────────────────────────────┘
```

Figure 62.   Orange surname note card for an LDS endowment (TIB) record.

```
┌─────────────────────────────────────────────────────────────────────┐
│ FORSSLING, Lars Fredrik (1803)              sealing                  │
│                                             to spouse                 │
│                                                                       │
│   #6965 Lars Frederick Forsling (d)                                   │
│      b. 1803 Sundsvall, Westerman, Sweden                             │
│      d. 22 Mar 1862                                                    │
│                                                                       │
│   Sealed 21 June 1894 to                                              │
│                                                                       │
│   Magdalena Sunman (d)                                                │
│   b. 16 Feb 1804 Sundsvall, Westerman, Sweden                         │
│   d. 4 Dec 1868                                                        │
│                                                                       │
│                                                                       │
│  S. L. Temple recs of sealings of dead couples                        │
│  GS F 184,587                                                         │
└─────────────────────────────────────────────────────────────────────┘
```

Figure 63.   Orange surname note card for an LDS sealing to spouse record.

```
┌─────────────────────────────────────────────────────────────────────┐
│ FORSSLING, Lars Fredrik (1803)              sealing                  │
│                                             to parents                │
│                                                                       │
│    Parents: Lars Forsling                                             │
│             Martha Stina Roberg Forsling                              │
│                                                                       │
│    Children: #3203 Per Olof Forsling                                  │
│              b. 1800 Sundsvall; d. 3 Sep 1809                         │
│              bap. 6-5-1939; endowed 30 Oct 1941                       │
│                                                                       │
│              #3204 Lars Fredric                                       │
│              b. 1803 Sundsvall; d. 22 May 1862                        │
│              bap 20 June 1894; endowed 21 June 1894                   │
│                                                                       │
│    Sealed 5 June 1942                                                 │
│                                                                       │
│                                                                       │
│  S. L. Temple recs of sealings of families                            │
│  GS F 184,722  p. 190                                                 │
└─────────────────────────────────────────────────────────────────────┘
```

Figure 64.   Orange surname note card for a sealing to parents record.

Information from other than a birth, marriage, death, or ordinance record is written on a white card, as illustrated in
Figures 65 and 66.

```
DOUD,  Jeremiah Osborne (1820)                    1860 census
                                              Albion, Jackson
                                                    Wisconsin

   167-138 Dowd,  Osborne    40 cooper  Penn
              "      Jermiah    13        Penn
              "      Olive        8        Penn




   Correspondence with Wisconsin State Historical Society
```

Figure 65. White surname note card for a census record.

```
DOUD,  Olive Jane (1852)                          1860 census
                                              Albion, Jackson
                                                    Wisconsin

   167-138 Dowd,  Osborne    40 cooper  Penn
              "      Jermiah    13        Penn
              "      Olive        8        Penn




   Correspondence with Wisconsin State Historical Society
```

Figure 66.   White surname note card for a census record.

Locality Note Cards

Information from gazetteers and call numbers for locality
records are written on white cards and filed in alphabetical
order in the locality section of the card file. Figures 67, 68, 69
and 70 are examples of information recorded on locality note
cards.

```
New York, Warren County

    Formed in 1813 from Washington County
    Washington County formed in 1772 from Albany County
    Albany County formed in 1683, original county

    County seat:  Lake George




Everton's Handy Book for Genealogists
```

Figure 67.   White locality note card for Warren County, New York.

```
Sweden, Örebro, Kvistbro

    Clerical survey    1800-1815  GS F 149,474
         "      "      1816-1830  GS F 149,475
         "      "      1831-1840  GS F 149,476
         "      "      1841-1845  GS F 202,879
         "      "      1846-1850  GS F 202,880
         "      "      1851-1855  GS F 424,177
         "      "      1856-1860  GS F 424,178
         "      "      1861-1865  GS F 424,179
         "      "      1866-1870  GS F 424,180
       " "      "      1871-1875  GS F 424,181
         "      "      1876-1880  GS F 424,182
         "      "      1881-1885  GS F 424,183
         "      "      1886-1890  GS F 424,184
         "      "      1891-1895  GS F 424,185
```

Figure 68.   White locality note card for Kvistbro, Sweden.

```
England, Hampshire (Southampton), Romsey

    Market town and parish
    Parish registers began 1569
    8 miles NW Southampton
    Population--5,432
    Separate jurisdiction
    Archdeaconry and Diocese of Winchester

    Nonconformist churches:  Baptist
                             Independent
                             Wesleyan Methodist
                             Sandemainians


Smith's Genealogical Gazetteer of England
GS Ref 942, E5g
```

Figure 69.   White locality note card for Romsey, England.

```
Denmark, Randers, Rosmus Parish

Rosmus Parish surrounded by parishes:
   Hyllested
   Tirstrup
   Lyngby
   Hoed




Genealogical Guidebook and Atlas of Denmark
GS Ref 948. 9, E6s
```

Figure 70.   White locality note card for Rosmus, Denmark.

Address Note Cards

Addresses of relatives, record searchers, libraries, etc., are recorded on white cards. The cards are filed in the address section of the file in alphabetical order by name of individual or by locality. Figure 71 illustrates an address note card.

```
HENINGER, Oscar
   8426 Longhurst Lane
   Houston, Texas

      Son of Uncle John Heninger.  Oscar is willing to
      search records of the area for the family.
```

Figure 71.   White address note card.

Search Note Cards

Note cards of the appropriate color are made in advance and filed in the search section of the file box until the search is completed. (See Figures 72 and 73.)

```
┌─────────────────────────────────────────────────────────────┐
│  BILLING, Carl Gustaf (1811)                      death       │
│                                                               │
│    died 16 Sep 1871                                           │
│                                                               │
│                                                               │
│                                                               │
│                                                               │
│                                                               │
│                                                               │
│                                                               │
│                                                               │
│  Check 1871 Vital Recs Extracts of Sundsvall, Västernorr-     │
│    land, Sweden--GS F 201,331                                 │
└─────────────────────────────────────────────────────────────┘
```

Figure 72.   Blue search note card.

```
┌─────────────────────────────────────────────────────────────┐
│  TREPASS, James (1833)                          marriage      │
│                                                               │
│    Married Mary about 1858                                    │
│    Search 1855-1859 in Warwickshire                           │
│                                                               │
│                                                               │
│                                                               │
│                                                               │
│                                                               │
│                                                               │
│                                                               │
│  Correspond with Registrar General, Somerset, England         │
└─────────────────────────────────────────────────────────────┘
```

Figure 73.   Pink search note card.

RESEARCH FOLDER

The research folder is a manila-type folder in which the following items are placed:

1. Copy of the objective family group record. (See Chapter 1.)

2. Copy of the corresponding pedigree chart. (See Chapter 1.)

3. Correspondence. (See Chapter 7.)

4. Maps. (See Chapter 10.)

5. Certificates of vital registration. (See Chapter 16.)

6. Copies of the objective family group record and pedigree chart from the Genealogical Society collection. (See Chapter 21.)

7
Correspondence

Correspondence as a genealogical research tool makes records available to those who choose not to travel to the record repository, thereby saving travel time and expense.

The genealogical researcher must determine which records to search, where these records are available, and the most efficient means for searching the records, either in person, by correspondence with the record repository, or by correspondence with an agent who will visit the record respository on behalf of the researcher.

SUGGESTIONS FOR CORRESPONDENCE

Suggestions for genealogical correspondence are essentially the same as for all correspondence:

1. Type or write legibly in black ink.
2. Use good quality paper and envelopes.
3. Make the request brief.
4. Limit the initial request to one item.
5. Enclose a stamped, self-addressed envelope or enclose sufficient money for postage.
6. Provide specific names, places, dates, and relationships.
7. Use the official title when writing to public officials, not the name of the public official; officers change and the letter may be forwarded to the individual.
8. When it is not possible to determine the exact address, a general address is acceptable:

> Local Library
> City or Town, State

> Minister, Name of church or denomination
> Town or City, State or Country

> National Archives
> Capital, Country

9. Request that the letter be referred to the proper authority if the individual receiving the letter does not have authority for the desired record.

10. Personal checks are not recommended. Enclose an American Express Money Order (from local businesses) for $2 as a deposit for each search or certificate, and return postage. Offer to pay any balance due; overpayment will be refunded.

11. Do not request a reply in English from individuals in foreign countries. If the official is familiar with English, he will reply in English. If the reply is in a foreign language, a translation by a research specialist or someone familiar with the language is more accurate than a letter or certificate written in incorrect English.

12. Make a notation of letter sent, money enclosed, addressee, etc., on the appropriate note card.

13. Make a carbon of each letter sent and file in the research folder until the reply is received.

14. Record information from the reply on the appropriate note card.

SAMPLE LETTERS

The following sample letters (Figures 74 through 97) may be used to obtain information by correspondence. The letters are included in this chapter as a convenience to the researcher. At the bottom of each letter, reference is made to the chapter in which the particular information is discussed.

Your Name
Your Address
Current Date

The Genealogical Society
50 East North Temple Street
Salt Lake City, Utah 84150

Gentlemen:

 Would you please send me the name and address of
the branch library nearest to my residence?

 Enclosed is a stamped self-addressed envelope for
your convenience.

 Thank you.

Sincerely yours,

Your Name (signed)

Encl: Stamped self-addressed envelope

Figure 74.   Letter to the Genealogical Society. (See Chapter 9.)

Your Name
Your Address
Current Date

The Genealogical Society
50 East North Temple Street
Salt Lake City, Utah 84150

Gentlemen:

Could you please tell me if the research account for
Margaret S. Olsen, Gunnison, Utah is in your files or if it
is available on microfilm?

Margaret S. Olsen is my grandmother, and she hired
the Research Department to do genealogical research on
our family lines in Denmark. The initials of the researcher
are LMT.

Enclosed is a note from my grandmother giving permission for me to obtain the original research file. If you
have the original file, please mail it to me. I will be happy
to pay for any expenses incurred through this request.

Thank you.

Sincerely yours,

Your Name (signed)

Encl: Note of permission

Figure 75.   Letter to the Genealogical Society. (See Chapter 9.)

Your Name
Your Address
Current Date

The Genealogical Society
50 East North Temple Street
Salt Lake City, Utah 84150

Gentlemen:

     Would you please send me the names and addresses
of the accredited researchers for the states of New York
and Pennsylvania?

     Enclosed is a stamped self-addressed envelope for
your convenience.

     Thank you.

Sincerely yours,

Your Name (signed)

Encl: Stamped self-addressed envelope

Figure 76.   Letter to the Genealogical Society. (See Chapter 9.)

Your Name
Your Address
Current Date

The Genealogical Society
50 East North Temple Street
Salt Lake City, Utah 84150

Gentlemen:

I am doing some genealogical research in Australia,
and would appreciate it if you could provide me with the
correct genealogical jurisdictions for Hungerford.

Could you also recommend a good gazetteer and map
to use for research in Australia?

I will be very grateful for any information you can
send to me, and I am enclosing a stamped self-addressed
envelope for your reply.

Thank you.

Sincerely yours,

Your Name (signed)

Encl: Stamped self-addressed envelope

Figure 77.   Letter to the Genealogical Society. (See Chapter 10.)

                                        Your Name
                                        Your Address
                                        Current Date

National Tourist Council
Antwerp, Belgium

Gentlemen:

        Would you please send me a copy of a road map for
Belgium?

        Enclosed is an American Express Money Order for
$2.00 to cover the cost of the map. I will be happy to send
more if necessary.

        Thank you.

                                Sincerely yours,

                                Your Name (signed)

Encl: $2.00

Figure 78.   Letter to a national tourist council. (See Chapter 10.)

                                        Your Name
                                        Your Address
                                        Current Date

Librarian
State Historical Library
Capital, State

Dear Sir:

    Family information indicates that my great grand-
father lived in Pine Creek, (State) in 1848. Could you please
tell me in which county Pine Creek was located at that time?

    I will be happy to pay for this service. Enclosed is a
stamped self-addressed envelope.

    Thank you.

                                        Sincerely yours,

                                        Your Name (signed)

Encl: Stamped self-addressed envelope

Figure 79.   Letter to a state historical library. (See Chapter 10.)

Your Name
Your Address
Current Date

State Department of Highways
State Capital, State

Gentlemen:

    Would you please send me a copy of a highway map
for the county of Saratoga? I am particularly interested
in a map which also shows cemeteries, schools, township
boundaries, and railroads.

    Enclosed is an American Express Money Order for
$2.00 to cover the cost of the map. I will be happy to send
more if necessary.

    Thank you.

Sincerely,

Your Name (signed)

Encl: $2.00

Figure 80.   Letter to a state department of highways. (See Chapter 10.)

GERALD ALDER FAMILY ORGANIZATION

For Descendants of Gerald Alder and Anna Sorenson

May, 1972

Dear Relative,

Several of the descendants of Gerald Alder are interested in forming a family organization and in compiling a
family history. To insure that information about you and
your family will be in this history, and also that it will be
complete and accurate, please complete the enclosed form
and return it within ten days in the enclosed stamped self-
addressed envelope.

Many family members have contributed towards the
family history, and their help certainly has been appreciated.
Aunt Martha Hixon and Uncle Dan Alder have spent many
years doing genealogical research on the Alder line and
deserve many thanks for their efforts.

Please come to the reunion at Lakeside Park on
Saturday, August 24, at 12:00 noon. Bring the entire family
and your own picnic lunch. At 2:00 p.m. a business meeting
will be held to bring you up to date on the genealogical
research and to present plans for further organizing the
family.

It is suggested that the annual family dues be $5.00
per married couple, payable at the reunion, or $6.50 if
paid at a later date. Those who pay dues this year will
receive a printed family group record for Gerald Alder and
his wife, Anna Sorenson.

Sincerely yours,

Henry S. Alder

Encls: Family group with questionnaire
        Stamped self-addressed envelope

Figure 81.   Letter to a relative for a family organization. (See Chapter 11.)

```
                                          Your Name
                                          Your Address
                                          Current Date




        Name of Agent
        Address of Agent

        Dear Sir:

              Thank you for your willingness to act as my agent in
        searching the records at the county courthouse in your town.
        Would you please search the marriage records from 1862
        to 1872 for the following marriages:

                    John H. Palmer to Anna Miller
                    Amos B. Richardson to Emily Stout

              I would like to have the information copied exactly as it is
        in the record or obtain a photocopy of the record.  Enclosed
        is an American Express Money Order for $5.00 as a deposit
        for this search and for copies of any information found.

              Thank you.

                                          Sincerely yours,




                                          Your Name (signed)


        Encl: $5.00
```

Figure 82.   Letter to a genealogical research agent. (See Chapter 13.)

Name of Agent
Address of Agent
Current date

Name of Patron
Address of Patron

Dear Sir:

    I have searched the marriage records at the local
courthouse for the years 1862 to 1875 for the marriage of
John Palmer to Anna Miller and the marriage of Amos B.
Richardson to Emily Stout.   The following is the only
information I could find:

      Married on 12 July 1867, John Palmer to
    Mrs. Anna Miller, widow. His age, 42; her age,
    37; both residents of Jackson County and the town
    of Albion. Minister, Rev. John R. Richards.
    Witnesses, Samuel H. Miller and George A.
    Richardson. License applied for 2 July 1867.

    The search required one hour of time, and the $5.00
deposit will be sufficient payment. If there are other
searches you would like in the courthouse or in local
cemeteries, I would be happy to do this for you.

                Sincerely yours,

                Name of Agent (signed)

Figure 83.   Letter from a genealogical research agent to a patron. (See Chapter 13.)

Your Name
Your Address
Current Date

Name of Accredited Researcher
Address of Accredited Researcher

Dear Sir:

You have been recommended as being qualified to
teach genealogical research procedures of Switzerland.
There are several of us with Swiss ancestry who are
desirous of taking a class in Swiss research. Would you
be willing to teach such a class, and if so, could you furnish
us the following information:

1. Minimum or maximum number of students.
2. Fee, including travel expense.
3. Number of weeks required for class.
4. Day of week and time for class.

We look forward to hearing from you. Enclosed is a
stamped self-addressed envelope for your convenience.

Thank you.

Sincerely yours,

Your Name (signed)

Encl: Stamped self-addressed envelope

Figure 84. Letter to a genealogical research specialist. (See Chapter 13.)

Your Name
Your Address
Current Date

Mrs. Molly Jones
225 South Meriam
Bronson, Indiana 46100

Dear Aunt Molly,

I am gathering information on our Coombs line of ancestry and am wondering if you have Great Grandfather Coombs' old family Bible. Mother remembers seeing some births, marriages, and deaths recorded in it; but, she doesn't remember where she saw it or whose names were recorded.

If you do not have it, can you tell me who has it?

I am compiling a family history which will eventually be made available to members of the family. Any information you can give me will be appreciated.

I am enclosing a stamped self-addressed envelope for your reply.

Thank you.

Sincerely yours,

Your Name (signed)

Encl: Stamped self-addressed envelope

Figure 85. Letter to a relative. (See Chapter 14.)

Your Name
Your Address
Current Date

Newspaper Office
Town, State or Country

Gentlemen:

I am compiling a family history of my relatives who
settled in your town. I would like to contact descendants,
relatives, or other persons who have any information about
my second great grandfather and his family:

Cyrus P. Coombs
Had two brothers: Samuel and Levi
Married Elizabeth
Lived about thirty years in Bellevue
Died in Bellevue about 1849
Had the following children: Cyrus, Thomas
John, Eliza, and Charlotte

If you would print this request for information in
your newspaper, it will be appreciated. I will be happy
to pay for this service.

Thank you.

Sincerely yours,

Your Name (signed)

Figure 86.   Letter to a newspaper office. (See Chapter 14.)

Your Name
Your Address
Current Date

Postmaster
Town, State or Country

Dear Sir:

   I am compiling a family history of my relatives who
settled in your town. I would like to contact descendants
or other relatives of my second great grandfather, Cyrus
P. Coombs.

   Would you be so kind as to refer this letter to anyone
with the surname of Coombs or anyone whom you know to
be a relative of the Coombs family?

   Enclosed is a stamped self-addressed envelope for
their convenience.

   Thank you.

                                        Sincerely yours,

                                        Your Name (signed)

Encl: Stamped self-addressed envelope

Figure 87.   Letter to a postmaster. (See Chapter 14.)

Your Name
Your Address
Current Date

Local Library
Town, State or Country

Gentlemen:

    Would you please search your index for [insert the
name of the applicable record: biographies, family histories,
locality histories, or obituaries] and if you find information
about Jonathan Bates, would you please send me a copy of the
information found? Jonathan Bates was born in 1810 in Pennsylvania and died 4 August 1882 in your town.

    If you do not provide these services in your library,
could you refer someone to me who would make the searches.
I will be happy to pay for the information.

    I am looking forward to hearing from you and am en-
closing a stamped self-addressed envelope for your convenience. Any information you can send to me will be very
much appreciated.

    Thank you.

Sincerely yours,

Your Name (signed)

Encl: Stamped self-addressed envelope

Figure 88.   Letter to a local library. (See Chapter 15.)

Your Name
Your Address
Current Date

Newspaper Office
Town, State or Country

Gentlemen:

Would you please search your newspaper obituaries
for information about my grandfather:

Louis William Johnson, died 10 February,
1925, in your city.

I understand he was very well known in the community
and lived most of his life there.

I would be most grateful for any information which
you could send to me, and would be happy to pay you for
your services. A stamped self-addressed envelope is
enclosed for your convenience.

Thank you.

Sincerely yours,

Your Name (signed)

Encl: Stamped self-addressed envelope

Figure 89.   Letter to a newspaper office. (See Chapter 15.)

Your Name
Your Address
Current Date

County Clerk
County Courthouse
County Seat, State

Dear Sir:

Would you please search your marriage indexes from
1882 to 1902 for the marriage of Jacob Mulford Lott and
Olive Jane Doud? If this record is found, I would appreciate
a photocopy of the record or an exact typewritten or handwritten copy of the information.

Enclosed is an American Express Money Order for
$2.00 to cover the cost of the search and the copy of the
record. I will be happy to send more if necessary.

Thank you.

Sincerely yours,

Your Name (signed)

Encl: $2.00

Figure 90. Letter to a county clerk. (See Chapter 16.)

Your Name
Your Address
Current Date

Office of the Mayor
Town, Country

Dear Sir:

 Would you please search your birth records from 1795 to 1799 for the following:

  Birth of Hans Peter Jaussi, August 1796 in your town; parents, Peter Jaussi and Benedicta Dousse.

 If this information is found, I would appreciate receiving an exact copy of the entry. If you do not have this information in your possession, would you please refer this letter to the proper record custodian?

 Enclosed is an American Express Money Order for $2.00 to cover the cost of the search, copy of the information found, and return postage by air mail. I will be happy to pay any balance due.

 Thank you.

Sincerely yours,

Your Name (signed)

Encl: $2.00

Figure 91. Letter to a foreign government official. (See Chapter 16.)

Your Name
Your Address
Current Date

National Archives
Capital City
Country

Gentlemen:

     Could you please tell me on which date your government began registration of births, marriages, and deaths, and the address to which I would write to request the birth, marriage, and death information?

     I am looking forward to hearing from you and am enclosing a stamped self-addressed envelope for your convenience.

     Thank you.

Sincerely yours,

Your Name (signed)

Encl: Stamped self-addressed envelope

Figure 92.   Letter to a national archives.

Your Name
Your Address
Current Date

Minister
Name of Church
Town, State or Country

Reverend and Dear Sir:

Would you please be so kind as to search your church
records from 1850 to 1854 for the christening of Henry John
Lott, son of Jacob S. Lott and Eliza Lowers? If the information is found, I would appreciate an exact copy of the entry.

If you do not have this information in your possession,
would you please refer this letter to the proper record
custodian?

Enclosed is an American Express Money Order for
$2.00 as a deposit for this search. I will be happy to send
any balance due.

Thank you.

Sincerely yours,

Your Name (signed)

Encl: $2.00

Figure 93.   Letter to a minister. (See Chapter 16.)

Your Name
Your Address
Current Date

Name of Accredited Researcher
Address of Accredited Researcher

Dear Sir:

Enclosed is a family group record. Please search
the Temple Records Index Bureau for TIB cards pertaining
to individuals on the family group record.

Enclosed is an American Express Money Order for
$5.00 as a deposit for this research.

Thank you.

Sincerely yours,

Your Name (signed)

Encls: 1 family group record
        $5.00

Figure 94.   Letter to an accredited researcher. (See Chapter 18.)

Your Name
Your Address
Current Date

Name of Accredited Researcher
Address of Accredited Researcher

Dear Sir:

    Enclosed is a family group record with photocopies of
some Temple Records Index Bureau (TIB) cards. Please
search the Computer File Index (CFI) for the names of the
parents and children listed on the family group record:

    Parents:
        Harry Martin born 1822 in Ohio--individual ordinances
        Jane Evans born 1832 in Penn.--individual ordinances
        Harry Martin and Jane Evans married 1850 in Ohio--
           marriage ordinance

    Children:
        Henry Martin born 1851 in Ohio--individual ordinances
        Margaret Martin born 1854 in Ohio--individual
           ordinances
        Esther Martin born 1856 in Ohio--individual ordinances
        Martha Martin born 1859 in Ohio--individual ordinances

    Enclosed is an American Express Money Order for
$5.00 as a deposit for this research.

    Thank you.

Sincerely yours,

Your Name (signed)

Encls: 1 family group record
        TIB cards
        $5.00

Figure 95.   Letter to an accredited researcher. (See Chapter 20.)

Your Name
Your Address
Current Date

Name of Accredited Researcher
Address of Accredited Researcher

Dear Sir:

     Enclosed is a family group record with photocopies of
some Temple Records Index Bureau (TIB) cards and some
extracts from the Computer File Index (CFI). Please search
the family group record sections at the Genealogical Society
for copies of the enclosed family group record and send me
a photocopy of each one found:

        Main Records Section Family Group Records
        Section #1, Patrons Family Group Records
        Section #2, Patrons Family Group Records

     Please search the pedigree chart sections at the Genea-
logical Society for the name of the husband listed on the
enclosed family group record and send me a photocopy of
each pedigree chart found:

        Card Indexed Pedigree Charts
        Section #1, Alphabetized Pedigree Charts
        Section #2, Alphabetized Pedigree Charts

     Enclosed is an American Express Money Order for
$5.00 as a deposit for this research.

     Thank you.

Sincerely yours,

Your Name (signed)

Encls: 1 family group record
       TIB cards
       CFI extracts
       $5.00

Figure 96.   Letter to an accredited researcher. (See Chapter 21.)

Your Name
Your Address
Current Date

Name of Accredited Researcher
Address of Accredited Researcher

Dear Sir:

Enclosed is a family group record with photocopies
of some Temple Records Index Bureau (TIB) cards and
some extracts from the Computer File Index (CFI). Please
search the following restricted sealing record for me:

The Manti Temple, sealings of living couples,
1892 to 1900, for the sealing of Andrew Phillips
and Barbara Martin.

I am a direct descendant of this couple, and I would
appreciate receiving an exact copy of the entry. Enclosed
is an American Express Money Order for $5.00 as a
deposit for this research.

Thank you.

Sincerely yours,

Your Name (signed)

Encl: 1 family group record
TIB cards
CFI extracts
$5.00

Figure 97.   Letter to an accredited researcher. (See Chapter 22.)

8
Libraries

Libraries, as repositories of source material, are aids to the genealogical researcher, who must be selective and determine the records to search prior to visiting the library. Libraries, including genealogical libraries, contain many records compiled from secondary sources or records that are of little value to the genealogical researcher. He must learn to sort out the library material of value and ignore the material that does not apply to the specific genealogical problem. He is most interested in locating records about a specific person or family, or records about a specific locality. In order to accomplish this he must understand the following:

1. Library call numbers
2. The library card catalog
3. Special library services

CALL NUMBERS

As books are acquired, they are assigned an identification number, which is written on the "spine" (back edge) of the book and which is known as the library call number. Call numbers are composed of two parts: (1) the Dewey classification number and the (2) Cutter number. The Dewey number indicates the subject of the book, and the Cutter number indicates the author of the book. See Figure 98 for an example of a complete call number on the spine of a book.

Books are shelved in the library stacks (shelves) in numerical order by call number, and one must have the complete call number to find the desired book. Books on similar subjects are assigned similar call numbers so that books on similar subjects are shelved together. Call numbers for the same book may be different in different libraries.

There may be symbols above or in front of the call number that indicate a special location in the library and/or the type of record:

1. Ref—indicates the book will be found in the reference section.

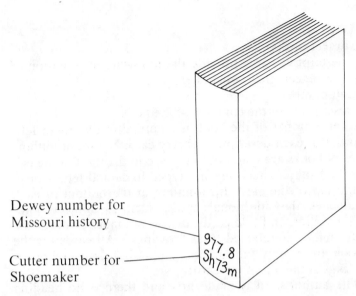

Dewey number for
Missouri history

Cutter number for
Shoemaker

Figure 98.   Call number on the spine of a book.

2. Reg—indicates call numbers will be found in a book called a register, usually located in the reference section.

3. Map—indicates the geographic reference will be found with the map collection.

4. Q—indicates an oversized book (*quarto*); usually shelved at the end of the regular stacks.

5. Micro or film—indicates a microfilm/microfiche and may be located in a special microforms area.

6. Leaf—indicates one piece of paper printed on only one side.

There may be other symbols peculiar to a particular library. If there is doubt concerning symbols in the call number, the librarian should be consulted.

CARD CATALOG

The card catalog is a file cabinet(s) with descriptive cards filed alphabetically by the first line of information, and is an index to the holdings of the library. One or more descriptive cards are made for each book:

1. Author card
2. Co-author or joint author cards where applicable

3. Title card

4. Subject card(s)

The descriptive cards provide the following information of value to the genealogical researcher:

1. Call number

2. Description of the contents of the book

The call number of the book is recorded in the upper left-hand corner of each descriptive library card. Names of authors and titles of books are typed in lowercase to the right of the call number, and subject headings are typed in capital letters or in red at the top of the card. Information at the bottom of each card indicates the additional cards, such as subject, joint author, co-author, and title cards, that were made for the book. This information is referred to as "tracings." All cards for the same book are exactly the same as the author card except for the headings at the top of the card:

1. The author card is made first and there is no heading added.

2. The heading added to the joint author or co-author card is the name of the joint or co-author.

3. The heading added to the title card is the title of the book.

4. The heading added to a subject card is the subject of the book.

Figures 99, 100, 101, 102, and 103 are illustrations of descriptive library catalog cards for the book *Missouri, Day by Day* by Floyd Calvin Shoemaker.

977.8
Sh73m   Shoemaker, Floyd Calvin, 1886
              Missouri, day by day. State Historical
          Society of Missouri, 1942-43.

              1. Missouri-History. 2. Missouri-
          Biography. I. Missouri State Historical
          Society. II. Title.

Figure 99.   Author card.

```
          Missouri State Historical Society
977. 8
Sh73m     Shoemaker, Floyd Calvin, 1886
               Missouri, day by day.  State Historical
          Society of Missouri, 1942-43.




               1. Missouri-History.  2. Missouri-
          Biography.  I. Missouri State Historical
          Society.  II. Title.
```

Figure 100.   Joint-author card.

```
          Missouri, day by day
977. 8
Sh73m     Shoemaker, Floyd Calvin, 1886
               Missouri, day by day.  State Historical
          Society of Missouri, 1942-43.



               1. Missouri-History.  2. Missouri-
          Biography.  I. Missouri State Historical
          Society.  II. Title.
```

Figure 101.   Title card.

```
          MISSOURI-HISTORY
977. 8
Sh73m     Shoemaker, Floyd Calvin, 1886
               Missouri, day by day.  State Historical
          Society of Missouri, 1942-43.



               1. Missouri-History.  2. Missouri-
          Biography.  I. Missouri State Historical
          Society.  II. Title.
```

Figure 102.   Subject card.

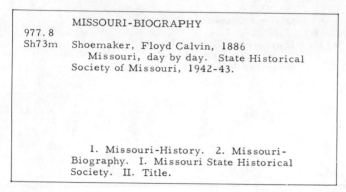

Figure 103.   Subject card.

Cards are filed alphabetically in the card catalog by the first line of information (author, title, or subject). The filing arrangement is usually word by word rather than letter by letter. For this reason, the card catalog is referred to as a dictionary-type card catalog. Compare the differences in the two filing arrangements in Figure 104.

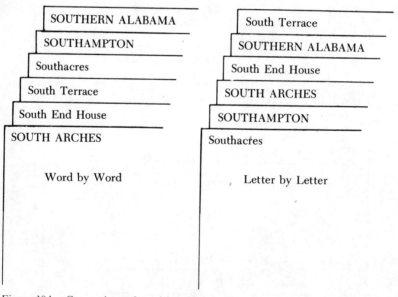

Figure 104.   Comparison of word-by-word and letter-by-letter filing.

Subject headings are standardized, and the same subject headings are generally used in all libraries. Standard subject headings may be further subdivided by placing a locality name after the subject. (See Figure 105.)

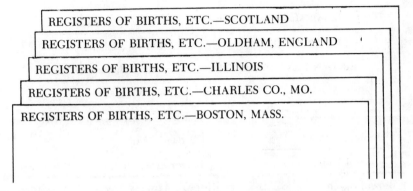

REGISTERS OF BIRTHS, ETC.—SCOTLAND

REGISTERS OF BIRTHS, ETC.—OLDHAM, ENGLAND

REGISTERS OF BIRTHS, ETC.—ILLINOIS

REGISTERS OF BIRTHS, ETC.—CHARLES CO., MO.

REGISTERS OF BIRTHS, ETC.—BOSTON, MASS.

Figure 105.   Standard subject heading subdivided by locality.

A locality is considered a subject and could be a town, parish, county, region, state, or country. Localities may be further subdivided by placing a standard subject heading after the name of the locality, as in Figure 106.

OHIO—MAPS

OHIO—HISTORY

OHIO—GENEALOGY

OHIO—GAZETTEERS

OHIO—DESCRIPTION AND TRAVEL—GAZETTEERS

OHIO—CENSUS

OHIO—BIOGRAPHY

Figure 106.   Locality subject heading subdivided by subject.

Cards that refer to individuals are filed before cards that refer to the surname as a subject. For example, all cards for individuals with the surname "Brown" are filed before the cards for "BROWN FAMILY HISTORY." (See Figure 107.)

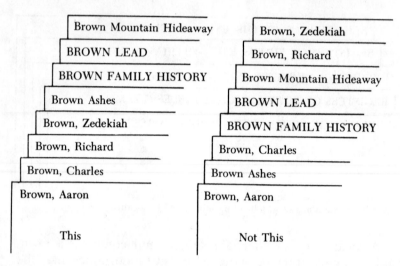

Figure 107. Individuals-before-subjects filing.

Cross-reference cards are used to refer library patrons from a subject that is not standard to a subject that is standard. These are referred to as "See" cards. (See Figures 108 and 109.)

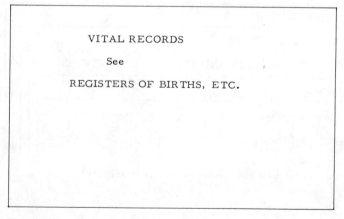

Figure 108. "See" card for vital records.

ATLASES, AMERICAN

See

ATLASES

Figure 109.   "See" card for atlases, American.

Cross-reference cards are made to refer library patrons
from one standard subject to another standard subject that
could give additional information. These are referred to as
"See also" cards. (See Figures 110 and 111.)

REGISTERS OF BIRTHS, ETC.

See also

OBITUARIES-INDEXES
VITAL STATISTICS
WILLS

Figure 110.   "See also" card for registers of births, etc.

```
ATLASES

See also

BIBLE-GEOGRAPHY
also subdivision MAPS under name of countries,
cities, etc., e.g.
GERMANY-MAPS
NEW YORK (CITY)-MAPS
```

Figure 111.   "See also" card for atlases.

SPECIAL SERVICES

There are different departments and services in libraries, depending upon their size and type. The following departments and special services are of benefit to the genealogical researcher:

1. Reading room
2. Circulation or loan department
3. Reference department
4. Microforms area
5. Map collection
6. Inter-library loan
7. Surname index
8. Special collections
9. Copying service
10. Correspondence

Reading Room

Each library has a reading room equipped with desks or tables for study purposes.

Circulation or Loan Department

In this department, one may check out books and learn the regulations governing the library. If the library has open stacks, the borrower finds the book he wants and checks it out at the loan desk. If it has closed stacks, the borrower presents a call slip properly filled out, and an attendant finds the book. Some libraries do not allow their books to circulate (be checked out), in which case there is no circulation or loan department.

Reference Department

Books that are consulted frequently for technical information are not allowed to circulate and are arranged in one central location, called the reference room, reference library, or reference shelves. Any book may be used as a reference book, but more specifically the term refers to encyclopedias, dictionaries, directories, gazetteers, bibliographies, indexes, almanacs, etc.

Microforms Area

Microfilm is a photographic reproduction of documents, printed pages, etc., that have been reduced in size through photographic means and printed on rolls of film. Microfiche is also a photographic reproduction of documents, printed pages, etc., that have been reduced in size, but printed on 4″ x 6″ cards. Both microfilm and microfiche can be enlarged and viewed on special reading machines.

Microfilm and microfiche are used to conserve space and to reproduce old, worn, or rare publications for more general use. In many libraries a special room is devoted to microforms storage and microfilm reading machines. There is no standard for the order in which the books or records appear on a roll of microfilm. More than one book or record may be reproduced on the same roll of film, or several rolls of film may be required to film one record.

In the microfilming process, it is possible that pages may be omitted, and sometimes these pages or cards that are out of place are filmed at the end of the roll of microfilm. For records that are kept current, particularly indexes, one should be aware of the microfilming date.

It requires practice to read microfilms. The researcher will find that if he focuses his eyes on one particular spot on the screen while turning the reel, he will not become dizzy. If the reproduction is small or of poor quality, a magnifying glass may be helpful, or one could consider searching the original record.

Map Collection

The map collection includes single maps, bound atlases, and gazetteers. These are often organized in a special location in the library because of their various sizes. A separate card catalog and technical assistance may be available.

Inter-Library Loan

The inter-library loan consists of borrowing library materials from one library for the use of patrons of another library. Attendants at the circulation desk can inform one if such service is available.

Surname Index

Some libraries, particularly genealogical libraries and historical societies, have a surname index that contains cards about individuals listed in periodicals, histories, biographies, newspapers. This is information that is not located easily through the card catalog. Libraries that have a surname index usually offer a search of this file through correspondence.

Indexes have the following advantages:

1. The alphabetical arrangement saves time because it is not necessary to search the entire record page by page.

2. An index makes reference to the original source, which should be searched since it may contain additional information.

Indexes have the following limitations:

1. There may be copying errors and omissions.

2. Names are listed alphabetically according to spelling in the record sources, and often no allowance is made for spelling variations and cross-references.

3. Errors may occur in alphabetizing.

4. Omissions may occur in indexing.

5. Females may be referred to by maiden and/or married surname(s).

6. The limitations established by the compiler may not be known.

Special Collections

Some libraries specialize in collecting information of particular interest to their patrons, such as historical data or geographic data about the locality or town in which the library is located. This information is organized into a special collections area. Rare books and restricted material are also available through special collections.

Copying Service

Most libraries have a copy service where library materials, including microfilms and microfiche, can be reproduced for the patron. A variety of processes are available for making these reproductions, and they vary with each library, as does the cost of the service.

Correspondence

Simple questions concerning services available to patrons via correspondence or general information about the library often can be answered by writing directly to a library. The majority of libraries are not equipped to answer large volumes of mail, nor do they undertake genealogical research for patrons; however, they often recommend individuals who will undertake searches in their records.

9
The Genealogical Society

The genealogical services of the LDS Church are combined under one organization known as the Genealogical Department of The Church of Jesus Christ of Latter-day Saints. This department includes five divisions:

1. Administrative Services Division
2. Priesthood Genealogy Division
3. Temple Services Division (see Chapter 17)
4. Acquisitions and Field Operations Division
5. Library Services Division

The Genealogical Society (50 East North Temple, Salt Lake City, Utah 84150) includes the Acquisitions and Field Operations Division and the Library Services Division. The Genealogical Society has two main purposes:

1. Collect genealogical records—Acquisitions and Field Operations Division.
2. Make the collection of records available to the public—Library Services Division.

The Genealogical Society is not an organization to teach one how to do genealogical research, nor is it an organization to censor, check for accuracy, and correct the records acquired. However, the Genealogical Society does offer some specialized research services:

1. Library of the Genealogical Society
2. Branch libraries
3. Surname Card Index
4. Pedigree Referral Service
5. Family Organization Card File
6. Research Department files
7. Research papers
8. Research survey
9. Research accreditation
10. Correspondence
11. Special Collections

LIBRARY OF THE GENEALOGICAL SOCIETY

The collection of the Library of the Genealogical Society represents records from many parts of the world and is of interest to all persons engaged in genealogical research. Often it is possible to accomplish more at this library, in less time, than in the original records of the specific locality, for the records are available in one central location.

The library contains two main types of records:
1. Books
2. Microforms

The books and microforms for specific geographic localities are grouped together with qualified personnel available to assist in each area. These reference personnel are willing to answer questions, assist in finding call numbers, recommend records to search, recommend reference books, assist in translating, and provide addresses for correspondence. The patron who is unfamiliar with the services of the Genealogical Society or is just beginning research should consult the General Reference Department.

Call Numbers

The books at the library are identified by the Dewey classification system of numbering. If the patron has a classification number from the old system, he can consult a register of changed call numbers for the particular country to obtain the new Dewey number. (See Figure 112.)

The following may be added as a prefix to call numbers and indicate a location in the library other than the regular library stacks:

C	Paperback Parish Printout (Controlled Extraction)
Chart	Chart Case
ES	Extra Surveillance
ESQ	Extra Surveillance, *Quarto* (large)
F	Microfilm
Folio	Larger than *Quarto* (too large for regular shelf)
Map	Map Case
Ms	Manuscript
P	Paperback Parish Printout (Record Tabulation)
PB	Pamphlet Box
PBA	Pamphlet Box, Small
PBQ	Pamphlet Box, *Quarto* (large)
Ped	Pedigree chart
Q	Quarto (too large for regular shelf)
Ref	Reference
Reg	Register
Staff	Reference desk
Supp	Supplement

CHANGED NUMBERS OF AMERICAN PUBLICATIONS
AND UNITED STATES

OLD &	NEW	OLD &	NEW	OLD &	NEW
Am. Pub. A	973 B2md	Am. Pub. K	929. 27305 L589L		
Am. Pub. B	973 D2d	Am. Pub. L	973 B2sa		
Am. Pub. C	973 B2dar	Am. Pub. M	973 B2ng		
F Am. Pub. D	974 B2ne	Am. Pub. N	974 B2n		
Am. Pub. D	976. 4 B2s	Am. Pub. O	974. 734 B2o		
Am. Pub. E	974 B2g	Am. Pub. P	974. 19 B2o		
F Am. Pub. F	973 B2t	Am. Pub. Q	974. 6 B2c		
Am. Pub. F	973 B2a	Am. Pub. R	974 B2m		
Am. Pub. G Extra Pub.	973 A3aa	Am. Pub. S	973 B2gm		
Am. Pub. G	973 C4aa	Am. Pub. T	973 B2gj		
Am. Pub. H	974 B2ne	Am. Pub. U	973 B2w		
F Am. Pub. H	973 B2df	Am. Pub. V	975. 5 B2v		
Am. Pub. I	974. 47 B2d	Am. Pub. W	973 B2t		
Am. Pub. J	977 B2o				

Figure 112.   Page from a register of changed call numbers. (*Changed Numbers of American Publications and United States*, Salt Lake City: The Genealogical Society, 1966, n.p.)

When assistance is needed to locate a particular item, the General Reference Department should be consulted.

Microfilms at the library are not assigned a Dewey classification number, but each roll of microfilm is assigned a chronological number in the order of acquisition beginning with number 1. Microfilms are arranged numerically and stored in metal cabinets. If the patron has a classification number from the old system, he can consult the register of changed film numbers, called the *Microfilm Number Index,* to obtain the new number. (See Figure 113.)

Card Catalog

The card catalog at the Library of the Genealogical Society consists of a dictionary type, or alphabetical arrangement. Each card is filed alphabetically word by word by the first line of information on the descriptive card. In addition to the dictionary arrangement typical of other libraries, there is a locality section for each of the following:

1. United States (general information) and Canada (general information)
2. States in the United States and provinces in Canada
3. Other countries

These sections are represented in the dictionary card catalog by guide cards arranged in alphabetical order. (See Figure 114.)

MICROFILM NUMBER INDEX

OLD SERIAL -PART NO.	NEW NUMBER	OLD SERIAL -PART NO.	NEW NUMBER	OLD SERIAL -PART NO.	NEW NUMBER
55304 - 612	422385	55309 - 2	422414	55313 - 30	422443
- 613	422386	- 3	422415	- 31	422444
- 614	422387	- 4	422416	- 32	422445
55305 - 1	422388	- 5	422417	- 33	422446
- 2	422389	- 6	422418	- 34	422447
- 3	422390	55310 - 1	422419	- 35	422448
- 4	422391	- 2	422420	- 36	422449
- 5	422392	- 3	422421	- 37	422450
- 6	422393	- 4	422422	- 38	422451
- 7	422394	- 5	422423	- 39	422452
- 8	422395	- 6	422424	- 40	422453
- 9	422396	- 7	422425	- 41	422454
- 10	422397	- 8	422426	- 42	422455
- 11	422398	- 9	422427	- 43	422456
- 12	422399	55311 - 1	422428	- 44	422457
- 13	422400	- 2	422429	- 45	422458
- 14	422401	- 3	422430	- 46	422459
- 15	422402	- 4	422431	- 47	422460
- 16	422403	- 5	422432	- 48	422461
- 17	422404	55312 - 1	422433	- 49	422462
- 18	422405	- 2	422434	- 50	422463
- 19	422406	- 3	422435	- 51	422464
- 20	422407	- 4	422436	- 52	422465
- 21	422408	- 5	422437	- 53	422466
- 22	422409	55313 - 25	422438	55314 - 1	422467
55306	422410	- 26	422439	- 2	422468
55307	422411	- 27	422440	- 3	422469
55308	422412	- 28	422441	- 4	422470
55309 - 1	422413	- 29	422442	- 5	422471

Figure 113.   Page from the Microfilm Number Index. (*Microfilm Number Index* [Changed Film Numbers], Salt Lake City: The Cataloging Department for the Genealogical Society of The Church of Jesus Christ of Latter-day Saints, 1967, vol. 14, p. 4857.)

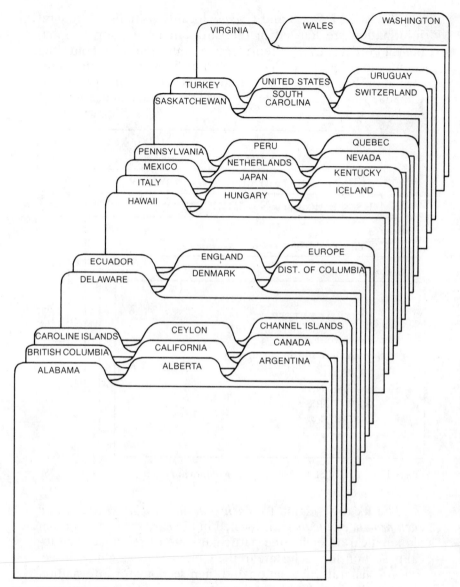

Figure 114.   Locality guide cards, Genealogical Society card catalog.

The *United States* and *Canada* locality sections for general information are located in the card catalog in proper alphabetical order. Cards representing information about the country in general are filed alphabetically by the first line of information behind the appropriate guide card: United States or Canada. For example, see Figure 115, United States general section.

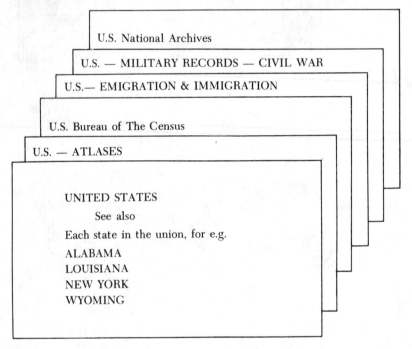

Figure 115.   United States general section of the card catalog.

The locality section for *each state in the United States* and *each province in Canada* is located in the card catalog in proper alphabetical order for the particular state or province. The locality section for each state in the United States includes a section for general information and then sections for information about each county, with information for each town or city filed behind the name of the appropriate county. Figure 116 illustrates the locality section for Ohio. The locality section for each province in Canada includes a section for general information and sections for each county if the province has counties, and then a section for information about each town or city.

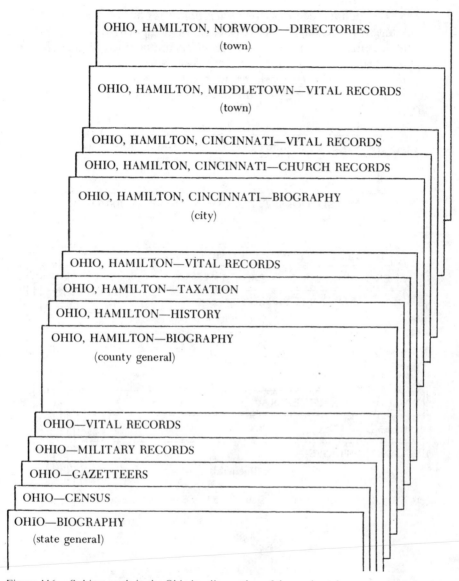

Figure 116.   Subject cards in the Ohio locality section of the card catalog.

The locality section for *other countries* is located in the catalog in proper alphabetical order for the particular country. The locality section for each country includes a section for general information and sections for information for each county (or foreign equivalent), with information for each town, city, or parish filed behind the name of the appropriate county. (See Figure 117.)

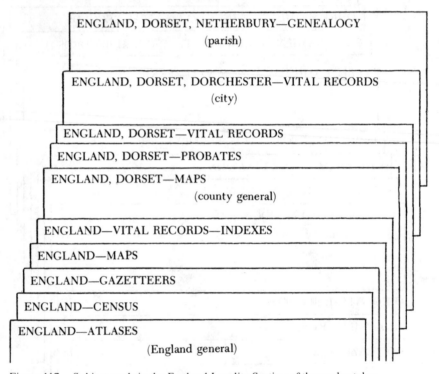

ENGLAND, DORSET, NETHERBURY—GENEALOGY
(parish)

ENGLAND, DORSET, DORCHESTER—VITAL RECORDS
(city)

ENGLAND, DORSET—VITAL RECORDS

ENGLAND, DORSET—PROBATES

ENGLAND, DORSET—MAPS
(county general)

ENGLAND—VITAL RECORDS—INDEXES

ENGLAND—MAPS

ENGLAND—GAZETTEERS

ENGLAND—CENSUS

ENGLAND—ATLASES
(England general)

Figure 117.   Subject cards in the England Locality Section of the card catalog.

Many records are not cataloged in sufficient detail to appear in all the sections. The patron should look first in the section for the specific town, city, or parish. If the desired record is not located, he should proceed to the general section of the larger jurisdictions: county, state, and country.

The call numbers for some records are available in books known as registers of call numbers. These call numbers may not be included in the card catalog, in which case a cross-reference card is made. (See Figure 118 for a cross-reference card and Figure 119 for a page from the corresponding register.)

```
REG          BELGIUM, BRABANT-REGISTERS
949.311
V26r     Genealogical Society of The Church of Jesus
             Christ of L.D.S. Cataloging Dept.
             Register of tables of births, marriages,
         and deaths of parishes in the province of Bra-
         bant, Belgium, 1792-1870.  Salt Lake City, 1968.
             1v unpaged.

         Alphabetically arranged by name of parish.

             1. Brabant province, Belgium-Vital Records.
         2.  Belgium, Brabant-Vital Records. 3. Brabant
         province, Belgium-Registers.  4. Belgium,
         Brabant-Registers.
```

Figure 118.   Cross-reference card for a register of call numbers.

INDEX TO

BIRTHS, MARRIAGES, AND DEATHS

1792-1870

Locality	Information	Period	Film No.	Item No.
Ixelles (Elsene)	Deaths	1813-1823	626,780	53
		1823-1832	626,782	53
		1833-1842	626,785	18
		1843-1850	626,787	52
		1851-1860	627,237	51
		1861-1870	627,241	18
		1861-1870	627,245	1
Jette (and Ganshoren)	Births	1792-1801	626,732	15
		1802-1813	626,736	8
		1813-1823	626,740	11
		1823-1832	626,742	25
		1833-1842	626,744	5
	Marriages	1792-1801	674,450	10
		1802-1813	626,759	44
		1813-1823	626,761	54
		1823-1832	626,763	50
		1833-1842	626,765	66
	Deaths	1792-1802	626,774	15
		1803-1813	626,778	8
		1813-1823	626,780	51
		1823-1832	626,782	51
		1833-1842	626,785	15

Jette - SEE ALSO - Jette-Saint-Pierre

Figure 119. Page from a register of call numbers. (*Register of Tables of Births, Marriages, and Deaths of Parishes in the Province of Brabant, Belgium, 1792-1870.* Salt Lake City: The Genealogical Society of The Church of Jesus Christ of Latter-day Saints Cataloging Department, 1968, n.p.)

BRANCH LIBRARIES

The Library of the Genealogical Society has been established for the purpose of collecting, compiling, and maintaining a reservoir of genealogical source material. Branch libraries have been established to make these resources available to individuals living outside the Salt Lake City area.

Microfilms, but not printed books, can be borrowed from the main library for the use of branch library patrons. These are available under three types of loans:

1. Two-week loan—may be extended to one- or two-week renewal or changed to six-month or indefinite loan.

2. Six-month loan—may be changed to indefinite loan.

3. Indefinite loan—microfilm is retained by the branch library, but the Genealogical Society retains the right to recall the film at any time. Indefinite loans are determined by, and/or rented with, the permission of the branch librarian and would include microfilms in frequent use.

A few records are restricted from circulating to branch libraries; if any one item on a roll of microfilm is restricted, the entire roll is restricted. These restrictions are for the following reasons:

1. Confidential information (example: temple sealing records)

2. Request of donor (example: South Carolina state records)

Call numbers for microfilms available for circulation can be obtained by consulting a microfilmed copy of portions of the main card catalog entitled Microfilmed Card Catalog (MCC). The Microfilmed Card Catalog was filmed in 1974-75 to replace the Dictionary Card Catalog (DCC), which was filmed in 1969 in three sections. The Microfilmed Card Catalog is available at branch libraries in four sections:

1. Locality Section (90 rolls English-speaking countries; 181 rolls other countries). Microfilms of the locality cards for English-speaking countries are available at all branch libraries: cards for each state in the United States, the United States general section, each province in Canada, the Canadian general section, British Isles, New Zealand, and the Channel Islands. (See Figure 120.) The microfilms of the locality cards for non-English speaking countries may be obtained through a special order at the branch library.

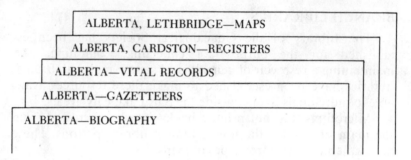

Figure 120.   Cards from the Locality Section of the Microfilmed Card Catalog.

2. Register Section. This section is available at all branch libraries and contains microfilmed copies of about 300 registers of call numbers. A few of these registers were filmed in the Locality Section (1969) and the Subject Section (1969), but this new filming includes many additional registers. (See Figure 121.)

8.

UNITED STATES 1870 CENSUS
GEORGIA

COUNTY	FILM NO.	COUNTY	FILM NO.
CLAYTON	545,643	HART	545,656
CLINCH		HEARD	
COBB		HENRY	
COFFEE			
COLQUITT		HOUSTON	545,657
		IRWIN	
COLUMBIA	545,644		
COWETA		JACKSON	545,658
		JASPER	
CRAWFORD	545,645		
DADE		JEFFERSON	545,659
DAWSON		JOHNSON	
DECATUR		JONES	
DE KALB	545,646	LAURENS	545,660
DOOLY		LEE	
DOUGHERTY			
		LIBERTY	545,661
EARLY	545,647	LINCOLN	
ECHOLS			
EFFINGHAM		LOWNDES	545,662
ELBERT		LUMPKIN	
EMANUEL		MACON	
FANNIN			
		MADISON	545,663
FAYETTE	545,648	MARION	
FLOYD		McINTOSH	
FORSYTH	545,649	MERIWETHER	545,664
FRANKLIN		MILLER	
		MILTON	
FULTON	545,650		
		MITCHELL	545,665
GILMER	545,651	MONROE	
GLASCOCK		MONTGOMERY	
GLYNN			
		MORGAN	545,666
GORDON	545,652	MURRAY	
GREENE		MUSCOGEE	
GWINNETT	545,653	NEWTON	545,667
HABERSHAM		OGLETHORPE	
		PAULDING	
HALL	545,654		
HANCOCK		PICKENS	545,668
		PIERCE	
HARALSON	545,655	PIKE	
HARRIS			

Figure 121. Page from a register of call numbers. (*United States Census*, 1870, compiled by the Cataloging Department for the Genealogical Society of The Church of Jesus Christ of Latter-day Saints, Salt Lake City, Utah, 1968, p. 8.)

3. Surname Section (52 rolls). The Surname Section is available at all branch libraries. It is a microfilmed copy of the Genealogical Society's Surname Subject File and includes all cards that were in the Family History Section (1969) plus many additional cards, but is still incomplete. (The Surname Subject File is a shelf list available to patrons of the Library of the Genealogical Society only through the microfilmed Surname Section.) (See Figure 122.)

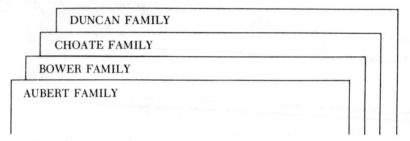

Figure 122.   Cards from the Surname Section of the Microfilmed Card Catalog.

4. Subject Section. This section is available at all branch libraries and contains call numbers for records of religious and ethnic groups, miscellaneous collections, and much secondary information. This section includes all cards in the Subject Section (1969) plus many additional entries. (See Figure 123.)

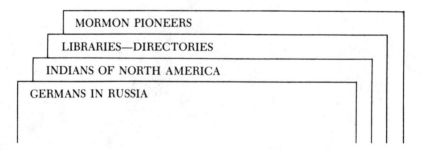

Figure 123.   Cards from the Subject Section of the Microfilmed Card Catalog.

Branch libraries are organized under the direction of the LDS Church genealogy leaders and are self-supporting. It is the responsibility of the local Church leaders to provide proper physical facilities consisting of recommended reference books, microfilms, tables, reading machines, and film cabinets. Upon request, the Genealogical Society will provide the name and address of the nearest branch library. (See sample letter, Figure 124.)

When employees of branch libraries are unable to answer a research question, the patron completes a "Branch Genealogical Library Reference Questionnaire" (Figure 125), which the branch librarian forwards to the Genealogical Society. Reference consultants analyze the research problem, obtain the desired information, and/or give suggestions for further research.

SURNAME CARD INDEX

Origin and Contents

The Surname Card Index (Index File or Surname File) is an index of names of persons compiled from books in the Library of the Genealogical Society. It is not possible to make a detailed card for the card catalog for each name that appears in each book; therefore, this index serves as a supplement to the card catalog. Information on the index card varies and may include the following (see Figure 126):

1. Surname or complete name
2. Date of birth
3. Place of birth
4. Date of marriage
5. Place of marriage
6. Name of spouse
7. Date of death
8. Place of death
9. Type of record indexed
10. Name of record indexed
11. Call number, Library of the Genealogical Society

```
                                          Your Name
                                          Your Address
                                          Current Date



        The Genealogical Society
        50 East North Temple Street
        Salt Lake City, Utah 84150

        Gentlemen:

             Would you please send me the name and address of
        the branch library nearest to my residence?

             Enclosed is a stamped self-addressed envelope for
        your convenience.

             Thank you.

                                  Sincerely yours,



                                  Your Name (signed)


        Encl:  Stamped self-addressed envelope
```

Figure 124.   Letter to the Genealogical Society.

Branch Genealogical Library   REFERENCE QUESTIONNAIRE

This form is intended to provide suggestions for further genealogical research by the patron. Due to staff limitations, the Genealogical Society cannot undertake actual research.

INSTRUCTIONS: Branch library staff member is to complete this form and submit it to the Genealogical Society, 50 East North Temple, Salt Lake City, Utah 84150 Attention: Patron Services Dept.

I. BRANCH AND PATRON DATA

BRANCH	Date Requested
Patron Name	Telephone
Street Address	Family Group Record enclosed ☐
City, State and ZIP Code	Pedigree chart enclosed ☐

II. STATEMENT OF PROBLEM OR QUESTION

a. Genealogical Data (Give all data pertinent to the problem)

Given Name(s)	Surname(s)	Sex
Birthplace or Residence (Parish or Town, County, State or Country)	Birthdate (Day, Month, Year)	
Spouse's Given Name and Surname	Marriage Date (Day, Month, Year)	
Father's Given Name and Surname	Death or Burial Date (Day, Month, Year)	
Mother's Given Name and Maiden Surname	Your Relationship to Individual	

Other Marriages

b. Sources Already Consulted (Check boxes and designate specific record searched, locality, time period etc.)

☐	Home Records	☐	Other L.D.S. Sources
☐	Temple Records Index Bureau	☐	Family Histories
☐	Church Records Archives	☐	Census
☐	Church Records	☐	Civil Vital Records
☐	Probate Records	☐	Land Records
☐	Military Records	☐	Other (Specify)

c. Patron's Question

SEE REVERSE SIDE FOR REPLY

PFGSO131 2/74 50M Printed in USA by Woodruff Printing Company

Figure 125.   Branch Genealogical Library Reference Questionnaire.

```
49062
F          Phipps Family
974. 8
V 29       Bible records from Pennsylvania.  Filmed
           by G. S. , at the Historical Society of
Pt. 1      Pennsylvania, 1964.
           7 rolls, 35 mm.  hand-typewritten



           1.  Pennsylvania-Vital Records.
```

Figure 126. Card from the Surname Card Index.

The following is an example of a surname note card made as a result of searching the Surname Card Index. (See Figure 127.)

```
PHIPPS FAMILY                    Surname Card Index
                                 Genealogical Society




Bible Records from Pennsylvania.
GS Ser. No.  49062, pt.  1.   GS F 382,722
```

Figure 127.   White surname note card for the Surname Card Index.

Genealogical Application

1. The Surname Card Index refers to the original record where more biographical information may be found.

Genealogical Limitations

1. Index cards have not been made for all books in the Genealogical Society Library.
2. There is uncertainty as to which books are indexed.

Availability

1. Original index—Library of the Genealogical Society.
2. Microfilmed copy—not microfilmed (scheduled for microfilming).

PEDIGREE REFERRAL SERVICE

Origin and Contents

The Pedigree Referral Service was initiated to help individuals and family organizations coordinate their genealogical research. Individuals registered each surname on their pedigree with the geographic location and the time period for the particular surname(s), and this information, along with the individual's name and address, was entered in a computer. The information is arranged by locality according to the same standards as the locality sections of the Library's card catalog and is available in computer printout books. (See Figure 128.)

Figures 129, 130, and 131 are examples of a surname note card and address note cards made as a result of searching the Pedigree Referral Service.

PRINTED JUN 1969   PEDIGREE REFERRAL SERVICE   PAGE 9436

FILING SPELLING	SURNAME	ACTUAL SPELLING	TOWN	LOCALITY	COUNTY	STATE	YEARS
DEPPE, LA VINA C. WINTLE	165 NORTH 1ST WEST WINTLE	SMITHFIELD, UTAH	YARMOUTH	84335	NRFLK	ENGL	1835-1860
ROSE, RAY HAVEN WINTLE	308 WEST AVENUE WINTLE	ALAMOSA, COLORADO 81101	YARMOUTH		NRFLK	ENGL	1846-1860
&STAY, RANDALL W. WOODBURY	763 ROANOKE ST. WOODBURY	WOODBRIDGE, VIRGINIA	YARMOUTH		NRFLK	ENGL	1618-1700
&LIVINGSTON, MRS. MARY H. WOOLSEY	5050 NORTH ELTON STREET WOOLSEY	BALDWIN PARK, CALIF.	YARMOUTH	91706	NRFLK	ENGL	1500-1623
PRICE, NORA W. WOOLSEY	KANOSH, UTAH WOOLSEY		YARMOUTH		NRFLK	ENGL	1586-1610
PINGREY, EASTER MARIE CHAMPERNOUN CHAMPERNOUNE	3105 S.E. 79th CHAMPERNOUN CHAMPERNOUNE	PORTLAND, OREGON	YARNSMOUTH YARNSMOUTH	97206	NRFLK NRFLK	ENGL ENGL	1480-1550 1480-1550
&ROBERTS, ALBERTA J. ALDOUS	3125 NO. 575 E. ALDOUS	NO. OGDEN, UTAH 84404	YAXHAM		NRFLK	ENGL	1870-1939
YARRINGTON, HELEN JEFFERIES	1128 SO. FORREST STREET JEFFERIES	WESTPORT, WASHINGTON	YAXHAM		NRFLK	ENGL	1780-1866
THOMAS, BARBARA G. JEFRIES	P.O. BOX 87 JEFRIES	STOCKTON, UTAH	YAXHAM		NRFLK	ENGL	1866-0000
&MANNING, GEORGIDA U. HERWIN	LEHI, UTAH HERWIN		YELVERTON		NRFLK	ENGL	1786-1810
&HEALD, DAVID M. ANDREW ANDROS	209 NORTH 4TH STREET ANDREW ANDROSS	GARDEN CITY, KANSAS			NRTHMB NRTHMB	ENGL ENGL	1622-1670 1622-1670
GARRISON, MARY JEAN N. BAINBRIDGE	1790 SOUTH 500 EAST BAINBRIDGE	OREM, UTAH 84057			NRTHMB	ENGL	1832-0000

Figure 128. Computer printout page from the Pedigree Referral Service. (*Pedigree Referral Service File,* Salt Lake City: The Genealogical Society of The Church of Jesus Christ of Latter-day Saints, 1969, vol. 31, p. 9436.)

```
WINTLE                          Pedigree Referral
                                Service

Yarmouth, Norfolk, England

   LaVina C. Deppe,         years 1835-1860
      165 N. 1st W.
      Smithfield, Utah 84335

   Ray Haven Rose,          years 1846-1860
      308 West Avenue
      Alamosa, Colorado 81101
```

Figure 129.   White surname note card for the Pedigree Referral Service.

```
DEPPE, LaVina C.                Pedigree Referral
                                Service

   165 North 1st West
   Smithfield, Utah 84335

   Working on Wintle line in Yarmouth, Norfolk, England
      1835-1860
```

Figure 130.   White address note card for the Pedigree Referral Service.

```
ROSE, Ray Haven                 Pedigree Referral
                                Service

   308 West Avenue
   Alamosa, Colorado  81101

   Working on Wintle line in Yarmouth, Norfolk, England
      1846-1860
```

Figure 131.   White address note card for the Pedigree Referral Service.

Genealogical Application

1. The Pedigree Referral Service provides names and addresses of relatives who may have additional information on the pedigree surnames.

Genealogical Limitations

1. Addresses may be out of date.

2. Individuals who registered may be deceased.

3. Indiscriminate registration was encouraged, and often the individual had no original information in his possession.

4. Many individuals with original information failed to register because they did not have time to answer requests.

5. There was duplication of registration because all members of the LDS Church were encouraged to register.

6. Registration of patronymic surnames is of no value.

Availability

1. Original computer printouts—Library of the Genealogical Society.

2. Microfilmed copy—Library of the Genealogical Society.

FAMILY ORGANIZATION CARD FILE

Origin and Contents

The Genealogical Society maintains a Family Organization Card File, which lists the names of family organizations, the date of the organization, date of registration, and the names and addresses of the officers. (See Figure 132.)

FAMILY ORGANIZATION FILE		
Name of Family Org.	George Diamond Family Organization	
Date Org. 10 July 1961	DATE REPORTED 4 Aug 1961	PRS NO. 0219-315
OFFICE	NAME	ADDRESS
PRES.	William E. Diamond	969 Whitney Drive Salt Lake City, Utah
SEC.	Jane D. Osgood	1499 Appleblossom Lane Salt Lake City, Utah
GEN.	David Diamond	739 Spruce Lane Orem, Utah 84057
FAMILY REP.	George Diamond	1690 Jubilee Street Logan, Utah
PRS REP.	David Diamond	

Figure 132.   Card from the Family Organization Card File.

Genealogical Application

1. The Family Organization Card File prevents unnecessary duplication of time and expense for individuals desiring to form or join a family organization.

2. The Family Organization Card File provides names and addresses of individuals who may have additional genealogical information.

Genealogical Limitations

1. The information may not be current; each family organization is responsible to register and provide the Genealogical Society with up-to-date information.

2. The office of family representative is obsolete.

Availability

1. Original card file—Library of the Genealogical Society.

2. Microfilmed copy—Not microfilmed.

RESEARCH DEPARTMENT FILES

Origin and Contents

For many years, the Genealogical Society maintained a Research Department where individuals or family organizations (clients) could establish an account and hire genealogical research. This service of the Research Department was discontinued in 1966. However, the files assembled by the Research Department are valuable and could contain the following information:

1. Pedigree charts and family group records compiled by the client and the researcher.

2. Correspondence between the researcher and the client with evaluation and suggestions for further searches.

3. Correspondence between the researcher and agents and record custodians.

4. Copies of information obtained from the records searched, such as certificates of vital registration and parish register extracts.

Genealogical Application

1. Information obtained from previous research will save time and money.

2. Information supplied to the Research Department by the client may be unknown to the present generation.

Genealogical Limitations

1. The research files are indexed by the name of the client and not by the names on the pedigree.

2. Access to the research files is legally restricted to the client or his heirs, and written permission from the client or his legal heir must be obtained and presented at the Genealogical Society.

3. It appears that some information has been removed from some of the files prior to microfilming.

Availability

1. Original files:
   a. Library of the Genealogical Society
   b. Client or his legal heir (if returned to the client)
2. Microfilmed copy of files—General Reference Department of the Genealogical Society Library.
3. Research files are available only to the client or his legal heir or with written permission of the client or his legal heir. (See sample letter, Figure 133.) Clues to the existence of a research file for a particular client may be obtained in the following ways:
   a. Check the microfilmed alphabetical list of clients (index), General Reference Department, Library of the Genealogical Society or through a branch library.
   b. Inquire of relatives and family organizations.
   c. Search the Main Records Section Family Group Records (see Chapter 21) and look for initials (LMT) of the employee of the Research Department or the notation "Gen. Soc."
   d. Search the Card Index to Heirs (see Chapter 22) for the name and address of persons submitting names for temple ordinances prior to 1941. These were often individuals who hired the Research Department, and often the Genealogical Society is indicated as having submitted names.

Your Name
Your Address
Current Date

The Genealogical Society
50 East North Temple Street
Salt Lake City, Utah 84150

Gentlemen:

Could you please tell me if the research account for
Margaret S. Olsen, Gunnison, Utah is in your files or if it
is available on microfilm?

Margaret S. Olsen is my grandmother, and she hired
the Research Department to do genealogical research on
our family lines in Denmark. The initials of the researcher
are LMT.

Enclosed is a note from my grandmother giving permission for me to obtain the original research file. If you
have the original file, please mail it to me. I will be happy
to pay for any expenses incurred through this request.

Thank you.

Sincerely yours,

Your Name (signed)

Encl: Note of permission

Figure 133.   Letter to the Genealogical Society.

RESEARCH PAPERS

The Research Department has prepared brief research papers on various subjects of interest in genealogical research. The majority of these papers pertain to research in specific countries. Research papers are available to library patrons at the General Reference Desk; a price list and mail order service is available through LDS Church Distribution Center, 1999 West 1700 South, Salt Lake City, Utah 84104.

RESEARCH SURVEY

Individuals can request a research survey through the personnel of the Genealogical Society for $10 per surname. The purpose of the research survey is to do the following:

1. Determine if other persons are working on the particular pedigree.

2. Determine what records are available at the Genealogical Society.

3. Recommend records to search.

The records consulted in a research survey are determined by the individual conducting the survey and usually include the following:

1. Temple Records Index Bureau (see Chapter 18)

2. The Computer File Index (see Chapter 20)

3. Patrons Family Group Records 1962-present (see Chapter 21)

4. Main Records Section Family Group Records (see Chapter 21)

5. A spot check in the Genealogical Society card catalog:
   a. Family histories (see Chapter 15)
   b. Locality histories (see Chapter 15)
   c. Other records for the localities

An individual can complete his own research survey by completing the research steps in the lesson assignments. (See Section IV.)

RESEARCH ACCREDITATION

The Genealogical Society administers examinations on research in various localities and furnishes upon request a list of accredited researchers for a particular state in the United States or other country. (See sample letter, Figure 134.) It is best to hire an accredited researcher to make specific searches only, rather than to allow the accredited researcher to assume full

Your Name
Your Address
Current Date

The Genealogical Society
50 East North Temple Street
Salt Lake City, Utah 84150

Gentlemen:

     Would you please send me the names and addresses
of the accredited researchers for the states of New York
and Pennsylvania ?

     Enclosed is a stamped self-addressed envelope for
your convenience.

     Thank you.

                 Sincerely yours,

                 Your Name (signed)

Encl: Stamped self-addressed envelope

Figure 134.   Letter to the Genealogical Society.

responsibility. The Genealogical Society does not guarantee the work of the accredited researcher, nor his honesty, but refers names of individuals who have shown a certain proficiency in research through examination. The Genealogical Society will remove a name from the list if complaints are received and not satisfied.

Applicants for the examination should meet the following requirements:

1. Have access to the Genealogical Society or a branch library.

2. Have 1,000 hours of research experience in a geographic locality of accreditation.

3. Have 100 hours of research experience in LDS Church records.

4. Be willing to do research for hire.

The examination consists of the following:

1. Written examination in the language for non-English-speaking localities.

2. Reading of early handwriting of the locality.

3. Tabulation of genealogical information on family group records and a pedigree chart.

4. Examination on LDS Church records and basic genealogical research.

5. Written examination on specific record sources and research procedures for the locality.

6. Oral examination on specific record sources and research procedures for the locality.

7. Presentation of a pedigree problem successfully solved by the accreditation applicant.

CORRESPONDENCE

The Library of the Genealogical Society answers brief requests by correspondence concerning research problems or answers questions concerning services of the Library. (See sample letters, Figures 124, 133, and 134.) If the request is too detailed or time consuming for a brief reply, the Genealogical Society will recommend that the individual request a paid research survey or consult an accredited researcher.

SPECIAL COLLECTIONS

The Special Collections at the Genealogical Society include rare books, valuable manuscripts, and records that are restricted in use.

10
Reference Books

Reference books are research tools that make it easier for the genealogical researcher to do the following:

1. Learn which genealogical records are available.
2. Obtain the genealogical records.
3. Interpret the genealogical information in the records.

The genealogical researcher will save time and money by consulting the best reference books and will have better success in using reference books if he reads, studies, and understands the various parts of a reference book.

1. *The title page* contains the title of the book, the name(s) of the author(s), editor(s) or compiler(s), name and address of the publisher, and date of publication. This is referred to as bibliographic information and is copied onto the card which is placed in the card catalog of the Library.

2. *The copyright page* is on the back of the title page and gives the Library of Congress Number, the date of copyright, and the name of the copyright holder. Persons who hold a copyright prior to 1978 have exclusive rights to all or part of their material for 28 years and may renew their copyright for an additional 28 years. As this book goes to press, the U.S. Congress has enacted a new law governing copyrights after 1978, extending copyright protection to the lifetime of the copyright holder plus an additional 50 years after his death. It is illegal and an infringement of copyright even to make a single copy of a map or a page from a book for personal or commercial use of any kind without permission from the copyright holder.

3. *The table of contents* is a brief listing of the subjects in the book in the order they appear.

4. *The preface or introduction* is an explanation of the purpose and use of the reference book, the reasons for compiling the reference, the limitations of the reference, and special acknowledgments.

5. *The keys* are guides or explanations of special symbols used in the book to save space and typesetting expense.

6. *The body* is the largest portion of the reference and contains the information for which the reference was compiled.

7. *The appendixes* contain special tables or items of information relating to, but not specifically part of, the main body of the reference. They are often additional information on a similar or related subject.

8. *The index* is an alphabetical list of names and/or subjects included in the body of the book with references to page numbers.

Some reference books have been compiled specifically for the genealogist and others have been compiled for other reasons, but have been found to be of value to the genealogist. These include the following:

1. Genealogical textbooks
2. Inventories of genealogical records
3. Registers of call numbers for genealogical records
4. Gazetteers
5. Maps and atlases

TEXTBOOKS

A basic genealogical textbook is a reference book that introduces the genealogical research method and its application. To accomplish this purpose, a basic genealogical textbook should include the following:

1. Definition of genealogical research terminology
2. Introduction to genealogical research tools
3. Description of basic genealogical records
4. Lesson assignments

INVENTORIES

Inventories are itemized lists of records. These could include inventories of government archives, church archives, and libraries, or a compilation of information from any or all of these. An inventory generally includes a description of the records, the time period, and the availability. (See Figure 135.)

REGISTERS OF CALL NUMBERS

A register of call numbers is a reference book that contains library call numbers and also may be an inventory. (See Figure 136.) The call numbers may or may not be included in the library card catalog. Printed registers of call numbers are an advantage to the genealogical researcher for the following reasons:

STATE OF KENTUCKY   79

Name of Church	Location by City	Kind of Record Years Included	Location of Records

STATE OF KENTUCKY

Calloway County —

| Bapt. - Locust Grove | Murray | Ch. Rec. 1841-1948 | HCSBC |

Campbell County —

Meth. Tayor Street	Newport	Bapt. 1869-1920	DSGRQ v. 6
Bapt. - Old Licking	Cold Spring	Burials	KYHS Reg. V. 45*
Bapt.	Flagg Spring	Rec. of	KYHS Reg. V. 45*
Bapt.	Persimmon Grove	Burials	KYHS Reg. V. 45*
Meth. - Asbury	Cold Spring	Burials	KYHS Reg. V. 45*

Christian County —

| Bapt. | Bethel | 1814-1871 | SBTS |

Cumberland County —

| Bapt. | Mt. Pleasant | Ch. Rec. 1850-1876 | HCSBC |
| Bapt. | Burkesville | 1893-1966 | HCSBC |

Daviess County —

Bapt.	Whitesville	Ch. Rec. 1878-1961	HCSBC
Bapt.	Owensboro	Ch. Rec. 1813-1833	HCSBC
Yelvington		1878-1883	
Bapt.	Owensboro	Ch. Rec. 1840-1963	HCSBCS

Fayette County —

Bapt. David's Fork	Reference: *Kentucky Pioneer and Court Records* by McAdams, pp. 177, 213.		
Cath. St. Peter's	Marriage records 1834-1855. See above reference.		
Bapt.	East Hickman	Min. 1787-1921	SBTS
Disciples	....	Ch. Rec. 1831-1870	Bosworth Mem. Library Lexington
Disciples	....	Reg. 1827-1889, etc.	Bosworth Mem. Library, Lexington
Presby. Bethel	....	Deaths & Bapt. 1823-+	See: Ky. Pioneer & Court Records
Presby. Walnut Hill	Lexington	Ch. Rec. 1822-1926	KHSRQ v. 54

Figure 135. Page from a published inventory. (E. Kay Kirkham, *A Survey of American Church Records*, Logan, Utah: Everton Publishers, 1971, p. 79.)

Family Group Records (Patrons Section, submitted 1966 [4th-gen])			
New No.	Beginning Name	New No.	Beginning Name
510,764	Diesing	510,804	McFate, Ja*
510,765	Duke, James A	510,805	Neilson, James P
510,766	Edward, Ell	510,806	Nielson, And
510,767	Ensign	510,807	North
510,768	Fancher	510,808	Olsen, Lars A
510,769	Fisch	510,809	Paasch
510,770	Fox	510,810	Parry, C
510,771	Gaarsoe	510,811	Peka
510,772	Gentry, Chr	510,812	Peterson, John D
510,773	Goddard, W	510,813	Price, Edw
510,774	Green, Charles H	510,814	Powell, Charles W
510,775	Gunderson, Er	510,815	Ramsburg
510,776	Halling, Jor	510,816	Reece, R
510,777	Hansen, Jan	510,817	Richardson, Che
510,778	Harp	510,818	Roberts, Cl
510,779	Hatch, Ray	510,819	Rogers, Ross W
510,780	Hellewell	510,820	Rumsey, S
510,781	Hickman, C	510,821	Schaal, Herman E
510,782	Hoffman, W	510,822	Sedlaczek
510,783	Horman, Charles G	510,823	Shorten, J
510,784	Hulse, H	510,824	Slaugh
510,785	Ians	510,825	Smith, Orv
510,786	Jarman, Cl	510,826	Sorensen, Leona
510,787	Jensen, Ole A	510,827	Stanley, W
510,788	Johnson, Jam	510,828	Stewart, W
510,789	Jones, Hyrum J	510,829	Strong, John A
510,790	Kaalstad	510,830	Tanner, Dav
510,791	Kibel, Alo	510,831	Terry, Thomas J
510,792	Knudsen, L	510,832	Thornley, John W
510,793	Lammers, W	510,833	Tranter, Thomas W
510,794	Laubscher, J*	510,834	Vallo
510,795	Lemmon, John Leo	510,835	Wakefield, Le
510,796	Little, Je	510,836	Warr, P
510,797	Lund, Wils	510,837	Weight, G
510,798	Mansfield	510,838	White, Charles A
510,799	Matthews, T	510,839	Wilde, William B
510,800	Meservy	512,500	Wilson, Car
510,801	Mitchell, Edward H	512,501	Wood, John A
510,802	Morris, John B	512,502	Wyer
510,803	Murphy, Hy		

*This name is also on different family group records on the preceding microfilm.

Figure 136.   Page from a register. (Laureen R. Jaussi and Gloria D. Chaston, *Register of L.D.S. Church Records*, Salt Lake City: Deseret Book Company, 1968, p. 42.)

1. Registers are easier for the researcher to use at a desk than card files.

2. Registers can be used at the reading machines to obtain follow-up call numbers.

3. Registers not under copyright can be photocopied for personal use more easily than card files.

4. Some registers are available for purchase, enabling the researcher to obtain the call numbers at home prior to visiting the library.

5. Copies of registers can be made available to more than one person at the same time, whereas only one person can use a drawer of the card catalog.

6. Registers are easier to use in the classroom than a microfilm copy of the card catalog and enable the student to obtain the call numbers prior to visiting the Library.

GAZETTEERS

Gazetteers are alphabetical dictionaries of place names and are used to obtain specific information about a particular locality. (See Figures 137, 138, 139, and 140.)

Genealogical Application

Each time genealogical research reveals a new place name, a gazetteer should be consulted for the following information:

1. Correct spelling
2. Change in spelling (ancient and modern)
3. Correct combination of town, parish, and/or county
4. Change in name
5. Change in boundary
6. Distinguish between two or more places with the same name
7. Meeting places for religious denominations
8. Names of near-by places
9. Maps that may be included in the gazetteer
10. The population of a locality at a given period of time

Genealogical Limitations

Few gazetteers are compiled and printed specifically for genealogical research; therefore, there are genealogical limitations:

1. Different editions of gazetteers contain different information.

State List of Post Offices   **Cherry Point   NORTH CAROLINA**

NORTH CAROLINA
(Abbreviation: N.C.)

ZIP code	Post office and county	Parcel post Unit Zone	
	(Abbottsburg, Ind. R. Sta. Bladenboro)	1229	....
28315	°Aberdeen, Moore, 1	1278	....
	(Acme, R. Sta. Riegelwood)	1180	....
28317	Addor, Moore	1278	....
27006	Advance, Davie, 3	1377	....
27910	Ahoskie, Hertford, 1 (GC)	1026	....
	(Akers Center, Sta. Gastonia)	1478	....
27201	Alamance, Alamance, 3	1276	....
28001	°Albemarle†, Stanly, 1 (GC)	1378	....
28508	Albertson, Duplin, 3	1128	....
28701	(Alexander, Buncombe, 3	1627	....
	(Alexander Mills, R. Sta. Forest City)	1528	....
28006	Alexis, Gaston	1478	....
28509	Alliance, Pamlico	1028	....
	(Alma, R. Sta. Maxton)	1279	....
28702	Almond, Swain	1728	....
27202	Altamahaw, Alamance, 2	1326	....
	(Altapass, R. Sta. Spruce Pine)	1577	....
	(Amity Gardens, Sta. Charlotte)	1428	....
	(Anderson‡, Ind. R. Sta. Kitty Hawk)	926	....
28801	°Andrews†, Cherokee, 2	1728	....
27501	Angier, Harnett, 2	1227	....
28007	Ansonville, Anson, 3	1378	....
27502	Apex, Wake, 2	1227	....
28802	Apple Grove, Ashe	1525	....
28703	Aquone, Macon	1728	....
28510	Arapahoe, Pamlico, 3	1028	....
27007	Ararat, Surry	1426	....
	Archdale (Br. High Point)	1377	....
	(Arcola, R. Sta. Warrenton)	1376	....
	Arden, Buncombe	1628	....
	(Ardmore, Sta. Winston-Salem)	1376	....
28420	Ash, Brunswick, 2	1230	....
27203	°Asheboro†, Randolph, 1 (GC)	1327	....
	Branch Post Office: North Asheboro. Station: Farmer (R).		
28801†	°Asheville†, Buncombe, 1 (GC)	1627	....
	Branch Post Office: Oteen z. Stations: Biltmore z. Court House z. Glenrock. Grace z. West Asheville z.		
28603	Ashford, McDowell, 3	1527	....
	(Atando, Sta. Charlotte)	1428	....
28421	Atkinson, Pender, 3	1179	....
28511	Atlantic, Carteret, 3	979	....
28512	Atlantic Beach, Carteret, 3	1029	....
	(Atlantic Christian College, Sta. Wilson)	1127	....
27805	Aulander, Bertie, 2	1074	....
27806	Aurora, Beaufort, 3	1028	....
28518	Autryville, Sampson, 3	1229	....
27915	Avon, Care	928	....
28008	Avondale, Rutherford, 3	1528	....
28513	°Ayden†, Pitt, 2 (C)	1078	....
27916	Aydlett, Currituck	926	....
	(Azalea, Sta. Wilmington)	1130	....
27809	Badin, Stanly, 2	1378	....
27503	Bahama, Durham, 3	1228	....
27807	Bailey, Nash, 3	1127	....
28705	Bakersville, Mitchell, 2	1576	....
	(Bald Creek, Ind. R. Sta. Burnsville)	1577	....
28706	Balfour, Henderson, 3	1578	....
28707	Balsam, Jackson, 3	1678	....
28708	Balsam Grove, Transylvania	1628	....
28604	Banner Elk, Avery, 2	1526	....
27808	Barber, Rowan	1427	....
27917	Barco, Currituck	926	....
28610	Barium Springs, Iredell, 3	1427	....
28709	Barnardsville, Buncombe, 2	1577	....

See first page of list for symbol identification.

ZIP code	Post office and county	Parcel post Unit Zone	
28319	Barnesville, Robeson	1280	....
28710	Bat Cave, Henderson, 3	1578	....
27808	Bath, Beaufort, 3	1028	....
27809	Battleboro, Nash, 3	1126	....
28515	Bayboro, Pamlico, 3	1028	....
27207	Bear Creek, Chatham, 3	1277	....
28011	Bear Poplar, Rowan	1427	....
28516	°Beaufort†, Carteret, 2 (GC)	1029	....
	(Beech Creek, Ind. R. Sta. Sugar Grove)	1526	....
	(Bee Log, R. Sta. Burnsville)	1577	....
27918	Belcross, Camden, 3	975	....
27009	Belews Creek, Forsyth	1376	....
27810	°Belhaven, Beaufort, 2 (C)	1027	....
	Station: Ransomville (R).		
27811	Bellarthur, Pitt	1127	....
28012	°Belmont†, Gaston, 1 (GC)	1478	....
	Branch Post Offices: Catawba Heights. North Belmont.		
27919	Belvidere, Perquimans, 3	1026	....
	(Belwood, R. Sta. Lawndale)	1528	....
27208	Bennett, Chatham, 3	1327	....
27504	Benson, Johnston, 2 (C)	1228	....
28016	°Bessemer City, Gaston, 2 (C)	1478	....
27010	Bethania, Forsyth	1376	....
27812	Bethel, Pitt, 2	1077	....
28518	Beulaville, Duplin, 2	1129	....
	(Biltmore, Sta. Asheville)	1627	....
27209	Biscoe, Montgomery, 2	1328	....
27813	Black Creek, Wilson	1127	....
28711	°Black Mountain†, Buncombe, 1 (C)	1577	....
	Stations: Black Mountain Sanatorium (R). Blue Ridge† (R).		
	(Black Mountain Sanatorium, R. Sta. Black Mountain)	1577	....
28520	¶Bladenboro, Bladen, 2	1229	....
	Station: Abbottsburg (Ind. R.).		
27212	Blanch, Caswell, 3	1275	....
27814	Blounts Creek, Beaufort, 3	1028	....
28605	Blowing Rock, Watauga, 2	1526	....
	(Blue Ridge†, R. Sta. Black Mountain)	1577	....
	Boger City (Br. Lincolnton)	1478	....
	(Boiling Spring Lakes, R. Sta. Southport)	1181	....
28017	Bolivia, Brunswick, 3	1528	....
28422	Bolivia, Brunswick, 3	1180	....
28423	Bolton, Columbus, 3	1180	....
27213	Bonlee, Chatham, 3	1277	....
	Bonnie Doone (Br. Fayetteville)	1228	....
28606	Boomer, Wilkes	1476	....
28607	¶Boone†, Watauga, 1 (GC)	1526	....
27011	Boonville, Yadkin, 2	1426	....
28018	Bostic, Rutherford, 3	1528	....
	(Boulevard, Sta. Leaksville)	1326	....
28322	Bowdens, Duplin	1178	....
28902	Brasstown, Clay, 3	1728	....
28712	°Brevard†, Transylvania, 1 (GC)	1628	....
27815	Bricks, Edgecombe	1126	....
28519	Bridgeton, Craven, 3	1078	....
27500	Broadway, Lee, 3	1278	....
	(Brookford, R. Sta. Hickory)	1477	....
	Brookside (Br. Goldsboro)	1128	....
27214	Brown Summit, Guilford, 3	1326	....
28424	Brunswick, Columbus, 3	1230	....
28713	Bryson City, Swain, 2	1678	....
27506	Buies Creek, Harnett, 2	1228	....
27507	Bullock, Granville	1226	....
27508	Bunn, Franklin, 3	1177	....
28323	Bunnlevel, Harnett, 3	1228	....
28425	Burgaw, Pender, 1	1129	....
27215†	°Burlington†, Alamance, 1 (GC)	1276	....
	Branch Post Office: Glen Raven z (Ind.).		

ZIP code	Post office and county	Parcel post Unit Zone	
28714	Burnsville, Yancey, 2	1577	....
	Stations: Bald Creek (Ind. R.). Bee Log (R). Cane River (Ind. R). Celo (R). Newdale (Ind. R).		
27509	Butner, Granville, 2	1226	....
28324	Butters, Bladen	1229	....
27920	Buxton, Dare, 3	928	....
27228	Bynum, Chatham	1277	....
28325	Calypso, Duplin, 3	1178	....
27921	Camden, Camden, 3	976	....
28226	°Cameron, Moore, 3	1278	....
	(Cameron Village, Sta. Raleigh)	1227	....
	Camp Lejeune (Ind. Br. Jacksonville)	1079	....
28715	Candler, Buncombe, 2	1627	....
27229	Candor, Montgomery, 2	1328	....
	(Cane River, Ind. R. Sta. Burnsville)	1577	....
28716	°Canton, Haywood, 1 (GC)	1627	....
	(Caraleigh, R. Sta. Raleigh)	1227	....
28019	°Caroleen, Rutherford, 3	1528	....
28425	Carolina Beach, New Hanover, 2	1130	....
	(Carolina Hills, R. Sta. Fletcher)	1628	....
27510	Carrboro, Orange, 2 (C)	1277	....
28327	°Carthage, Moore, 2	1278	....
27511	Cary, Wake, 2 (C)	1227	....
28020	Casar, Cleveland, 3	1527	....
28717	Cashiers, Jackson, 3	1678	....
27616	Castalia, Nash, 3	1176	....
28718	Castle Hayne, New Hanover, 3	1130	....
	(Caswell (Br. Kinston)	1128	....
28609	Catawba, Catawba, 2	1477	....
	(Catawba Heights (Br. Belmont)	1478	....
27512	Ca-vel, Person, 2	1226	....
27239	Cedar Falls, Randolph	1327	....
27231	Cedar Grove, Orange, 3	1276	....
28520	Cedar Island, Carteret	979	....
28718	Cedar Mountain, Transylvania, 3	1628	....
	(Celo, R. Sta. Burnsville)	1577	....
	(Centerville, R. Sta. Louisberg)	1176	....
27232	Central Falls, Randolph, 3	1327	....
28430	Cerro Gordo, Columbus, 3	1230	....
28431	Chadbourn, Columbus, 2 (C)	1230	....
	(Chadwick, Sta. Charlotte)	1428	....
28513	Chalybeate Springs, Harnett	1227	....
27514†	°Chapel Hill†, Orange, 1 (GC)	1277	....
	Branch Post Office: Eastgate. Station: Glen Lennox.		
28201†	°Charlotte†, Mecklenburg, 1 (GC)	1428	....
	Branch Post Offices: Derita z. Hickory Grove. Municipal Airport.		
	Stations: Amity Gardens. Atando. Chadwick. Charlottetown r. Dilworth r. Downtown. Elizabeth. Freedom, z. Mint Hill (R). Myers Park. North 26. North Charlotte z. Park Road z. Plaza z. Randolph z. Sedgefield. Shamrock. Wilkinson Boulevard. University Park.		
	(Charlottetown, Sta. Charlotte)	1428	....
28719	Cherokee, Swain, 2	1678	....
28533	Cherry Point (Ind. Br. Havelock)	1029	....

Figure 137.   Page from a gazetteer [postal directory]. (*Directory of Post Offices*, United States Postal Service, Washington, D.C., July 1963, p. 177.)

NORTH CAROLINA 165

Name	Map Index	Date Created	Pop. By M 1960	U.S.Census Reports Available	Parent County or Territory From Which Organized	County Seat
Cabarrus	D2	1792	68	1800–80	Mecklenburg . . . . Concord 28025
				(CH burned 1874; Clk Sup Ct has div, pro & civ ct rec)		
• Caldwell	E1	1841	50	1850–80	Burke, Wilkes . . . . Lenoir 28645
				(Reg Deeds has b, m, d & lnd rec; Clk Sup Ct has div, civ ct & pro rec from 1841)		
• Camden	A1	1777	6	1790–80	Pasquotank . . . . Camden 27921
				(Clk Sup Ct has div ?, civ ct rec from 1896, pro rec from 1912)		
• Carteret	B2	1722	31	1790–80	Bath . . . . Beaufort 28516
				(Reg Deeds has b, m, d & lnd rec; Clk Sup Ct has div, pro & civ ct rec)		
Caswell	D1	1777	20	1800–80	Orange . . . . Yanceyville 27379
				(Clk Sup Ct has div, pro & civ ct rec)		
• Catawba	E2	1842	73	1850–80	Lincoln . . . . Newton 28658
				(Clk Sup Ct has div, pro & civ ct rec from 1843)		
• Chatham	D2	1770	27	1790–80	Orange . . . . Pittsboro 27312
				(Reg Deeds has b & d rec from 1913, m & lnd rec from 1771; Clk Sup Ct has div rec from 1913, pro rec from 1771 & civ ct rec from 1869)		
• Cherokee	G2	1839	16	1840–80	Macon . . . . Murphy 28906
				(Clk Sup Ct has div, pro & civ ct rec)		
• Chowan	B1	1670	12	1790–80	Prec. Albermarle . . . . Edenton 27932
• Clay	G2	1861	6	1870–80	Cherokee . . . . Hayesville 28904
				(Reg Deeds has b, m, d, pro & lnd rec)		
• Cleveland	E2	1841	66	1850–80	Rutherford, Lincoln . . . . Shelby 28150
				(Reg Deeds has b & d rec from 1913, m rec from 1851, also lnd rec; Clk Sup Ct has div, pro & civ ct rec from 1841)		
Columbus	C3	1808	49	1810–80	Bladen, Brunswick . . . . Whiteville 28472
				(Reg Deeds have b & d rec from 1913, m rec from 1867; Clk Sup Ct has div & civ ct rec from 1868, pro rec from 1817)		
• Craven	B2	1705	59	1790–80	Prec. Bath Co. . . . . New Bern 28560
				(1810 census missing) (Reg Deeds has b & d rec from 1914, m & pro rec from 1780, civ ct rec from 1915 & lnd rec from 1710; City Clk has bur rec from 1800; Clk Sup Ct has div rec from 1915)		
• Cumberland	C2	1754	149	1790–80	Bladen . . . . Fayetteville 28301
				(Reg Deeds has b, m, d & bur rec; Clk Sup Ct has div rec from 1930, pro rec from 1850 & civ ct rec from 1900)		
• Currituck	A1	1671	7	1790–80	Albemarle . . . . Currituck 27929
				(1820 census missing; CH burned 1842) (Reg Deeds has b, m, d & lnd rec; Clk Sup Ct has div, pro & civ ct rec)		
Dare	A2	1870	6	1870–80	Currituck, Tyrell, Hyde . . . . . . Manteo 27954
				(Reg Deeds has b & d rec from 1913, m rec from 1870; Clk Sup Ct has div, pro & civ ct rec from 1870)		
• Davidson	D2	1822	79	1830–80	Rowan . . . . Lexington 27292
				(Reg Deeds has b, m, d, bur & lnd rec from 1823; Clk Sup Ct has div, pro & civ ct rec from 1823)		
• Davie	D1	1836	17	1840–80	Rowan . . . . Mocksville 27028
				(Reg Deeds has b rec from 1913, m & bur rec combined from 1913 & m & lnd rec from 1836; Clk Sup Ct has div rec from 1831, civ ct & pro rec from 1837)		
Dobbs		1758			Johnston, discontinued 1791
• Duplin	C2	1749	40	1790–80	New Hanover . . . . Kenansville 28349
				(Reg Deeds has b & d rec from 1913, m rec from 1749, wills & lnd divisions, maps, deeds, lnd grants & deeds of trust from 1749, corporations, assumed names & partnerships from 1899)		
• Durham	C1	1881	112		Orange, Wake . . . . Durham 27701
				(Co Health Dept has b, d & bur rec; Reg Deeds has m & lnd rec; Clk Sup Ct has div, pro & civ ct rec from 1881)		
• Edgecombe	B1	1741	54	1790–80	Bertie . . . . Tarboro 27886
• Forsyth	D1	1849	189	1850–80	Stokes . . . . Winston–Salem 27102
				(Reg Deeds has b, m, d & lnd rec; Clk Sup Ct has div, pro & civ ct rec from 1849)		
Franklin	C1	1778	29	1800–80	Bute . . . . Louisburg 27549
				(1820 census missing) (Reg Deeds has b & d rec from 1913, m rec from 1869, lnd rec from 1779 & pro rec; Clk Sup Ct has div rec)		
• Gaston	E2	1846	127	1850–80	Lincoln . . . . Gastonia 28052
				(Reg Deeds has b rec from 1846, m, d, notary & lnd rec; Clk Sup Ct has div rec)		
Gates	B1	1778	9	1790–80	Chowan, Hertford . . . . Gatesville 27938
				(Reg Deeds has b, m, d, bur & lnd rec; Clk Sup Ct has div, pro & civ ct rec from 1780)		
Glasgow		1791			Discontinued 1799
Graham	G2	1872	6	1880	Cherokee . . . . Robbinsville 28771
				(Reg Deeds has b & d rec from 1913, m & lnd rec from 1873, div & civ ct rec from 1875 & pro rec from 1910)		
Granville	C1	1746	33	1800–80	Edgecombe, Orig. Glasgow . . . Oxford 27565
Greene	B2	1799	17	1800–80	Dobbs or Glasgow . . . . Snow Hill 28580
				(CH burned 1876) (Reg Deeds has b, m, d, bur & lnd rec; Clk Sup Ct has div & civ ct rec from 1874 & pro rec)		
• Guilford	D1	1770	247	1790–80	Rowan, Orange . . . . Greensboro 27402
				(Reg Deeds has b, d & bur rec from 1913, m rec from 1872, lnd rec from 1771; Clk Sup Ct has div, pro & civ ct rec from 1940; CH burned 1872, many older rec still available)		

Figure 138. Page from a gazetteer. (George B. Everton, Sr., *The Handy Book for Genealogists,* revised and enlarged, Logan, Utah: Everton Publishers, 1971, p. 165.)

Waco, *Ky.*, p.v., Madison co., 5 m. E. of Richmond.✝

Waco, *Miss.*, p.o., Marshall co.

Waco, *Mo.*, p.o., Jasper co.

Waco, *Neb.*, p.v.◆, York co., 19 m. W. of Seward by B.&M.R.RR. Pop. 127.

Waco, *N.C.*, p.o., Cleveland co.

Waco, *Tex.*, a thriving city◆, cap. of McLennan co., situated nearly in the centre of the State, on both sides of the Brazos R., which is spanned by a handsome suspension bridge, and on the H.&T.C., the M. P. and the T.&St.L.RRs., 186 m. N.W. Houston. The city is regularly laid out and remarkably well built, and contains a substantial stone court house, 9 churches, and a number of flourishing educational institutions, of which Waco University is the principal. Waco is the commercial centre of a rich and fertile country, which is rapidly filling up with immigrants, and has a number of manufacturing establishments, 1 nat. and 2 State banks, 2 daily, 1 tri-wkly, 3 wkly and 2 monthly papers. Pop. 7,296.

Waco'nia, *Minn.*, p.v. and tp., Carver co., on a lake of the same name, 8 m. N.W. Chaska. Pop. 218; of tp. 1,288.

Wacoo'chee, *Ala.*, p.o., Lee co.

Wacoochee Valley, *Ala.*, tp., Lee co. Pop. 1,571.

Wacous'ta, *Iowa*, p.tp., Humboldt co. P. 213.

Wacousta, *Mich.*, p.v. in Watertown tp., Clinton co., on Looking Glass R., 5 m.N.E. Eagle. P. 225.

Wacou'ta, *Minn.*, p.tp., Goodhue co. Pop. 88.

Wad'dams, *Ill.*, tp., Stephenson co. P. 1,436.

Wad'dam's Grove, *Ill.*, p.o.,Stephenson co.

Wad'dells, *N.C.*, p.o.. Rockingham co.

Wad'dill, *Mo.*, p.o., Newton co.

Wad'dington, *N.Y.*, p.v.◎ and tp., St. Lawrence co., on St. Lawrence R., which here supplies great water-power, 18 m. N.E. Ogdensburg. It has several mills and factories. Pop. 977; of tp. 2,609.

Wade, *Kan.*, p.o., Miami co.

Wade, *Me.*, tp., Aroostook co. Pop. 131.

Wade, *Ill.*, tp., Clinton co. Pop. 750.

—tp., Jasper co. Pop. 2,969.

Wade, *Mich.*, p.o., Clare co.

Wade, *N.C.*, p.o., Harnett co.

Wade, *O.*, p.o., Washington co.

Wad'ena, *Iowa*, p.v. in Illyria tp., Fayette co., on Volga R. and C.,M.&St.P.RR., 7 m. N.W. Volga City. Pop. 128.

Wadena, *Minn.*, a W. central co., drained by Crow Wing R.; area, 540 sq. m. The surface is rolling and consists chiefly of prairies. The chief prod. In 1880 were 47,634 bush. of wheat, and 17,924 of oats. Cap., Wadena. Val. of taxable prop. abt. $175,000. Pop. 2,080 (of whom 334 for.).

—p.v.◆ and tp., Wadena co., on N.P.RR., 47 m. W. by N. from Brainerd. Pop. 307; of tp. 737.

Wades, *Va.*, p.o., Bedford co.

Wades'borough, *Ky.*, p.h. and tp., Calloway co., 10 m. N. of Murray. Pop. 175; of tp. 1,626.

Wadesborough, *N.C.*, p.v.◆ and tp., cap. of Anson co., 18 m. N.W. Rockingham by C.C.RR. It has an institute, a bank, and a wkly paper. Pop. 800; of tp. 3,327.

Wades'burg, *Mo.*, p.o., Cass co.

Wade's Mill, *Ky.*, p.o., Clark co.

Wades'town, *W.Va.*, p.h., Monongalia co., 5 m. E. of Burton. Pop. 78.

Wades'ville, *Ind.*, p.v. in Centre tp., Posey co., 16 m. N.E. Mount Vernon. Pop. 101.

Wadesville, *Va.*, p.v., Clarke co., 10 m. E.N.E. Winchester. Pop. 100.

Wadeville, *Ind.*, p.o., Choctaw Nation.

Wadeville, *N.C.*, p.o., Montgomery co.

Wadham's Mills (wäd'amz), *N.Y.*, p.v. in Westport tp., Essex co., on D.&H.C.Co's.RR., 4 m. N.W. Westport. Pop. 165.

Wa'ding River, *N.J.*, p.h. in Bass River tp., Burlington co., on a small river of same name, 13 m. S.W. Egg Harbor City. Pop. 35.

Wading River. *N.Y.*, p.v. in Brookhaven and Riverhead tps., Suffolk co., near Long Island Sound, and 10 m. N.W. Riverhead. Pop. 397.

Wad'ley, *Ga.*, p.v.◆, Jefferson co., on C.RR. of Ga., 86 m. W. by N. from Macon. It has a high school. Pop. 281.

Wadley's Falls, *N.H.*, p.v. in Lee tp., Strafford co., on Lamprey R., 4 m. N.W. New Market.✝

Wad'malaw Island, *S.C.*, tp., Charleston co., consisting of one of the sea islands. Pop. 4,000.

Wadsworth, *Ala.*, p.o., Autauga co.

Wadsworth, *Ill.*, p.h. in Newport tp., Lake co., on Des Plaines R., 43 m. N. of Chicago by C.,M.&St.P.RR. Pop. 64.

Wadsworth, *Nev.*, p.v.◆, Washoe co., on Truckee R., 189 m. N.E. Sacramento, Cal. by C.P.RR. Pop. 661.

Wadsworth, *O.*, p.v.◆ and tp., Medina co., 53 m. E. of Mansfield by N.Y.,P.&O.RR. It has a Mennonite College, excellent schools, a bank, a wkly paper, and several factories. Pop. 1,219; of tp. 2,837.

Wad'y Petra, *Ill.*, p.h., Stark co., on R.I.& P.RR., 10 m. S.E. Toulor. Pop. 85.

Wael'der, *Tex.*, p.v.◆, Gonzales co., 80 m. E. by N. from San Antonio by G.,H.&S.A.RR. Pop. 225.

Wager, *Ark.*, p.o., Benton co.

Wag'gaman, *La.*, p.o., Jefferson parish.

Wag'goners, *W.Va.*, tp., Mason co. P. 4,585.

Wag'goners Ripple, *O.*, p.h. in Green tp., Adams co., on Brush Creek, 2 m. from the Ohio R., and 8 m. S.E. West Union. Pop. 60.

Wag'ner, *Iowa*, p.h.and tp.,Clayton co.,on Roberts Creek, 6 m. S. of Luana Station. P. 40; of tp. 997.

Wagner, *Oreg.*, p.o., Grant co.

Wagner, *Pa.*, p.v. in Decatur tp., Mifflin co., on a div. of Penn. RR., 12 m. N.E. Lewistown. P. 125.

Wagner, *S.C.*, tp., Oconee co. Pop. 3,247.

Wag'nerville, *Kan.*, p.o., Phillips co.

Wag'oner, *Ind.*, p.o., Miami co.

Wagon Landing, *Wis.*, p.o., Polk co.

Wagon Mound, *N.Mex.*, p.o., Mora co.

Wag'ontown, *Pa.*, p.h. in West Calin tp., Chester co., 15 m. N.W. West Chester. Pop. 80.

WagonWheel Gap, *Col.*,p.o.,Rio Grande co.

Wagon Works, *O.*, p.v.◆, Lucas co., within Toledo City limits.

Wa'gozn, *Ind.*, p.o., Pottawattamie co.

Wag'rum, *O.*, p.h. in Etna tp., Licking co., 14 m. E. of Columbus. Pop. 75.

Wagrum, *Va.*, p.o., Accomack co.

Wahu, *Ind.T.*, p.o., Nez Percés Nat.

Wahal'ak, *Miss.*, p.v. in Scooba tp., Kemper co., 48 m. N. of Meridian by M.&O.RR. Pop. 115.

Wah'buy, *Dak.*, p.o., Day co.

Wahee', *S.C.*, tp., Marion co. Pop. 1,998.

Wah'jamega, *Mich.*, p.v., Tuscola co., on Cass R., and on M.C.RR., 24 m. S.E. Bay City. P. 100.

Wahkink'um, *Wash.*, a S.W. co., bounded S. by Columbia R.; area, 150 sq. m. The surface is rough and mountainous, and generally covered with forests. Lumber is the chief wealth. Cap., Cathlamet. Pop. 1,600 (of whom 898 for., 559 Chinese, and 56 Indians).

Wahoo', *Ga.*, p.tp., Lumpkin co. Pop. 320.

Wahoo, *Neb.*, p.v.◆ in Stocking tp., cap. of Saunders co., at the confluence of Cottonwood and Wahoo Creeks, 39 m. N.E. Lincoln by U.P.RR. It has a graded school, a nat. and 2 private banks, and 3 wkly papers. Pop. 1,064.

—tp., Saunders co. Pop. 627.

Wahoo, *Tenn.*, p.o., Sullivan co.

Wah'peton, *Dak.*, p.v.◆, cap. of Richland co., on Red R. of the North, 1 m. W. of Breckenridge. Minn., by St.P.,M.&M.RR. Pop. 400.

Figure 139. Page from a gazetteer. (Leo de Colange, *The National Gazetteer: A Geographical Dictionary of the United States*, London. England: Hamilton, Adams, and Co., 1884, p. 1039.)

Names of Places.	Class.	County.	State.	Ref. Letters	Popula- tion.	D. fr. Wash.	D. fr. Cap.
CONSULTING INDEX.							15
Barkhamstead,......	t.........	Litchfield, ...	Ct.	V e	1,715	349	23
Barlow, ...	tsh.	Washington, ..	O.	M g	452	314	96
Barnard,.........	t.........	Windsor, ...	Vt.	V c	1,881	455	87
Barnardstown, ...	t.........	Franklin, ...	Mas.	V d	918	403	91
Barnegat, ...	t.........	Dutchess, ...	N. Y.	U e	......	297	79
Barnet, ...	t.........	Caledonia, ...	Vt.	V b	1,764	529	43
BARNSTABLE, ...	County,...	....	Mas.	X e	28,514	....	....
Barnstable,........	t.........	Barnstable,....	Mas.	X e	3,974	466	68
BARNWELL, ...	District, ...	....	S. C.	M m	19,236	....	....
Barnwell, C. H......	c. t.......	Barnwell, ...	S. C.	M m	......	562	62
Barnstead,........	t.........	Strafford, ...	N. H.	W c	2,047	492	18
Barnsville, ...	t.........	Belmont, ...	O.	M f	408	297	128
Barr,............	tsh.	Daviess, ...	In.	G h	......	666	128
Barre,............	t.........	Washington, ..	Vt.	V b	2,012	521	5
Barre, ...	t.........	Worcester,....	Mas.	V d	2,503	399	61
Barre, ...	tsh.	Orleans, ...	N. Y.	P c	4,768	386	260
Barre, ...	tsh.	Huntingdon, ..	Pa.	Q f	1,770	170	93
BARREN,........	County....	....	Ken.	I i	15,079	....	....
Barrington, ...	t.........	Stafford, ...	N. H.	W c	1,895	499	33
Barrington, Great,...	t.........	Berkshire, ...	Mas.	......	2,264	349	135
Barrington, ...A.	t.........	Bristol, ...	R. I.	W e	612	402	8
Barrington, ...A.	tsh. and t...	Yates,........	N. Y.	Q d	1,354	320	193
Barry, ... A.	tsh.	Schuylkill, ...	Pa.	R f	443	182	75
BARRY,..........	County....	....	M. T.	I d	......	....	....
Bart, ...A.	tsh.	Lancaster, ...	Pa.	R g	1,750	110	54
BARTHOLOMEW,	County,....	....	In.	H g	5,476	....	....
Bartlett,..........	t.........	Coos, ...	N. H.	W b	644	556	79
Barton, ...	t.........	Orleans, ...	Vt.	V b	729	568	45
Barton, ...	tsh.	Tioga, ...	N. Y.	R d	982	260	181
Bartonville, ...	t.........	Gasconade,...	Mo.	C h	......	945	35
Baskenridge, ...	t.........	Somerset, ...	N. J.	T f	......	213	47
Batavia, ...	tsh. and c. t.	Genesee,.....	N. Y.	P d	4,264	370	244
Batavia, ...	t.........	Greene,......	N. Y.	T d	......	349	44
Batavia, ...	tsh.	Clermont,.....	O.	J g	1,712	476	109
Batavia, ...	c. t.	Clermont,.....	O.	J g	426	476	109
Batavia, ...	tsh.	Geauga,......	O.	M e	336	320	164
Batesville,........	c. t.	Independence, .	A. T.	C k	......	1,044	102
Bath,............	t.........	Lincoln, ...	Me.	Y c	3,773	576	37
Bath,............	t.........	Grafton, ...	N. H.	V b	1,628	523	81
Bath,............	t.........	Rensselaer, ...	N. Y.	U d	......	374	1
Bath,............	tsh. and c. t.	Steuben, ...	N. Y.	Q d	3,387	299	216
BATH,...........	County....	....	Va.	O h	4,002	....	....
Bath, ...	c. t.	Morgan, ...	Va.	P g	......	93	186
Bath, ...	t.........	Beaufort, ...	N. C.	R k	......	318	138
BATH,...........	County....	....	Ken.	K h	8,799	....	....
Bath, ...	tsh.	Allen, ...	O.	J f	410	509	112
Bath,............	tsh.	Green, ...	O.	J g	1,534	452	56
Bath,............	tsh.	Medina, ...	O.	M e	374	344	123
Bath,............	tsh.	Franklin, ...	In.	J g	......	520	82
BATON ROUGE, E.	Parish, ...	....	La.	C p	6,698	....	....
BATON ROUGE,W.	Parish, ...	....	La.	B n	3,084	....	....
Baton Rouge,......	c. t.	E. Baton Rouge,	La.	C p	......	1,237	117
Battle Town, ...	t.........	Frederick, ...	Va.	Q g	......	59	160
Baughman, ...	tsh.	Wayne, ...	O.	M f	1,231	346	115
Bay, ...	tsh.	Sandusky, ...	O.	K e	149	442	117
Bayard's Town,*....	Borough,...	Allegany, ...	Pa.	N f	2,118	....	....
Bazetta, ...	tsh.	Trumbull, ...	O.	N c	539	302	162
Bazil, ...a.	t.........	Fairfield, ...	O.	L g	73	377	32

* Bayard's Town Borough is in the vicinity of Pittsburgh, and is considered a suburb of that city.

Figure 140. Page from a gazetteer. (Samuel Augustus Mitchell, *An Accompaniment to Mitchell's Reference and Distance Map of the United States*, Philadelphia: Mitchell and Hinman, 1834, p. 15.)

2. Some gazetteers do not distinguish between a church parish and a government parish.

3. The name of a particular locality may not be listed in the gazetteer:

    a. The gazetteer may cover too large an area to include small place names.

    b. The name of the locality may not be the name of a town, city, or parish, but the name of a river, lake, or landmark that is not included in the gazetteer.

    c. The gazetteer includes only place names that existed at the time of publication.

    d. Some place names may be omitted because of oversight.

4. Gazetteers do not always include all the desired genealogical information, and it may be necessary to search more than one gazetteer. (Information not pertinent to genealogical research need not be copied.)

MAPS AND ATLASES

Maps and atlases (bound book of maps) are used in genealogical research to obtain visual pictures of specific localities or places.

Genealogical Application

Each time genealogical research reveals a new place name, a map should be consulted for the following information:

1. Geographic location in relation to other localities

2. Size in relation to other localities

3. Nearness to borders of other countries, counties, townships, parishes, etc.

4. Nearness to lakes, rivers, oceans, railroads, cemeteries, etc.

5. Distance from one town to another by using the "scale," which is a relationship of inches to miles, or foreign equivalent

6. Boundary outlines

Genealogical Limitations

Few maps are designed and published specifically for genealogical research; therefore, there are genealogical limitations:

1. Not all places may be shown.

2. The map may cover too large an area to show special details, such as churches, schools, cemeteries, etc.

3. The map will show only localities that existed at the time of publication of the map.

4. Some maps are not indexed or are indexed poorly.

5. A printed place name may cross over a boundary line, causing difficulty in determining the correct boundary.

AVAILABILITY

There are various ways in which genealogical reference books can be obtained:

1. Books in print (note date on title page) are available through the publisher.

2. Books in print are available through genealogical mail-order service. Write and request a specific reference and the price, since prices vary:

> Deseret Book Company
> 44 East South Temple
> P.O. Box 659
> Salt Lake City, Utah 84111

> The Genealogy Tree
> 1348 North 380 West
> Provo, Utah 84601

3. Some books are available at local libraries.

4. Some books are available at the Library of the Genealogical Society.

5. Some books that are out of print are available on microfilm at branch libraries of the Genealogical Society.

6. Some books that are out of print are available through bookstores that specialize in used books, such as the following:

> Genealogical Publishing Co., Inc.
> 521-532 St. Paul Place
> Baltimore, Maryland 21202

> Goodspeed's Book Shop, Inc.
> 18 Beacon Street
> Boston, Massachusetts 02108

GENEALOGICAL RESEARCH JURISDICTIONS

A genealogical jurisdiction is the authority or governing body that initiates the keeping of genealogical records. The genealogical jurisdictions most frequently used are the government (civil) jurisdiction and the church (ecclesiastical) jursidiction. (See Chapter 3.) Genealogical or record-keeping jurisdictions generally coincide with geographic jurisdictions, and the Genealogical Society uses the name of the geographic jurisdiction for the genealogical jurisdiction.

The name of the genealogical jurisdiction is determined by the Genealogical Society through the use of *The Statesman's Year-Book* (S.H. Steinberg, ed., London: Macmillan & Co. Ltd., 1956, 1638 pp.). Figure 141 illustrates the names of the genealogical jurisdictions for various countries, and Figures 142 and 143 illustrate the order in which to record the genealogical jurisdictions on locality note cards.

The Genealogical Society has established a standard with which to record the genealogical jurisdictions for each Genealogical Society program, and this standard varies with different programs; therefore, there is some inconsistency. For an illustration of the various Genealogical Society programs, the time period used to establish the genealogical jurisdiction, the order in which the jurisdiction is recorded, and an example of the jurisdictions, see Figure 144.

Country	Genealogical Jurisdictions		
ARGENTINA	Argentina	Federal District or Province	Town
ATLANTIC ISLANDS	Atlantic Islands	Island	Town
AUSTRALIA	Australia	State, Territory, or Island	Town
AUSTRIA	Austria	Administrative State	Town
AUSTRIA- HUNGARY	Not to be used		
BELGIUM	Belgium	Province	Town
BOLIVIA	Bolivia	Department	Town
BRAZIL	Brazil	Federal District, State, or Territory	Town
BULGARIA	Bulgaria	Department (*Oblast*)	Town
CANADA	Province	County (if no county, repeat province)	Town
CANAL ZONE	See Panama		
CARIBBEAN ISLANDS	Caribbean Islands	Island	Town
CHANNEL ISLANDS	Channel Islands	Island	Town
CHILE	Chile	Territory or Province	Town
CHINA	China	Province	Town
COLOMBIA	Colombia	Department (*Comisarias, Intendencias*)	Town
COSTA RICA	Costa Rica	Province	Town
CUBA	See Caribbean Islands		
CZECHOSLO- VAKIA	Czechoslovakia	County	Town
DENMARK	Denmark	County (*Amt*)	Town, Parish
ECUADOR	Ecuador	Province or Territory	Town
EL SALVADOR	El Salvador	Department	Town
ENGLAND	England	County or Shire	Town, Parish
FINLAND	Finland	County (*Laani*)	Town, Parish
FRANCE	France	Department	Town

Figure 141.   Genealogical jurisdictions for locality note cards. (Continued on next page)

Country	Genealogical Jurisdictions		
GERMANY	Germany	Minor States: Anhalt Brunswick Lippe-Detmold Oldenburg Schaumburg-Lippe Waldeck Mecklenburg-Schwerin Mecklenburg-Strelitz	Town
		Free Cities: Bremen Hamburg Luebeck	Town
	Major States: Baden Bavaria	County (*Kreis*) Government District (Regierungsbezirk)	Town Town
	Hesse- Darmstadt	Government District (*Provin*)	Town
	Prussia	Administrative Province (*Provinz*)	Town
	Saxony	Government District (*Kreishauptmannschaft*)	Town
	Thuringia Württemberg	Former Duchy Government District (*Kreis*)	Town Town
GERMANY, WEST	West Germany	State (*Laender*)	Town
GERMANY, EAST	East Germany	District (*Bezirke*)	Town
GIBRALTAR	Gibraltar	Gibraltar	Gibraltar
GUAM	See Pacific Islands		
GUATEMALA	Guatemala	Department	Town
HONDURAS	Honduras	Department or Territory	Town
HUNGARY	Hungary	District (Megye)	Town
ICELAND	Iceland	County (Sysla)	Town
INDIAN OCEAN ISLAND	Indian Ocean	Island	Town
INDONESIA	Indonesia	Province	Town
IRELAND	Ireland	County	Town, Parish
ISLE OF MAN	England	Isle of Man	Town
ITALY	Italy	Province (*Provincia*)	Town
JAPAN	Japan	Prefecture (*Ken*)	Town

Figure 141. Genealogical jurisdictions for locality note cards. (Continued on
next page)

Country	Genealogical Jurisdictions		
KOREA	Korea	Province	Town
LUXEMBOURG	Luxembourg	Administrative Co. (*Canton*)	Town
MEXICO	Mexico	Federal District	Town
NETHERLANDS	Netherlands	Province (*Provincia*)	Town
NEW ZEALAND	New Zealand	Province or County	Town
NICARAGUA	Nicaragua	Department or Territory	Town
NORWAY	Norway	County (*Amt, Fylke*)	Town, Parish
PANAMA	Panama	Province	Town
PARAGUAY	Paraguay	Department or Fed. Dist.	Town
PERU	Peru	Department or Constitutional Province	Town
POLAND	Poland	Voivodship	Town
PORTUGAL	Portugal	District (*Regiao*)	Town
PUERTO RICO	See Caribbean Islands		
RHODESIA	Rhodesia	District	Town
SAMOA	See Pacific Islands		
SCOTLAND	Scotland	County or Shire	Town, Parish
SOUTH AFRICA	South Africa	Province	Town
SPAIN	Spain	Province	Town
SURINAM	Surinam	District	Town
SWEDEN	Sweden	County (*Lan*)	Town, Parish
SWITZERLAND	Switzerland	District (*Canton*)	Town
UNITED STATES	Alaska	Alaska	Town
	Hawaii	Island	Town
	State	County from which created	Ind. City
	Other states	County	Town
URUGUAY	Uruguay	Department	Town
USSR	USSR	County (Soviet Republic)	Town
VENEZUELA	Venezuela	Fed. District, State, or Territory	Town
WALES	Wales	County or Shire	Town, Parish
YUGOSLAVIA	Yugoslavia	Federated Republic	Town
ZAMBIA	Zambia	Province	Town

Figure 141.   Genealogical jurisdictions for locality note cards. (Concluded)

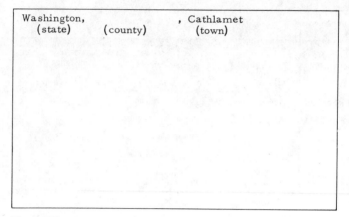

Figure 142.   White locality note card for Cathlamet, Washington.

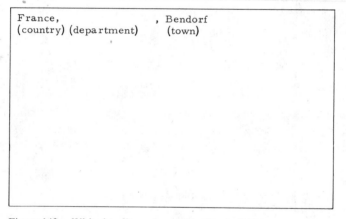

Figure 143.   White locality note card for Bendorf, France.

Genealogical Society Program	Time Period	Order to Record Jurisdiction	Example of Order to Record Jurisdiction
Family Group Record	Time of Recording	Smallest to largest	Portland, Multnomah, Oregon
Dictionary Card Catalog (locality section)	Time of cataloging	Largest to smallest	Oregon, Multnomah, Portland
Dictionary Card Catalog (alphabetical section)	Time of cataloging and/or time of event	Smallest to largest	Portland, Multnomah, Oregon
The Name Tabulation Program	Time of event	Smallest to largest	Portland, Multnomah, Oregon
Computer File Index	Time of event	Largest to smallest	Oregon, Multnomah, Portland

Figure 144.   Genealogical Society programs and jurisdictions.

BIBLIOGRAPHY—GAZETTEERS AND MAPS

The following gazetteers and maps are recommended for identifying place names and establishing genealogical jurisdictions on the first four-generation family group records. Many of these references are available for purchase for home use; others are available on microfilm through branch libraries. The countries are arranged alphabetically and are those most often of interest in genealogical research. When it is impossible to obtain a recommended reference or impossible to interpret a recommended reference, or when the country of interest is not listed, one can write to the Genealogical Society. (See sample letter, Figure 145.)

Your Name
Your Address
Current Date

The Genealogical Society
50 East North Temple Street
Salt Lake City, Utah 84150

Gentlemen:

    I am doing some genealogical research in Australia, and would appreciate it if you could provide me with the correct genealogical jurisdictions for Hungerford.

    Could you also recommend a good gazetteer and map to use for research in Australia?

    I will be very grateful for any information you can send to me, and I am enclosing a stamped self-addressed envelope for your reply.

    Thank you.

Sincerely yours,

Your Name (signed)

Encl: Stamped self-addressed envelope

Figure 145.   Letter to the Genealogical Society.

References at the Genealogical Society Library were used to determine bibliographic data, and the bibliographic format has been established as follows:

1. Gazetteers for each country are listed in the recommended order for research before the list of maps for each country.

2. English translation for foreign titles is word for word and in parentheses after the title.

3. A description is included to assist in determining the usefulness of the reference book.

4. The limitations and intent of the compiler are not included, and the genealogical researcher must read the preface and/or introduction of each reference to determine this.

5. If the reference is in print or available through used book dealers, the name and the address of the publisher is included so one may obtain a copy for home use.

6. The title of the book, the compiler, and/or the name and address of the publisher may have changed with different editions.

7. For references in print, no publication date is included unless the reference has been available for more than fifty years, in which case a time period is indicated. (The most recent edition is not always the best genealogical reference.)

8. For references out of print, the date of publication or approximate time period is indicated.

9. The Genealogical Society call number is provided to save time when using the reference at the Library of the Genealogical Society or when corresponding with the Genealogical Society concerning the specific reference.

10. Genealogical Society call numbers may or may not have a prefix. Additional copies may be located in the reference section, map collection, regular stacks, oversized collection, extra surveillance area.

11. The year for various editions and additional copies is not provided. Various editions may not be shelved together.

12. The Genealogical Society microfilm number is included so one can determine the availability through branch libraries.

13. The edition date is provided for microfilmed copies.

14. Sample locality cards are included as guides for extracting genealogical information. Additions and English translations of foreign terms are included in brackets.

BELGIUM—GAZETTEER

Dictionnaire Historique et Geographique des Communes Belges
(Historic and Geographic Dictionary of the Communities
of Belgium). 2 vols. In print.
Compiler: Eugene De Seyn.
Publisher: Établissements Brepols S. A., Turnhout, Belgium.
Description: Historical gazetteer which gives names of towns
and the province in which the town is located; includes
general reference maps of the nine provinces; not indexed.
GS call number: Ref 949.3, E2s.
GS film number: Not microfilmed.
Example of genealogical information, Figure 146.

```
Belgium, Flandre Occidentale, Aalbeke
(country)    (province)          (town)


   Aalbeke, community in the
      province of Flandre Occ [Occidentale]




Dictionnaire Historique et Geographique des Communes
   Belges.  GS Ref 949.3, E2s  1947 edition
```

Figure 146. Locality note card for Aalbeke, Belgium.

BELGIUM—MAP

Road Map, write (see sample letter, Figure 147):
National Tourist Council
Antwerp, Belgium

                                                Your Name
                                                Your Address
                                                Current Date

National Tourist Council
Antwerp, Belgium

Gentlemen:

    Would you please send me a copy of a road map for
Belgium?

    Enclosed is an American Express Money Order for
$2.00 to cover the cost of the map. I will be happy to send
more if necessary.

    Thank you.

                                        Sincerely yours,

                                        Your Name (signed)

Encl: $2.00

Figure 147.   Letter to a national tourist council.

CANADA—GAZETTEERS

Gazetteer of Canada. A series; one volume for each province.
   In print.
Author: Canadian Permanent Committee on Geographic
   Names.
Publisher: Queen's Printer, Ottawa, Canada.
Description: Gives names of places and a description of the
   place.
GS call numbers:

Ref 971.42, E5c	Alberta
Ref 971.1, E5c	British Columbia
Ref 971.46, E5c	Manitoba
Ref 971.72, E5c	New Brunswick
Ref 971.8, E5ca	Newfoundland and Labrador
Ref 971.25, E5c	Northwest Territories and Yukon
Ref 971.74, E5c	Nova Scotia
Ref 971.76, E5c	Prince Edward Island
Ref 971.44, E5c	Saskatchewan
Ref 971.5, E5c	Southwestern Ontario

GS film number: Not microfilmed.
Example of genealogical information, Figure 148.

```
British Columbia, Alberni
   (province)       (city)


   Alberni, a city north of Alberni Inlet in Alberni Dist.










Gazetteer of Canada British Columbia
GS Ref 971. 1, E5c  2d. ed. 1966
```

Figure 148.   White locality note card for Alberni, Canada.

Bullinger's Postal and Shippers Guide for the United States and Canada. In print.
Publisher: Bullinger's Guide, Inc., 63 Woodland Avenue, Westwood, New Jersey 07675.
Description: Gives names of places and the province in which the place is located.
GS call number: Ref 970, E8b.
GS film number: 1951 edition, 483,709.
Example of genealogical information, Figure 149.

```
British Columbia, Alberni
   (province)        (city)


   Alberni, B.C. [British Columbia]






Bullinger's Postal and Shippers Guide
GS Ref 970, E8b  1970 edition
```

Figure 149.   White locality note card for Alberni, Canada.

CANADA—MAP

Rand McNally Road Atlas. No. 3285. In print.
Publisher: Rand McNally & Company, P. O. Box 7600, Chicago, Illinois 60680.
Description: General reference maps; indexed.
GS call number: Not available at the Genealogical Society.
GS film number: Not microfilmed.

DENMARK—GAZETTEERS

Post-Og Telegraf Adressebog for Kongeriget Danmark (Post Telegraph Address Book for the Kingdom of Denmark). In print.
Publisher: Generaldirektoratet for Post-Og Telegrafvaesenet., Copenhagen, Denmark.

Description: Alphabetical list of place names which gives the name of the parish in which the place is located; separate section gives the name of the parish and the county in which the parish is located.

GS call number: Ref 948.9, E8g.

GS film numbers:

    1909 edition, 041,040

    1948 edition, 255,804

Example of genealogical information, Figure 150.

```
Denmark, Vejle, Jerlev, Mejsling
(country) (county)(parish) (village)


    Mejsling, Jerlev S [parish], Vejle




    Post-Og Telegraf Adressebog for Kongeriget Danmark
    GS Ref 948. 9, E8g  1960 edition
```

Figure 150.   White locality note card for Mejsling, Denmark.

J. P. Trap Kongeriget Danmark (J. P. Trap, Kingdom of Denmark). 5 vols. Out of print.

Compiler: H. Weitemeyer.

Publisher: Universitetsboghandler G. E. C. Gad, Copenhagen, Denmark.

Publication date: 1898-1909.

Description: Gives names of places and the parish, judicial district, and county in which the place is located; gives names of villages within each parish; information arranged by county; indexed in volume 5.

GS call number: Ref 948.9, E2t.

GS film numbers:
    1898-1909   599,364 vol. 1, Copenhagen City
    (3rd edition)   Frederiksberg Suburb
                     599,365 vol. 2, Frederiksborg Amt
                                      Kjøbenhavns Amt
                                      Holbæk Amt
                                      Sorø Amt
                                      Præstø Amt
                     599,366 vol. 3, Bornholms Amt
                                      Maribo Amt
                                      Odense Amt
                                      Svendborg Amt
                     599,367 vol. 4, Hjørring Amt
                                      Thisted Amt
                                      Aalborg Amt
                                      Viborg Amt
                                      Randers Amt
                     599,368 vol. 5, Aarhus Amt
                                      Vejle Amt
                                      Ringkjøbing Amt
                                      Ribe Amt
                                      Faerø Islands
                                      Index to parishes and villages

Example of genealogical information, Figure 151.

```
Denmark, Vejle, Jerlev, Mejsling
(country) (county)(parish)(village)

   Jerlev Sogn [parish]
   Jerlev Herred [judicial district]
   Vejle Amt [county]

   Byerne [villages]
      Jerlev              Smalle-Jerlev
      Mejsling            Jerlevgaard
      Jerlev Engmark      Tvedgaard
      Søndermark




Trap's Kongeriget Danmark
GS F 599,368,  vol. 5, 3d. edition 1898-1909
```

Figure 151.   White locality note card for Mejsling, Denmark.

DENMARK—MAPS

Genealogical Guidebook and Atlas of Denmark. In print.

Authors: Frank Smith and Finn A. Thomsen.

Publisher: Bookcraft, Inc., 1848 West 2300 South, Salt Lake City, Utah 84119.

Description: A book of black and white maps; similar to *Kort Over Danmark:* Lutheran (state church) parish boundaries are indicated; indexed.

GS call number: Ref 948.9, E6s.

GS film number: Not microfilmed.

Kort Over Danmark (Map of Denmark). In print.

Publisher: Geodaetisk Instituts Generalstabskort, Copenhagen, Denmark.

Description: A book of colored maps; similar to *Genealogical Guidebook and Atlas of Denmark;* Lutheran (State Church) parishes are indicated, but no parish boundaries; indexed. 2 scales: 3 vol. set 1:100,000; 1 vol., 1:200,000.

GS call number: Ref 948.9, G29g.

GS film number: Not microfilmed.

ENGLAND—GAZETTEERS

A Genealogical Gazetteer of England. In print.

Author: Frank Smith.

Publisher: Genealogical Publishing Co., Baltimore, Maryland.

Description: Gives names of places and the parish and county in which the place is located; gives names of chapelries within each parish; gives non-conformist churches; gives earliest date of Church of England parish registers; information extracted from Lewis's *A Topographical Dictionary of England,* 1831 and 1833 editions, and Arthur M. Burke's *Key to the Ancient Parish Registers of England and Wales* (London: Sackville Press, 1908).

GS Call number: Ref 942, E5g.

GS film number: Not microfilmed.

Example of genealogical information, Figure 152.

```
England, Nottingham, Edwinstow, Ollerton
(country)  (county)     (parish)    (town)

  Ollerton, market town and
     chapelry 1592 [date registers began]
  In parish of Edwinstow, Notts [Nottingham]

  Non-conformist Church:  Wesleyan Methodist




  Smith's Genealogical Gazetteer of England
  GS Ref 942, E5g  1968 edition
```

Figure 152.   White locality note card for Ollerton, England.

A Topographical Dictionary of England. 4 vols. Out of print.
Author: Samuel Lewis.
Publisher: S. Lewis and Company.
Publication date: 1831-1850.
Description: Gives names of places and the parish and county
    in which the place is located; gives names of chapelries
    within each parish; gives non-conformist churches.
GS call number: Ref 942, E5L.
GS film numbers:

1831 ed.	413,519	vol. 1, A-C
	413,520	vol. 2, D-K
	413,521	vol. 3, L-R
	413,522	vol. 4, S-Z
1842 ed.	496,543	vol. 1, A-C
	"	vol. 2, D-K
	823,621	vol. 3, L-R
	496,544	vol. 4, S-Z
1845 ed.	496,541	vol. 1, A-C
	"	vol. 2, D-K
	496,542	vol. 3, L-R
	"	vol. 4, S-Z
1845 ed.	412,147	vol. 1, A-C
	412,148	vol. 2, D-K
	412,149	vol. 3, L-R
	412,150	vol. 4, S-Z

1848 ed.   599,117   vol. 1, A-C   1st item on film
            496,481   vol. 2, D-K   2nd item on film
            496,482   vol. 3, L-R   1st item on film
              ''   vol. 4, S-Z   2nd item on film

Example of genealogical information, Figure 153.

England, Nottingham, Bilborough, Broxtowe
(country) (county)   (parish)   (town)

   Broxtowe not listed.

   Lewis' Topographical Dictionary of England
   GS Ref 942, E5L 1831 edition

Figure 153.   White locality note card for Broxtowe, England.

Imperial Gazetteer of England and Wales. 6 vols. Out of print.
Author: John Marius Wilson.
Publisher: A. Fullarton & Co., Edinburgh, Scotland.
Publication date: No date. [1860s]
Description: Gives names of places and the parish and county
   in which the place is located; includes many small places;
   gives non-conformist churches.
GS call number: Ref 942, E5i.
GS film numbers:

897,325   vol. 1, Aaron End–Chartley
             Holme   1st item on film
   ''   vol. 2, Chart-Grasmere   2nd item on film
897,326   vol. 3, Grasmoore-Lees   1st item on film
   ''   vol. 4, Leescourt-Mounton   2nd item on film
897,327   vol. 5, Mount Pellon-Sheffield 1st item on film
   ''   vol. 6, Sheffield-Zouch and 2nd item on film
             Summary

Example of genealogical information, Figure 154.

England, Nottingham, Bilborough, Broxtowe
(country) (county)   (parish)   (town)

  Broxtow, a hamlet in Nottingham in the parish of
    Bilbrough; [Broxtow] was once a parish.

Imperial Gazetteer of England and Wales
GS Ref 942, E5i

Figure 154.   White locality note card for Broxtowe, England.

Gazetteer of the British Isles (formerly Survey Gazetteer of the
British Isles). In print.
Publisher: John Bartholomew & Son, Ltd., Edinburgh, Scot-
land.
Publication date: 1904 to present.
Description: Gives names of small places and county in which
the place is located; no distinction is made between civil
and ecclesiastical parish.
GS call number: Ref 942, E5ba.
GS film number: 1904 edition 599,554.
Examples of genealogical information, Figures 155 and 156.

England, Warwickshire, Foleshill, Foleshill
(country) (county)   (parish)   (village)

  Foleshill, a parish and village in Warwickshire
  Church of England Churches: St. Laurence
                               St. Paul

Bartholomew's Gazetteer of the British Isles
GS Ref 942, E5ba 9th edition 1943 reprinted 1966

Figure 155.   White locality note card for Foleshill, England.

```
England, Nottingham, Bilborough, Broxtowe
(country) (county)      (parish)      (town)


  Broxtowe, hamlet and seat, in county and 3 m. NW of
  Nottingham.




Bartholomew's Gazetteer of the British Isles
GS Ref 942, E5ba 9th edition 1943  reprinted 1966
```

Figure 156.   White locality note card for Broxtowe, England.

ENGLAND—MAPS

Bartholomew Road Atlas Britain. In print.
Publisher: John Bartholomew & Son, Ltd., Edinburgh, Scotland.
Description: A book of modern general reference maps with index.
GS call number: Not available at the Genealogical Society.
GS film number: Not microfilmed.

A Genealogical Atlas of England and Wales. In print.
Compilers: David E. Gardner, Derek Harland, and Frank Smith.
Publisher: Deseret Book Company, 44 East South Temple Street, Salt Lake City, Utah 84111.
Description: A reproduction of 100-year-old maps; Church of England parishes are indicated, but no parish boundaries; not indexed.
GS call number: Ref 942, E3g.
GS film number: Not microfilmed.

A Series of Parish Outline Maps for the Counties of England and Wales. In print.
Publisher: A. Fullarton & Co., Edinburgh, Scotland.
Publication date: No date. [1860s]
Description: Church of England parish outline maps for the counties of England; detailed map for the city of London; maps for East Riding, North Riding, and West Riding of Yorkshire.

GS call number: Map, E7in.
GS film number: Not microfilmed.

Atlas to the Topographical Dictionaries of England and Wales.
   Out of print.
Publisher: S. Lewis and Company, London, England.
Publication date: 1831-1850.
Description: General reference maps of the counties of England and Wales; Church of England parishes are indicated, but no parish boundaries; not indexed.
GS call number: Ref Q 942, E5L.
GS film numbers:
   1845 edition 496,476 5th item on film
   1849 edition 496,477 2nd item on film

FRANCE—GAZETTEER

Dictionnaire National des Communes de France (National Dictionary of the Communities of France). In print.
Publisher: Editions Albin Michel, 22 Rue Huyghens, Paris, France.
Description: Gives towns with name of department; alphabetical list of departments at front of book.
GS call number: Ref 944, E5di.
GS film number: Not microfilmed.
Example of genealogical information, Figure 157.

```
France, Haut-Rhin, Bendorf
(country) (department) (town)


   Bendorf, Haut-Rhin [department]




Dictionnaire des Communes de France
GS Ref 944, 35di  1965 edition
```

Figure 157.   White locality note card for Bendorf, France.

FRANCE—MAP

Road Map, write (see sample letter, Figure 147):
    National Tourist Council
    Paris, France

GERMANY—GAZETTEERS

Meyer's Orts un Verkehrslexikon (Meyer's Town and Traffic
    Dictionary). Out of print.
Compiler: Dr. E. Uetrecht.
Publisher: Bibliographisches Institut, Leipzig, Germany.
Publication date: 1912.
Description: Gives names of places and parish and state in
    which the place is located as of 1871; gives names of
    churches and denominations.
GS call number: Ref 943, E5mo.
GS film numbers:
    1912 edition   496,640 vol. 1, A-K
                        496,641 vol. 2, L-Z
Example of genealogical information, Figure 158.

```
Prussia, Rheinland, Belgweiler
 (state) (province)   (village)


   Belgweiler
      D [village]
      Pr Rheinl [Province Rheinland]
      RB [district] Coblenz
      Kr A.G. [district court] Simmern
      Std A [civil registrar] Ohlweiler
      [no parish, look under Ohlweiler for parish]



   Meyer's Orts und Verkehrslexicon
   GS F 496,640  1912 edition
```

Figure 158.   White locality note card for Belgweiler, Prussia.

Müllers Grosses Deutsches Ortsbuch (Müller's Great German
    Gazetteer). In print.
Author: Fritz Müller.
Publisher: Post-und Ortsbuchverlag, Postmeister A. D.
    Friedrich Müller, Wuppertal-Barmen 10, Germany.
Description: Gives names of places and modern state in which

the place is located. Supplement gives modern names of places formerly in Germany, but now in other countries.
GS call number: Ref 943, E5m.
GS film number: Not microfilmed.
Example of genealogical information, Figure 159.

```
Germany West  Rheinland Pfalz,  Belgweiler
(country)        (state)          (village)


  Belgweiler, Rhein Pfalz [Rheinland Pfalz]




  Müllers Grosses Deutsches Ortsbuch
  GS Ref 943, E5m  1958 edition
```

Figure 159.   White locality note card for Belgweiler, West Germany.

GERMANY—MAPS

The German Empire of 1871. In print.
Publisher: Larry O. Jensen and Norman J. Storrer, P.O. Box 502, Pleasant Grove, Utah 84062.
Description: A Set of 21 different maps covering each kingdom, province, principality, duchy, etc.; includes 1 general map of the entire German Empire; establishes boundaries as of 1871.
Publication date: 1975.
GS call number: Ref 943 E7j.
GS film number: Not microfilmed.

Map of the German Empire. Out of print.
Publisher: No publisher indicated; filmed by the Genealogical Society at Berlin-Dahlem.
Description: Detailed map of German Empire in scale 1:100,000; 674 pages.
Publication date: About 1914.
GS call number: Original not available at the Genealogical Society.
GS film number: 068,814.

Der Grosse ADAC General Atlas The Giant ADAC General Atlas). In print.

Publisher: Mairs Geographischer Verlag, 7000 Stuttgart, Germany.

Description: Modern road map indicating boundaries.

Publication date: 1974.

GS call number: Staff 943,E3dg.

GS film number: Not microfilmed.

IRELAND—GAZETTEERS

The Parliamentary Gazetteer of Ireland. 10 vols. Out of print.

Publisher: A. Fullarton, Dublin, Ireland.

Publication date: 1844.

Description: Gives names of small places and the name of the parish, county, and barony in which the place is located; some maps; not indexed.

GS call number: Ref 941.5, E5p.

GS film numbers:

1844 edition

824,043	pt. 1, Abbert-Armagh	4th item on film
''	pt. 2, Armagh-Carragh	5th item on film
824,044	pt. 3, Carragh-Cushleak	1st item on film
''	pt. 4, Dalradia-Galway	2nd item on film
''	pt. 5, Galway-Killineen	3rd item on film
''	pt. 6, Killinegaruff-Magherafelt	4th item on film
824,045	pt. 7, Magherahall-Raphoe	1st item on film
''	pt. 8, Raphoe-Tibohine	2nd item on film
''	pt. 9, Tibohine-Youghal	3rd item on film
''	pt. 10, Youghal-Z and index	4th item on film

Example of genealogical information, Figure 160.

```
Ireland, Kildare, Belan, Belan
(country)(county) (parish) (town)


   Belan, a parish in the barony of Kilkea and Moone,
      County Kildare, Leintster [province]








   Parliamentary Gazetteer of Ireland
   GS F 824,043  1844 edition
```

Figure 160.   White locality note card for Belan, Ireland.

A Topographical Dictionary of Ireland. 2 vols. Out of print.
Author: Samuel Lewis.
Publisher: S. Lewis and Company, 87 Aldersgate Street, London, England.
Publication date: 1837-1850.
Description: Gives names of places and the name of the parish and county in which the place is located; gives names of non-conformist churches.
GS call number: Ref 941.5, E5L.
GS film numbers:

1837 edition	599,557	vol. 1, A-G	
	''	vol. 2, H-Z	
	413,528	vol. 2, H-Z	
	496,572	vol. 2, H-Z	3rd item on film
1847 edition	496,478	vol. 1, A-J	
	''	vol. 2, K-Z	
1849 edition	496,479	vol. 1, A-J	
	496,480	vol. 2, K-Z	
1850 edition	413,526	vol. 1, A-J	

Example of genealogical information, Figure 161.

```
Ireland, Kildare, Belan
(country)(county)  (parish)


    Belan, a parish in the barony of Kilkea and Moone,
        County of Kildare and province of Leinster






Lewis' Topographical Dictionary of Ireland
GS F 599, 557  1837 edition
```

Figure 161.   White locality note card for Belan, Ireland.

*The General Alphabetical Index to the Townlands and Towns of
    Ireland, Published with the Census of Ireland.* Out of print.
Publisher: Her Majesty's Stationery Office, Dublin, Ireland.
Publication date: 1861-1901.
Description: Gives names of places with the name of the
    parish, county, and barony in which the place is located.
GS call number: Ref 941.5, X2Ci.
GS film numbers:
    1871 edition   476,999   2nd item on film
    1901 edition   865,092
Example of genealogical information, Figure 162.

```
Ireland, Kildare, Belan
(country)(county)  (parish)


    Belan, a parish, Co. Kildare, Barony of Kilkea and
        Moone






Index to the Townlands and Towns of Ireland
GS F 476, 999   1871 edition
```

Figure 162.   White locality note card for Belan, Ireland.

Gazetteer of the British Isles (formerly *Survey Gazetteer of the British Isles*). In print.

Publisher: John Bartholomew & Son, Ltd., Edinburgh, Scotland.

Publication date: 1904 to present.

Description: Gives names of small places and county in which the place is located; no distinction is made between civil and ecclesiastical parish.

GS call number: Ref 942, E5ba.

GS film number: 1904 edition 599,554.

Example of genealogical information, Figure 163.

```
Ireland, Kildare, Belan
(country)(county)  (parish)


   Belan, parish and seat in County Kildare






Bartholomew's Gazetteer of the British Isles
GS Ref 942, E5ba 9th edition  1943   reprinted 1966
```

Figure 163.   White locality note card for Belan, Ireland.

IRELAND—MAPS

Genealogical Atlas of Ireland. Out of print.

Compilers: David E. Gardner, Derek Harland, and Frank Smith.

Publisher: Deseret Book Company, 44 East South Temple Street, Salt Lake City, Utah 84111.

Description: A book of black and white maps which have been reproduced from maps in *Philips' Handy Atlas of the Counties of Ireland, 1885,* and *Lewis's Atlas Comprising the Counties of Ireland, 1846.* Church of Ireland parishes are indicated, but no parish boundaries. Baronies are indicated. Index to *Philips* only.

GS call number: Ref 941.5, E3.

GS film number: Not microfilmed.

Lewis's Atlas Comprising the Counties of Ireland and a General Map of the Kingdom. Out of print.

Publisher: S. Lewis and Co., London, England.

Description: A book of general reference maps; Church of Ireland parishes are indicated, but no parish boundaries; boundaries of baronies are indicated; not indexed.

Publication date: 1846.

GS call number: Ref 941.5, E5L.

GS film numbers:

    1846 edition   496,477 1st item on film

           ''   ''   599,866 3rd item on film (film indicates 2nd item)

Philips' Handy Atlas of the Counties of Ireland. Out of print.

Publisher: George Philips and Son, 32 Fleet Street, London, England.

Publication date: 1884.

Description: A book of colored general reference county maps; boundaries of baronies are indicated; indexed by names of small places.

GS call number: 941.5, E3b.

GS film number: Not microfilmed.

ITALY—GAZETTEER

Nuovo Dizionario Dei Communi e Frazioni di Commune

(New Dictionary of the Municipal Divisions of the Communities). In print.

Publisher: Societá Editrice Dizionario Voghera Dei Communi, Rome, Italy.

Description: Section I gives names of municipalities and name of the province in which the municipality is located; Section III gives names of small towns (hamlets) with reference to municipality.

GS call number: Ref 945, E5n.

GS film number: Not microfilmed.

Examples of genealogical information, Figures 164 and 165.

Italy, Perugia, Preci, Abeto
(country)(province) (municipality)(hamlet)

    Abeto in municipality of Preci

Nuovo Dizionario dei Communi e Frazioni di Commune
GS Ref 945, E5n 1954 edition   Section III

Figure 164.   White locality note card for Abeto, Italy.

Italy, Perugia, Preci
(country)(province)(municipality)

    Preci in province of Perugia

Nuovo Dizionario dei Communi e Frazioni di Commune
GS Ref 945, E5n 1954 edition Section I

Figure 165.   White locality note card for Preci, Italy.

ITALY—MAP

Road Map, write (see sample letter, Figure 147):
    National Tourist Council
    Rome, Italy

NETHERLANDS—GAZETTEER

Repertorium DTB (Inventory [of] Baptisms, Marriages, and
Burials). In print.
Compiler: W. Wijnaendts van Resandt.
Publisher: Centraal Bureau Voor Genealogie, Nassaulaan 18,
Den Haag, Netherlands.
Description: Gives names of cities and province in which the
city is located; inventory of available church records.
GS call number: 949.2, A5w.
GS film number: Not microfilmed.
Example of genealogical information, Figure 166.

```
Netherlands, Friesland, Gorredijk
(country)      (province) (city)


  Gorredijk, Fr [Friesland]
    ref: [Reformed]
    D [baptisms] 1698
    T [marriages] 1699-1704, 1713-
    L [burials] 1698-1731, 1772-ra [Provincial
        Archives]
    men [Mennonite] T 1796-; L 1707-ra
    isr [Jewish] C [circumcision] 1775-ra
    civ [Civil] zie [see] Opsterland


Repertorium DTB
GS 949.2, A5w  1969 edition
```

Figure 166.   White locality note card for Gorredijk, Netherlands.

NETHERLANDS—MAP

Road Map, write (see sample letter, Figure 147):
National Tourist Council
The Hague, Netherlands

NORWAY—GAZETTEERS

Norsk Stedfortegnelse Postadressebog for Norge (Place Names
Post Address Book for Norway). In print.
Publisher: Postal Service, Norwegian Government, Oslo,
Norway.
Description: Gives names of places and name of parish and
county in which the place is located.

GS call number: Ref 948.1, E5h.
GS film number: 1901 edition 123,205.
Example of genealogical information, Figure 167.

```
Norway, Jarlsberg og Larvik, Konnerud, Blankenborg
(country)(old name of county)  (parish)    (farm)


  Blankenborg, Konnerud, Skoger [district]
    JL [ Jarlsberg og Larvik]






Norsk Stedfortegnelse
GS Ref 948. 1, E5h  1903 edition
```

Figure 167.   White locality note card for Blankenborg, Norway.

Norske Gaaranavne (Norwegian Farm Names). Out of print.
Compiler: O. Rygh.
Publisher: W.C. Fatritius & Sønners, Bogtrykkeri, Oslo, Norway.
Publication date: 1897-1924.
Description: Volume for each county; old designation of county; each volume indexed by farm name; names of parishes and names of farms within each parish.
Examples of genealogical information, Figures 168 and 169.

```
Norway, Jarlsberg og Larvik, Konnerud, Blankenborg
(country) (old name of county)   (parish)    (farm)


  Blankenborg, Konnerud Sogn [parish]






Norske Gaardnavne
GS Ref 948. 1, B4r  1907 edition
```

Figure 168.   White locality note card for Blankenborg, Norway.

```
Norway, Jarlsberg og Larvik, Konnerud
(country) (old name of county)      (parish)


Konnerud, Sogn [parish] in Jarlsberg og Larvik

   Farm names:    Svarterud
                  Sagbakken
                  Holland
                  Loventspladsen
                  Haugen
                  Vestmandsbraaten
                  Ulverud
                  [and others]



Norske Gaardnavne
GS Ref 948.1, B4d
```

Figure 169.   White locality note card for Konnerud, Norway.

GS call number: 948.1, B4r.
GS film numbers:

1897-1924 Edition

	Old Designation	Modern
908,594	vol. 1. Smaalenenes Amt	Østfold
"	vol. 2, Akershus Amt	Akershus
908,595	vol. 3, Hedemarkens Amt	Hedmark
"	vol. 4, Pt. 1, Kristians Amt	Oppland
"	vol. 4, Pt. 2, Kristians Amt	Oppland
908,596	vol. 5, Buskeruds Amt	Buskerud
"	vol. 6, Jarlsberg og Larviks Amt	Vestfold
908,597	vol. 7, Bratsberg Amt	Telmark
"	vol. 8, Nedenes Amt	Aust-Agder
"	vol. 9, Lister og Mandal Amt	Vest-Agder
908,598	vol. 10, Stavanger Amt	Rogaland
"	vol. 11, Søndre Bergenhus Amt	Hordaland
908,599	vol. 12, Nordre Berhenhus Amt	Sogn og Fjordane
"	vol. 13, Romsdale Amt	Møre & Romsdale
908,600	vol. 14, Søndre Trondhjems Amt	Sør-Trøndelag
"	vol. 15, Nordre Trondjhems Amt	Nord-Trøndelag

924,001	vol. 16, Nordlands Amt	Nordland
''	vol. 17, Tromsø Amt	Troms
''	vol. 18, Finmarkens Amt	Finnmark
908,594	Supplement	

NORWAY—MAPS

Cappelens Bilkartbok (Cappelen's Road Atlas). In print.
Publisher: J. W. Cappelen, Oslo, Norway.
Description: Colored general reference maps; 1:325,000 scale; indexed.
GS call number: Ref 948.1, E3c.
GS film number: Not microfilmed.

Kartbok for Norge (Mapbook of Norway). In print.
Compiler: Kongelig Norsk Automobilklub.
Publisher: Norges Geografiske Oppmålings, Oslo, Norway.
Description: Colored general reference road maps; parishes indicated; no parish boundaries; scale 1:500,000; indexed.
GS call number: Ref 948.1, K836k.
GS film number: Not microfilmed.

SCOTLAND—GAZETTEERS

Ordnance Gazetteer of Scotland: A Survey of Scottish Topography, Statistical, Biographical, and Historical. 6 vols.
Out of print.
Editor: Francis H. Groome.
Publisher: Thomas C. Jack, Grange Publishing Works, Edinburgh, Scotland.
Publication date: 1882-1885.
Description: Gives names of places and parish and county in which the place is located; county general reference maps with parish boundaries; not indexed.
GS call number: Ref 941, E5g.
GS film numbers:
1882-1885 edition

599,340	vol. 1, Aan-Corvichen	3rd item on film
599,341	vol. 2, Corwar-Ednam	1st item on film
''	vol. 3, Edrachillis-Harthill	2nd item on film
''	vol. 4, Hartree-Libberton	3rd item on film
599,347	vol. 5, Libberton-Petty	1st item on film
''	vol. 6, Petty-Zetland	2nd item on film

Example of genealogical information, Figure 170.

```
Scotland, Stirlingshire, Airth, Dunmore
(country) (county)      (parish)  (village)


  Dunmore, a village in Airth Parish, Stirlingshire
  A village on the right shore of the forth
  8 m ESE of Stirling




Groome's Ordnance Gazetteer
GS F 599,341  1883 edition
```

Figure 170.   White locality note card for Dunmore, Scotland.

A Topographical Dictionary of Scotland. 2 vols. Out of print.
Author: Samuel Lewis.
Publisher: S. Lewis and Company, London, England.
Publication date: 1846-1851.
Description: Gives names of places with name of parish and
    county in which the place is located; gives names of
    nonconformist churches.
GS call number: Ref 941, E5L.
GS film numbers:
1846 edition 413,523 vol. 1, A-J
             413,524 vol. 2, K-Z
1849 edition 496,480 vol. 1, A-J 2nd item on film
             496,481 vol. 2, K-Z 1st item on film
Example of genealogical information, Figure 171.

```
Scotland, Stirlingshire, Airth, Dunmore
 (country)  (county)     (parish) (village)

  Airth, a parish in County of Stirling
  6 1/2 m N from Falkirk
  Contains the village of Dunmore
  On the shore of the Forth
  Harbours:  Newmiln
             Airth
             Dunmore
  Size:  6 1/2 by 3 1/2 miles
  Non-conformists:  Burgher


Lewis'  Topographical Dictionary of Scotland
GS F 496,480  1849 edition
```

Figure 171.   White locality note card for Dunmore, Scotland.

A Genealogical Gazetteer of Scotland. In print.

Author: Frank Smith.

Publisher: Everton Publishers, P.O. Box 368, Logan, Utah 84321.

Description: Gives names of places with the name of the parish and county in which the place is located; date of earliest entry for each parish; names of non-conformist churches. Information extracted from *A Topographical Dictionary of Scotland, 1851,* and *Detailed List of the Old Parochial Registers of Scotland, 1872* (Edinburgh, Scotland: Printed by Murray and Gibb for the Registrar General of births, deaths, and marriages, 1872).

GS call number: Ref 941, E5fs.

GS film number: Not microfilmed.

Example of genealogical information, Figure 172.

```
Scotland, Stirlingshire, Airth, Dunmore
(country)  (county)     (parish) (village)


   Dunmore, a village in the parish of Airth, Stirling
      8 m E of Stirling




Smith's Genealogical Gazetteer of Scotland
GS Ref 941, E5fs  1971 edition
```

Figure 172.   White locality note card for Dunmore, Scotland.

Gazetteer of the British Isles (formerly *Survey Gazetteer of the British Isles*). In print.

Publisher: John Bartholomew & Son, Ltd., Edinburgh, Scotland.

Publication date: 1904 to present.

Description: Gives names of small places and county in which the place is located; no distinction is made between civil and ecclesiastical parish.

GS call number: Ref 942, E5ba.

GS film number: 1904 edition 599,554.

Example of genealogical information, Figure 173.

```
Scotland, Stirlingshire, Airth, Dunmore
(country)    (county)    (parish) (village)


   Dunmore, village, a small harbour on River Forth
   8 m SE of Stirling




Bartholomew's Gazetteer of the British Isles
GS Ref 942, E5ba 9th edition 1943  reprinted 1966
```

Figure 173.   White locality note card for Dunmore, Scotland.

SCOTLAND—MAPS

A Genealogical Atlas of Scotland. In print.

Compilers: David E. Gardner, Derek Harland, and Frank Smith.

Publisher: Bookcraft, Inc., 1848 West 2300 South, Salt Lake City, Utah 84119.

Description: A book of black and white maps reproduced from original old maps; appear to be same maps as those in *Philips' Handy Atlas, 1882,* but not quite as clear; Church of Scotland parishes are indicated; parish boundaries are difficult to determine; indexed.

GS call number: Ref 941, E3g.

GS film number: Not microfilmed.

Philips' Handy Atlas of the Counties of Scotland. Out of print.

Compiler: John Bartholomew.

Publisher: George Philip and Son, London, England.

Publication date: 1882.

Description: A book of county maps; very clear and easy to use; Church of Scotland parish boundaries are indicated; indexed.

GS call number: E.S.Q., 941, E3p.

GS film number: 1882 edition 423,175.

SWEDEN—GAZETTEERS

Svenska Orter (Swedish Places). 3 vols., 3 parts each vol. Out of print.

Publisher: Generalstabens Litografiska Anstalt, Stockholm, Sweden.

Publication date: 1932-1952

Description: Southern Sweden only; gives names of places and parish and county in which the place is located, gives names of villages and farms in each parish; general reference maps.

GS call number: Ref 948.5, E5so.

GS film numbers:

1932 edition vol. 1, South of Göteborg
  874,376 pt. 1, maps; indexed
  " pt. 2, A-K
  " pt. 3, L-Ö

1934 edition vol. 2, Between Göteborg and Stockholm
  874,377 pt. 1, A-K
  " pt. 2, L-Ö
  " pt. 3, maps; indexed

1952 edition vol. 3, Between Stockholm and Gävle
  874,378 pt. 1, maps; indexed
  " pt. 2, A-K
  " pt. 3, L-Ö

Example of genealogical information, Figure 174.

```
Sweden, Alvsborg, Kvinnestad, Kvinnestad
(country)(county)   (parish)      (village)

  Kvinnestad, Kommun [parish] i [in]
  Alvsb. [Alvsborg] län [county]
  Gäsene hd [judicial district]

  Byar: [villages]
    Grutlanda, Hagaskog, Hjälmeryd, Kvinnestad,
    Ramnaklev (delvis belägen inom Asklanda och
    Ornunga k:34), Riddartorp, Skinte, Stockabo,
    Tormundgärde, Uddetorp och Äne

  Hemman: [farms]
    Baggebol

Svenska Orter
GS Ref 948. 5, E5so vol. 2, pt. 1
```

Figure 174.   White locality note card for Kvinnestad, Sweden.

Geografiskt-Statistiskt Handlexikon Öfver Sverige (Geograph-
ical-Statistical Dictionary of Sweden). 2 vols. Out of print.
Author: Carl Martin Rosenberg.
Publisher: A. V. Carlsson, Stockholm, Sweden.
Publication date: 1882, 1883.
Description: Gives names of places with parish and county in
which the place is located.
GS call number: Ref 948.5, E5r.
GS film numbers:
    1882 edition 873,678 vol. 1, A-K
    1883 edition 873,679 vol. 2, L-Ö
Example of genealogical information, Figure 175.

```
Sweden, Alvsborg, Kvinnestad
(country)(county)    (parish)


Qvinnestad Sn [parish] in
  Elfsborgs län [county]
  Gäsene hd [judicial district]




Geografiskt-Statistiskt Handlexikon Öfver Sverige
GS 873,679 vol. 2, 1883 edition
```

Figure 175.   White locality note card for Kvinnestad, Sweden.

SWEDEN—MAPS

Kaks Bilatlas Över Sverige (Kak's Auto Atlas of Sweden). In
print.
Publisher: Generalstabens Litografiska Anstalt, Stockholm,
Sweden.
Description: General reference maps indicate small places;
indexed.
GS call number: Ref 948.5, E3k.
GS film number: Not microfilmed.

Domsaga Kartor (Judicial District Maps). In print.
Publisher: Generalstabens Litografiska Anstalt, Stockholm,
Sweden.

Description: Outline maps for each county indicating civil and
ecclesiastical parish boundaries.
GS call number: Map 948.
GS film number: Not microfilmed.

SWITZERLAND—ORIGIN OF FAMILIES

Familiennamenbuch der Schweiz (Family [Sur]name Book of
Switzerland). 1940 ed., 2 vols.; 1968-71 ed., 6 vols. In print.
Publisher: Polygraphischer Verlag AG, Zürich, Switzerland.
Description: Gives Swiss surnames alphabetically; gives name
of town where clan (*Geschlecht*) has rights of citizenship.
GS call number: Ref 949.4, D4f.
GS film number: 1940 edition 475,787.
Examples of genealogical information, Figure 176 and 177.

```
MAISSEN

  GR [Canton Grisons (Graubünden)]

    [originated from:]
       Brigels a [before 1800]
       Disentis a [before 1800]
       Somvix a [before 1800]
       Truns a [before 1800]

  ZH [Canton Zürich]

    [originated from:]
       Wädenswil c [after 1901]


Familiennamenbuch der Schweiz
GS F 475,787 1940 edition, vol. 2
(GS Ref 949.4, D4f)
```

Figure 176.   White surname note card for Maissen.

```
MAISSEN

  BS [Canton Baselstadt]
     Basel 1952 (Somvix)

  GR [Canton Grisons (Graubünden)]
     Breil/Brigels a [before 1800]
     Disentis/Mustér a [before 1800]
     Somvix a [before 1800]
     Trun a [before 1800]
     Zizers 1953*

  ZH [Canton Zürich]
     Wädenswil 1926 (Trun)
     Zürich 1949, 1957 (Disentis/Mustér)

Familiennamenbuch der Schweiz
GS Ref 949.4, D4fa 1968-1971 edition vol. 4
```

Figure 177.   White surname note card for Maissen.

SWITZERLAND—GAZETTEERS

Schweizerisches Ortslexikon (Swiss Gazetteer). In print.

Author: Arthur Jacot.

Publisher: C. J. Bucher AG, Luzern, Switzerland.

Description: Gives names of cities and towns and the name of the civil parish and canton in which the cities and towns are located. Editions prior to 1969 give the name of the town in which the civil registrar is located. Editions since 1969 include zip code equivalent. General reference maps indexed from gazetteer.

GS call number: ref 949.4, E8s.

GS film number: Not microfilmed.

Examples of genealogical information, Figures 178 and 179.

```
Switzerland, Bern, Diemtigen, Zwischenflüh
  (country)  (canton) (parish)     (village)


  Zwischenflüh, Bn [Bern]
  Diemtigen [civil parish]
  Oey [civil registrar]




Schweizerisches Ortslexikon
GS Ref 949. 4, E8s  1949 edition
```

Figure 178.   White locality note card for Zwischenflüh, Switzerland.

```
Switzerland, Bern, Diemtigen, Zwischenflüh
  (country)  (canton) (parish)     (village)


  Zwischenflüh, BE [Bern]
  Diemtigen [civil parish]
  3753 [postal zip code equivalent]




Schweizerisches Ortslexikon
GS Ref 949. 4, E8s  1969 edition
```

Figure 179.   White locality note card for Zwischenflüh, Switzerland.

Geographisches Lexikon der Schweiz (Geographical Dictionary of Switzerland, German ed.). 6 vols. Out of print.

Publisher: Verlag von Gebrüder Attinger, Neuenberg [Neuchâtel] Switzerland.

Publication date: 1902-1910.

Description: Gives name of canton, district, civil parish, and names of hamlets within boundaries of the civil parish; tells whether or not there is a Swiss Reformed and/or a Catholic ecclesiastical parish within the civil parish. There are district maps which show hamlets and small communities; general reference maps of cantons; not indexed.

GS call number: Ref 949.4, E5g.

GS film numbers:

1902-1910 edition	599,323	vol. 1, A-Emmeng
	''	vol. 2, Emmenh-Kraia
	599,324	vol. 3, Krail-Plen
	''	vol. 4, Ples-Schweiz
	599,326	vol. 5, Schweiz-Tavetsch
	599,325	vol. 6, Tavetsch-Z and Supplement

Example of genealogical information, Figure 180.

```
Switzerland, Bern, Diemtigen, Zwischenflüh
  (country) (canton) (parish)    (village)


  Zwischenflüh,
     Canton: Bern
     District: Nieder Simmenthal
     Civil parish: Diemtigen
     Ecclesiastical parish: Diemtigen

  At Diemtigen there is a Swiss Reformed Church

  Hamlets:
     Innetkirel, Narrenbach, and Oeien



  Geographisches Lexikon der Schweiz
  GS F 599,325 vol. 6  1902-1910 edition
```

Figure 180.   White locality note card for Zwischenflüh, Switzerland.

SWITZERLAND—MAPS

Karte Der Schweiz in 4 Blätter (Map of Switzerland in 4 Pages). In print.

Publisher: Kümmerley & Frey, Bern, Switzerland.

Description: Excellent colored maps with canton boundaries and location of towns, hamlets, and groups of houses; not indexed.

GS call number: Q949.4, E7ca.

GS film number: No date. 599,704.

UNITED STATES—GAZETTEERS

Directory of Post Offices (formerly *United States Official Postal Guide*). In print.

Publisher: United States Post Office Department, Government Printing Office, Washington, D.C.

Description: Post offices arranged alphabetically within each state; gives county in which post office is located. Section at the back lists each post office in each county by state and indicates the county seat.

GS call number: Ref 973, E8U.

GS film number: Not microfilmed.

Example of genealogical information, Figure 181.

```
Washington,  Wahkiakum,  Skamokawa
  (state)       (county)      (town)


  Skamokawa, a town in the County of Wahkiakum,
    State of Washington




  Directory of Post Offices
  GS Ref 973, E8u
```

Figure 181.   White locality note card for Skamokawa, Washington.

Bullinger's Postal and Shippers Guide for the United States and Canada. In Print.

Publisher: Bullinger's Guide, Inc., 63 Woodland Avenue, Westwood, New Jersey 07675.

Description: Gives names of places and the county and state in which the place is located; indicates whether there is a post office.

GS call number: Ref 970, E8b.

GS film number: 1951 edition 483,709.
Example of genealogical information, Figure 182.

```
Washington, Wahkiakum, Skamokawa
  (state)      (county)    (town)


  Skamokawa, a town in the County of Wahkiakum,
  State of Washington

  Indicates there is a post office




  Bullinger's Postal and Shippers Guide
  GS Ref 970, E8b
```

Figure 182.   White locality note card for Skamokawa, Washington.

The National Gazetteer: A Geographical Dictionary of the United States. Out of print.
Author: Leo de Colange.
Publisher: Hamilton, Adams, and Co., London, England.
Publication date: 1884.
Description: Gives names of places with the county and state in which the place is located; gives township where applicable; indicates whether there is a post office.
GS call number: Ref 973, E5c.
GS film number: 1884 edition 845,264.
Example of genealogical information, Figure 183.

```
Washington, Wahkiakum County
  (state)        (county)


  Wahkiakum, Wash., a SW county, bounded S by the
  Columbia River

  Capital:  Cathlamet

  Population of 1600 of whom 898 are foreigners
                             559 Chinese
                              56 Indians



  Colange's National Gazetteer
  GS F 845,264  1884 edition
```

Figure 183.   White locality note card for Wahkiakum County, Washington.

A Gazetteer of the United States of America. Out of print.
Author: John Hayward.
Publisher: Case, Tiffany, and Co., Hartford, Connecticut.
Publication date: 1853.
Description: Gives names of places with county and state in
    which the place is located.
GS call number: Ref 973, E5h.
GS film number: 1853 edition 599,735.
Examples of genealogical information, Figures 184 and 185.

```
Washington,  Wahkiakum County
  (state)           (county)


   Wahkiakum County not mentioned; too early








Hayward's Gazetteer of the U.S.
GS F  599,735  1853 edition
```

Figure 184.   White locality note card for Wahkiakum County, Washington.

```
Vermont,  Caledonia,  Barnet,  McIndoes Falls
 (state)    (county)  (township)    (village)

   McIndoes Falls, Vt.  In the town[ship] of Barnet.
     Caledonia County.






Hayward's Gazetteer of the U.S.
GS F 599,735  1853 edition
```

Figure 185.   White locality note card for McIndoes Falls, Vermont.

Fanning's Illustrated Gazetteer of the United States. Out of
   print.
Publisher: Ensign, Bridgman, & Fanning, New York, New
   York.
Publication date: 1855.
Description: Gives names of places with the township, county,
   and state in which the place is located; 31 state maps, 14
   city maps; not indexed.
GS call number: Ref 973, E5f.
GS film number: 1855 edition 599,773 2nd item on film.
Example of genealogical information, Figure 186.

```
Vermont, Caledonia, Barnet
 (state)     (county)    (town)



   Barnet, p. t. [post town]
     Caledonia County, Vermont






Fanning's Gazetteer of the United States
GS F 599,773  1855 edition
```

Figure 186.   White locality note card for Barnet, Vermont.

*An Accompaniment to Mitchell's Reference and Distance Map of
   the United States.* Out of print.
Author: Samuel Augustus Mitchell.
Publisher: Mitchell and Hinman, Philadelphia, Pennsylvania.
Publication date: 1834.
Description: Gives names of places with the county and state in
   which the place is located.
GS call number: Ref 973, E5m.
GS film number: 1834 edition 845,264 2nd item on film.
Example of genealogical information, Figure 187.

```
Vermont, Caledonia, Barnet
(state)   (county)   (town)


  Barnet, t. [town], Caledonia County, Vermont.










Mitchell, Accompaniment to Reference and Distance Map
  of the U.S.  GS F 845, 264   1834 edition
```

Figure 187.　White locality note card for Barnet, Vermont.

The United States Gazetteer: Containing an Authentic Description of the Several States. Out of print.

Author: Joseph Scott.

Publisher: F. and R. Bailey, Philadelphia, Pennsylvania.

Publication date: 1795.

Description: Gives names of places and the county and state in which the place is located; 19 maps of states with county boundaries.

GS call number: Not available at the Genealogical Society.

GS film number: 1795 edition 570,810 2nd item on film.

Example of genealogical information, Figure 188.

```
Vermont, Chittenden, Burlington
(state)    (county)    (town)


  Burlington, a post town and capital of Chittenden Co.,
    Vermont, on Lake Champlain
  Contains 30 houses compactly built








Scott's United States Gazetteer
GS F 570, 810  1795 edition
```

Figure 188.　White locality note card for Burlington, Vermont.

GAZETTEERS FOR PARTICULAR STATES, write (see
sample letter, Figure 189):
Librarian
State Historical Library
Capital, State

Your Name
Your Address
Current Date

Librarian
State Historical Library
Capital, State

Dear Sir:

Family information indicates that my great grandfather lived in Pine Creek, (State) in 1848. Could you please
tell me in which county Pine Creek was located at that time?

I will be happy to pay for this service. Enclosed is a
stamped self-addressed envelope.

Thank you.

Sincerely yours,

Your Name (signed)

Encl: Stamped self-addressed envelope

Figure 189. Letter to a state historical library.

UNITED STATES—ORIGIN OF COUNTIES

The Handy Book for Genealogists. In print.
Editor: George B. Everton, Sr.
Publisher: Everton Publishers, P.O. Box 368, Logan, Utah 84321.
Description: Counties arranged alphabetically within each state; gives date of formation and parent county; gives county seat; county outline map for each state.
GS call number: Ref 929.1, Ev27h.
GS film number: Not microfilmed.
Example of genealogical information, Figure 190.

```
Washington, Wahkiakum County
  (state)        (county)


Wahkiakum Co. formed in 1854 from Lewis Co.
Lewis Co. formed in 1845, original county.

County seat:  Cathlamet




The Handy Book for Genealogists
GS Ref 929.1, Ev27h  6th edition  1971
```

Figure 190.   White locality note card for Wahkiakum County, Washington.

UNITED STATES—MAPS

Rand McNally Road Atlas, No. 3285. In print.
Publisher: Rand McNally & Company, P.O. Box 7600, Chicago, Illinois 60680.
Description: General reference road maps; indexed.
GS call number: Not available at the Genealogical Society.
GS film number: Not microfilmed.

The Handy Book for Genealogists. In print.
Editor: George B. Everton, Sr.
Publisher: Everton Publishers, P.O. Box 368, Logan, Utah 84321.
Description: County outline map for each state.

GS call number: Ref 929.1, Ev27h.
GS film number: Not microfilmed.
Example of genealogical information, Figure 162.

County maps with township boundaries, write (see sample letter, Figure 191):

> State Department of Highways
> State Capital, State
> or
> County Clerk
> County Seat, State

WALES—GAZETTEERS

A Topographical Dictionary of Wales. 2 vols. Out of print.
Author: Samuel Lewis.
Publisher: S. Lewis and Company, London, England.
Publication date: 1833-1850.
Description: Gives names of places and the parish and county in which the place is located; gives names of chapelries within each parish; gives non-conformist churches.
GS call number: Ref 942.9, E5L.
GS film numbers:

1844 edition	496,477	vol. 1, A-L	3rd item on film
	''	vol. 2, L-Z	4th item on film
1850 edition	413,527	vol. 1, A-L	

Your Name
Your Address
Current Date

State Department of Highways
State Capital, State

Gentlemen:

Would you please send me a copy of a highway map for the county of Saratoga? I am particularly interested in a map which also shows cemeteries, schools, township boundaries, and railroads.

Enclosed is an American Express Money Order for $2.00 to cover the cost of the map. I will be happy to send more if necessary.

Thank you.

Sincerely,

Your Name (signed)

Encl: $2.00

Figure 191. Letter to a state department of highways.

Example of genealogical information, Figure 192.

```
Wales, Anglesey, Llangwyllog, Llangwyllog
(country)(county)   (parish)        (town)


   Llanvallog [ancient spelling] a parish in the County of
   Anglesey, North Wales

   Non-conformists:  Independents
                     Calvinistic
                     Wesleyan Methodists




   Lewis' Topographical Dictionary of Wales
   GS Ref 942.9, E5L 1833 edition
```

Figure 192.   White locality note card for Llangwyllog, Wales.

Gazetteer of the British Isles (formerly *Survey Gazetteer of the British Isles*). In print.
Publisher: John Bartholomew & Son, Ltd., Edinburgh, Scotland.
Publication date: 1904 to present.
Description: Gives names of small places and the county in which the place is located; no distinction is made between civil and ecclesiastical parish.
GS call number: Ref 942, E5ba.
GS film number: 1904 edition 599,554.
Example of genealogical information, Figure 193.

```
Wales, Anglesey, Llangwyllog,
(country)(county)   (parish)


   Llangwyllog, parish in Anglesey






   Bartholomew's Gazetteer of the British Isles.
   GS Ref 942, E5ba 9th edition 1943 reprinted 1966
```

Figure 193.   White locality note card for Llangwyllog, Wales.

WALES—MAPS

Bartholomew Road Atlas Britain. In print.

Publisher: John Bartholomew & Son, Ltd., Edinburgh, Scotland.

Description: A book of modern general reference maps with index.

GS call number: Not available at the Genealogical Society.

GS film number: Not microfilmed.

A Genealogical Atlas of England and Wales. In print.

Compilers: David E. Gardner, Derek Harland, and Frank Smith.

Publisher: Deseret Book Company, 44 East South Temple Street, Salt Lake City, Utah 84111.

Description: A reproduction of 100-year-old maps; Church of England parishes are indicated, but no parish boundaries; not indexed.

GS call number: Ref 942, E3g.

GS film number: Not microfilmed.

A Series of Parish Outline Maps for the Counties of England and Wales. In print.

Publisher: The Institute of Heraldic and Genealogical Studies, 58 Northgate, Canterbury, England.

Publication date: 1962-1966.

Description: Three parish and county outline maps for Wales: North Wales, South Wales, and Central Wales.

GS call number: Map 942, E7in.

GS film number: Not microfilmed.

Atlas to the Topographical Dictionaries of England and Wales. Out of print.

Publisher: S. Lewis and Company, London, England.

Publication date: 1831-1850.

Description: General reference maps of the counties of England and Wales; Church of England parishes are indicated, but no parish boundaries; not indexed.

GS call number: Ref Q942, E5L.

GS film numbers:

1845 edition	496,476	5th item on film.
1849 edition	496,477	2nd item on film.

OTHER COUNTRIES—GAZETTEERS

Dictionnaire des Bureaux de Poste (Dictionary of Post Offices).
  2 vols. In print.
Publisher: Bureau International de L'Union Postale Univer-
  selle, Berne, Switzerland.
Description: Worldwide index to post offices listing town, state,
  and/or province, and country with French spelling.
GS call number: Ref 910, D561.
Example of genealogical information, Figure 194.

```
USSR, Ukraine, Odessa, Blagoevo
(country)(state) (county)   (town)


  Blagoevo [town]
    URSS [USSR country]
    Ukraine [state]
    Odessa [district or county]




Dictionnaire des Bureaux de Poste
GS Ref 910, D561
```

Figure 194.   White locality note card for Blagoevo, USSR.

Place Names for Particular Countries, write (see sample letter,
  Figure 145):

The Genealogical Society
50 East North Temple
Salt Lake City, Utah 84150

OTHER COUNTRIES—MAPS

Continental Atlas. In print.
Publisher: Kartographischer Verlag, Continental Gummi-
  Werke Aktiengesellschaft, 3 Hannover, Germany.
Description: Colored general reference maps for Europe;
  indexed.
GS call number: Ref 943, E3c.
GS film number: Not microfilmed.

Road Atlas Europe. In print.
Publisher: John Bartholomew & Son, Ltd., Edinburgh, Scot-
    land.
Description: Colored road atlas of Europe; indexed.
GS call number: Not available at the Genealogical Society.
GS film number: Not microfilmed.

Road Map, write (see sample letter, Figure 147):
    National Tourist Council
    Capital City, Country

11
Family Organizations

A family organization is a research tool that provides assistance to the genealogical program of the family and helps accomplish the following objectives:

1. Extend the pedigree of the common ancestral couple and complete a family group record for each couple on the pedigree.

2. Complete a family group record for each married descendant.

3. Disseminate information in pedigree and family group form and publish family histories.

4. Hold annual reunions to which all family members are invited.

ADVANTAGES

An efficient family organization will provide its members with the following advantages:

1. Members of the family can share the genealogical research time, thereby accomplishing more genealogical research.

2. Members of the family can share the financial expenses for genealogical research.

3. Family organization finances can be used to train many family members in correct genealogical research procedures.

4. Family members can coordinate and organize research assignments to avoid duplication of time and money.

5. Family members generally donate their research time.

6. Family members can each assume responsibility for a different ancestral family group record.

LIMITATIONS

Family organizations may experience the following limitations:

1. One or two outspoken family members may try to control the organization to which many have contributed financially.

2. Family members who know little about genealogical research may donate a large sum and thereby control the genealogical research.

3. Family members may feel no responsibility toward the genealogical research when their financial contribution to the overall program is a relatively small sum.

4. Family organization funds are often paid to unqualified researchers who have only a monetary interest in the family's genealogical research.

5. Family members may try to obtain family organization funds for unnecessary research trips for themselves.

6. Most often only a few family members do the majority of the work.

7. Family members who donate research time are often assigned tedious and uninteresting tasks.

8. Family members who donate research time are often unqualified to do research.

9. Family genealogists may be pressured to meet reunion deadlines and to prepare detailed research reports, time that could better be spent in actual research.

10. Genealogical information provided by a family organization is only as reliable as the individual who did the research.

11. Very few family members are interested or qualified to judge the quality of the genealogical research results.

12. Family organizations can easily become too large to administer efficiently, and only a few individuals may be interested in assisting with large mailing lists, voluminous secretarial work, and family bulletins.

SELECTING A COMMON ANCESTRAL COUPLE

The first step in organizing a family is to select an ancestral couple whose descendants may become members of the organization. If deceased, or if because of age, the couple is unable to call their descendants together and organize the family, other family members act in their stead, selecting those best qualified for leadership rather than following the patriarchal order.

Some suggestions for selecting the common ancestral couple follow:

1. The first couple to immigrate to the United States.

2. The first couple to settle in the locality of interest.

3. The first couple to join The Church of Jesus Christ of Latter-day Saints.

It is best to select a couple born after 1800, or the task of contacting and organizing descendants could be difficult. Selecting a couple born much earlier would require genealogical research on the part of the descendants to prove their eligibility for membership.

FAMILY ORGANIZATION CARD FILE

Once the ancestral couple has been selected, it is necessary to check the Family Organization Card File (see Chapter 9) to determine if a family organization exists for the particular ancestral couple. Information obtained from the Family Organization Card File should be copied onto a surname note card. (See Figure 195.)

```
DIAMOND                  ·        Family Organization Card File

George Diamond Family Organization
    Organized:  10 July 1961
    Date Reported:  4 Aug 1961
    Pres:  William E. Diamond, 969 Whitney Drive,
        Salt Lake City, Utah
    Sec:  Jane D. Osgood, 1499 Appleblossom Lane,
        Salt Lake City, Utah
    Genealogy:  David Diamond, 739 Spruce Lane, Orem,
        Utah
    PRS Rep:  David Diamond
    PRS No.:  0219-315
    Fam Rep:  George Diamond, 1690 Jubilee Street,
        Logan, Utah
```

Figure 195.   White surname note card for the Family Organization Card File.

CONTACTING FAMILY MEMBERS

Once the ancestral couple has been selected and it is determined that no family organization exists, a letter should be composed to inform the couple's descendants of the purposes of the organization, what they must do to join, and when the first meeting will be held. (See sample letter, Figure 196.)

GERALD ALDER FAMILY ORGANIZATION

For Descendants of Gerald Alder and Anna Sorenson

May, 1972

Dear Relative,

Several of the descendants of Gerald Alder are interested in forming a family organization and in compiling a family history. To insure that information about you and your family will be in this history, and also that it will be complete and accurate, please complete the enclosed form and return it within ten days in the enclosed stamped self-addressed envelope.

Many family members have contributed towards the family history, and their help certainly has been appreciated. Aunt Martha Hixon and Uncle Dan Alder have spent many years doing genealogical research on the Alder line and deserve many thanks for their efforts.

Please come to the reunion at Lakeside Park on Saturday, August 24, at 12:00 noon. Bring the entire family and your own picnic lunch. At 2:00 p.m. a business meeting will be held to bring you up to date on the genealogical research and to present plans for further organizing the family.

It is suggested that the annual family dues be $5.00 per married couple, payable at the reunion, or $6.50 if paid at a later date. Those who pay dues this year will receive a printed family group record for Gerald Alder and his wife, Anna Sorenson.

Sincerely yours,

Henry S. Alder

Encls: Family group with questionnaire
Stamped self-addressed envelope

Figure 196. Letter to a relative for a family organization.

Since the family organization will want to gather information on the living as well as the deceased, a blank family group form to be completed by each married couple might be included in the letter. A biographical questionnaire could be added on the back of the family group record, on which space is provided for the names and addresses of brothers, sisters, and children. (See Figures 197 and 198.)

Please Print in Ink or Type

		Town	County	State
HUSBAND(full name)				
Birth date	Place			
Marriage date	Place			
Death date	Place			
Burial date	Place			
Father(full name)	Mother(maiden name)			

Other Wives of the Husband (If any, list in order with marriage date first)

		Town	County	State
WIFE(full maiden name)				
Birth date	Place			
Death date	Place			
Burial date	Place			
Father(full name)	Mother(maiden name)			

Other Husbands of the Wife (If any, list in order with marriage date first)

Please check the sources for information given:
Marriage certificates ☐
Birth certificates ☐
Church records ☐
Written family records ☐
Memory only ☐ Other sources (please list):

This sheet filled in by:
Name:
Address:

Sex. M or F	CHILDREN (Full names in order of birth)	WHEN BORN Day Mo. Yr.	WHERE BORN Town County	State	DIED Day Mo. Yr.	MARRIED (First husband or wife). List additional marriages with dates on reverse side of sheet.
	1					Date To
	2					Date To
	3					Date To
	4					Date To
	5					Date To
	6					Date To
	7					Date To
	8					Date To
	9					Date To
	10					Date To
	11					Date To
	12					Date To
	13					Date To

Figure 197. Request for family group information.

1. Your full name _____ Correct Mailing Address _____ Date _____

2. Your height _____ Weight _____ Color of eyes _____ Color of hair _____

3. Schools attended or other special training (name & dates)_____

_____

_____

_____

4. Occupation(s) (Please list where you have worked and give approximate dates)_____

_____

_____

_____

5. Occupation of your husband or wife_____

6. Hobbies or free time activities, interests, etc._____

_____

_____

7. Positions held (Church, civic, etc.)_____

_____

8. Military Service (Where and when, etc.)_____

_____

9. Missionary work or other special church work (Where & when, etc.)_____

_____

10. Achievements, recognitions, talents, honors, etc. (in sports, music, art, education, drama, business, vocation, etc.[where & when received])_____

_____

_____

11. Please list the name and address of (1) your brothers & sisters (2) your adult children.

NAME	Full Mailing Address (if known)
1.	
2.	
3.	
4.	
5.	
6.	
7.	
8.	
9.	
10.	
11.	
12.	
13.	
14.	

Copyright 1955 & 1958 by J. Grant Stevenson

Figure 198.   Biographical questionnaire.

When names and addresses are received, an address note card is made for each relative. (See Figure 199.) (The pedigree line to the common ancestor may be added on the address note card.) The address note cards are alphabetized by surname and placed in the address section of the file box to be used for mailing reunion notices, family newsletters, etc.

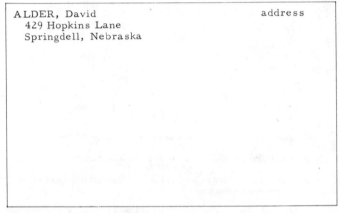

Figure 199.   White address note card for a relative.

SAMPLE CONSTITUTION

Each family organization needs a constitution or set of rules by which to govern its members. (See Figure 200.) It is important that the constitution be flexible to provide for the continued growth of the family, and be brief to provide for ease in interpretation and enforcement. A lengthy discussion of the constitution should be avoided at the reunion; instead, those assisting in the initial organization should prepare beforehand a constitution they feel is suitable and present it for approval.

It is possible to qualify a family organization as a nonprofit organization for tax-exempt status under the Internal Revenue Code. (See Chapter 12.)

CONSTITUTION

OF THE

GERALD ALDER FAMILY ORGANIZATION

ARTICLE I

Name

The name of this organization shall be the Gerald Alder
Family Organization.

ARTICLE II

Objectives

The objectives of this organization shall be as follows:

(1) Promote genealogical research and activity.

(2) Prevent duplication of effort by combining research
time and financial resources.

(3) Disseminate genealogical data to all family members.

(4) Maintain family unity by holding an annual reunion and
publishing an annual newsletter.

ARTICLE III

Membership

This organization shall be composed of the descendants of
Gerald Alder and the husband or wife of any of his descendants.

ARTICLE IV

Officers and Committees

The business of this organization shall be conducted by the
following officers and committees:

(1) Board of Directors.
(2) President.
(3) Vice President.
(4) Genealogical Chairman.
(5) Genealogical Committee.
(6) Secretary.

Figure 200. Constitution of the Gerald Alder Family Organization. (Continued
on next page)

2

(7)   Treasurer.
(8)   Historian.

ARTICLE V

Selection of Officers

(1)   Board of Directors--shall be elected for a three-year term by members attending the reunion and shall include:

(a)   A representative from each of the six families of the sons and daughters of Gerald Alder, and

(b)   One representative from the general membership.

The terms of office shall be rotated so that two directors shall be elected every year, and each third year three directors shall be elected.

(2)   President--shall be appointed by the Board of Directors from among their membership for a two-year term.

(3)   Vice President--shall be appointed by the Board of Directors from among their membership for a two-year term.

(4)   Genealogical Chairman--shall be appointed by the Board of Directors from the general membership for a term as designated by the Board of Directors.

(5)   Genealogical Committee--shall be appointed by the Board of Directors with at least one representative from each of the six families of the sons and daughters of Gerald Alder. The term of office shall be designated by the Board of Directors.

(6)   Secretary--shall be appointed by the Board of Directors from the general membership for a term as designated by the Board of Directors.

(7)   Treasurer--shall be appointed by the Board of Directors from the general membership for a term as designated by the Board of Directors.

(8)   Historian--shall be appointed by the Board of Directors from the general membership for a term as designated by the Board of Directors.

ARTICLE VI

Duties of Officers and Committees

(1)   Board of Directors--shall conduct and be responsible for the affairs of the organization; shall have power to appoint as many

Figure 200.   Constitution of the Gerald Alder Family Organization. (Continued on next page)

3

committees and individuals as necessary to fill offices outlined in the constitution and to carry out the objectives of the organization; shall assess dues; shall give the membership a report of the previous year's activities at each reunion; and shall act as nominating committee to select incoming directors.

(2) President--shall preside and conduct Board of Director meetings; and shall preside and conduct the annual family reunion.

(3) Vice President--shall act in the absence of the president.

(4) Genealogical Chairman--shall supervise all genealogical research done by committee members; shall supervise submission of names to the Genealogical Society; and shall have authority to call genealogical committee meetings or special family genealogical meetings, the latter with permission of the Board of Directors.

(5) Genealogical Committee--shall coordinate all genealogical research activity; shall compile family group records for each ancestral and each descendant couple; shall disseminate all information obtained through genealogical research.

(6) Secretary--shall secure and maintain an up-to-date record of membership and those eligible for membership; shall inform the membership of all activities through an annual family newsletter.

(7) Treasurer--shall keep and maintain a record of finances.

(8) Historian--shall be responsible for a history of the organization; shall cooperate with the genealogical committee in compiling family histories for publication; and shall be responsible for obtaining a history of each ancestor and each descendant.

ARTICLE VII

Amendments

This constitution may be amended at any announced reunion by a two-thirds vote of the members present.

Figure 200.   Constitution of the Gerald Alder Family Organization. (Concluded)

GENEALOGICAL RESEARCH

As the organization grows, it may become necessary to hold special genealogical meetings in conjunction with, or separate from, the annual reunion. These meetings could be training sessions in genealogical research where specific assignments are made to committee members.

The most efficient method for training family members in genealogical research is to encourage them to complete the lesson assignments in Section IV for each of their first four-generation family group records. When these assignments are completed, they will have the training and background necessary for undertaking more specific research assignments for the family organization.

Members of a family organization would be wise in expending a portion of their funds to train family members as research specialists. The genealogical chairman should continually increase his knowledge of proper techniques and available sources. Any money invested by the family in educating its own members toward this goal would be more than repaid through the superior services rendered by these individuals to the family genealogical program.

As the pedigree is proven and complete family group records are obtained, copies of the extended pedigree and family group records should be disseminated at the reunion to family members who pay their dues. There can be no guarantee of the quantity of research information to be distributed, but each family member should be entitled to a guarantee of the quality of the research.

The pedigree lines of the common ancestral couple will eventually join those of other active family organizations. A decision should be made by the board of directors concerning the pro-rating of funds for work on other pedigree lines or in combining with other families who may eventually be interested in the same pedigrees.

One family organization will not solve all research problems. Each person is a member of many families and may join more than one organization. In a well-organized family there is a place for each individual to use his talents, whether searching original records, writing biographies, collecting photographs, doing secretarial work, or supervising reunions.

REORGANIZING A FAMILY

The task of reorganizing an already existing family organization is more difficult than effecting a new organization. There are many family organizations in existence that are not functioning satisfactorily for several reasons:

1. Not all descendants are contacted annually.

2. Dues are too expensive, and young couples and older couples often cannot afford to join, leaving the responsibility to a few. (Donations above the set dues can be encouraged for those who can afford it.)

3. Each branch of the family is not represented on the board of directors.

4. Too much time is spent discussing genealogical research during the reunion. The details of genealogical research should be discussed in genealogical committee meetings and not before the entire group.

5. Genealogical research is either neglected or some descendants do not receive a report of the research.

6. Genealogical research is of poor quality. When family group records are printed, the sources are not documented, and often the ordinance dates are incorrect and incomplete.

7. Family funds are wasted by hiring unqualified researchers.

The problems seem to fall into two groups: (1) poor organization and (2) unsatisfactory genealogical research. When officers are already functioning, it may be difficult to give constructive criticism, but often the officers would welcome suggestions for a better organization. Perhaps changing the date or place of the annual reunion would result in a larger attendance. If some descendants are not being contacted, then one could suggest a means of doing it and volunteer to help with the project. Whenever criticism is offered, it is well to give the reasons for the criticism, and then suggest ways to correct the problem.

The problem of unsatisfactory genealogical research can be solved when those skilled in genealogical research are appointed to the family genealogical committee.

Those who show interest in genealogical research are frequently the ones who are appointed to do the family research. However, often those who show interest are not skilled or experienced, and those who may be well qualified are not always known to the officers of the family organization. Those with special genealogical skill should make themselves known to the family, and the best way to do this is by showing the results of their research. One might prepare accurate family group records and take them to the reunion to be displayed where relatives could view the work and copy information. Family members soon find it impossible to copy all they would like, and this offers an opportunity for suggestions concerning the family organization's research problems.

12
Tax-Exempt Organizations

A tax-exempt organization for religious, scientific, educational, literary, and/or charitable purposes provides an incentive for individuals to contribute financially to the genealogical research activity of a family organization. It is suggested that a tax-exempt organization be established in addition to the family organization, and that the responsibility and activity of each be separated as follows:

1. Family organization—coordinate social activities. (See Chapter 11.)

2. Tax-exempt organization—coordinate genealogical research for living and deceased ancestral families. (Social activities must not become a major function of the tax-exempt organization, or the tax-exempt privilege could be jeopardized.)

APPLICATION

1. Individuals who donate to the tax-exempt organization can deduct the donation from their income tax as a charitable donation. (Donations made between the date of incorporation and the date of tax-exempt approval are deductible.)

2. Those individuals most interested and knowledgeable in genealogical research can organize and direct the tax-exempt organization.

LIMITATIONS

1. Individuals who direct the tax-exempt organization must conform to all rules and regulations of the state in which they are organized.

2. Individuals who direct the tax-exempt organization must conform to all rules and regulations of the Internal Revenue Code governing such organizations.

HOW TO ORGANIZE

The family organization should first organize in the state in which the home address is located and then apply for tax-exempt status from the Internal Revenue Service. Corporations, trusts, funds, foundations, and community chests are among the different types of family organizations available for tax-exempt status. The following steps for forming a tax-exempt organization are those applicable to a corporation in Utah; requirements may vary somewhat in each state:

1. Write to the Secretary of State, State Capital, in the state in which incorporation is desired and request a copy of the "Non-Profit Corporation Laws" of the particular state.

2. Write to the nearest Internal Revenue Service office, or telephone by using the service's toll-free number, and request the following publications:

      a. "How to Apply for Recognition of Exemption for an Organization" (Publication 557).

      b. "Application for Employer Identification Number" (Form SS-4).

      c. "Application for Recognition of Exemption, Under Section 501 (c) (3) of the Internal Revenue Code; (Form 1023).

3. Select the name of the corporation; it must be different from the name of any other corporation in the state.

4. Determine the type of tax-exempt organization that best meets the objectives of the family organization (see Figure 201, "Two Types of Tax-Exempt Organizations"):

      a. Public charity

      b. Private foundation

5. Draft articles of incorporation that meet the state laws of incorporation and the Internal Revenue Service requirements for the particular type or organization selected. For a sample of articles of incorporation for an organization that qualifies as a public charity, see Figure 202. Some states do not require by-laws for incorporation; however, by-laws or other rules of operation, such as the family organization constitution (see Figure 200), are required by the Internal Revenue Code.

6. Submit two original copies of the articles of incorporation to the Secretary of State with the filing fee ($5 in Utah); if it is a stock corporation, include a sample of the stock certificate.

Public Charity	Private Foundation
1. Contributions to the organization qualify for income tax deduction.	1. Contributions to the organization qualify for income tax deduction.
2. Must have a religious or charitable purpose.	2. Need not have a religious or charitable purpose; educational, scientific, or literary purpose will qualify.
3. More than one-third of the organization's financial support must come from the general public.	3. No public support requirement.
4. Requirements regulating prohibitive activities of disqualified persons are not as stringent as a private foundation.	4. Stringent requirements regulating prohibitive activities of disqualified persons.
5. Do not need to utilize income earned from investments within the subsequent year.	5. Must utilize income earned from investments within the subsequent year.
6. Individuals can contribute up to 50% of their adjusted gross income and obtain a tax deduction.	6. Individuals can contribute up to 20% of their adjusted gross income and obtain a tax deduction.
7. Contributions in excess of the 50% limitation may be carried over and utilized during the next five years.	7. Contributions in excess of the 20% limitation may not be carried over and utilized during subsequent years.
8. In some states, may be exempt from paying state sales tax.	8. In some states, may be exempt from paying state sales tax.
9. Qualify for bulk mailing rates.	9. Qualify for bulk mailing rates.
10. Must file Form 990 within 4½ months after the close of each taxable year.	10. Must file Form 990-PF within 4½ months after the close of each taxable year; also Form 990-AR if assets exceed $5,000.
11. Subject to tax on unrelated business income.	11. Subject to tax on unrelated business income.
12. Not subject to investment income tax.	12. Subject to investment income tax.

Figure 201.   Two types of tax-exempt organizations.

ARTICLES OF INCORPORATION

OF THE

GERALD ALDER FAMILY ORGANIZATION

The undersigned, desiring to form a non-profit corporation under the Utah Non-Profit Corporation Cooperative Act, do hereby certify:

ARTICLE I

Corporate Name

This family organization shall be known as the Gerald Alder Family Organization.

ARTICLE II

Period of Duration

The period of duration for the corporation shall be perpetual unless sooner terminated by law.

ARTICLE III

Purposes of Corporation

This corporation is organized as a non-profit corporation, exclusively for religious, scientific, educational, literary, and charitable purposes, including for such purposes the following:

(1) Distribute contributions and genealogical data to organizations that qualify as exempt organizations under Section 501(c)(3) of the Internal Revenue Service Code of 1954 (or the corresponding provision of any future United States Internal Revenue law).

(2) Perform genealogical research to identify individuals and to qualify names of individuals for certain temple ordinances, in accordance with the religious precepts of The Church of Jesus Christ of Latter-day Saints, Inc.

(3) Prepare accurate and complete genealogical forms to submit to The Church of Jesus Christ of Latter-day Saints, Inc., in compliance with the standards established by said Church for completion of temple ordinances.

Figure 202.   Articles of Incorporation of the Gerald Alder Family Organization.
(Continued on next page)

2

(4)   Prepare accurate and complete genealogical records to submit to The Church of Jesus Christ of Latter-day Saints for filing in the Library of the Genealogical Society of said Church.

(5)   To preserve the genealogical and historical records pertaining to Gerald Alder, his ancestors, and descendants.

(6)   Combine the resources of any and all interested persons so that accurate genealogical records may be made available to the general public through depositing copies of said records in local record repositories.

(7)   Engage in any other religious, scientific, educational, literary, or charitable purpose permitted to be performed by the following:

   (a)   A corporation exempt from federal income tax under Section 501(c)(3) of the Internal Revenue Code of 1954 (or the corresponding provisions of any future United States Internal Revenue law).

   (b)   A corporation, contributions of which are deductible under Section 170(c)(2) of the Internal Revenue Code of 1954 (or the corresponding provisions of any future United States Internal Revenue law).

ARTICLE IV

Members

The corporation shall have members. All of the descendants of Gerald Alder and the husband or wife of any of these descendants are eligible for membership in this corporation. Each descendant (or the husband or wife of any descendant) may become a member thereof by submitting to the Secretary a written statement containing his name, address, and evidence of relationship to Gerald Alder and the payment of annual dues.

ARTICLE V

Shares of Stock

Shares of stock evidencing membership in the corporation shall not be issued or required.

ARTICLE VI

Annual Meeting

An annual meeting of the members of the corporation shall be held. The time and place of such meeting shall be determined each year by the Governing Board.

Figure 202.   Articles of Incorporation of the Gerald Alder Family Organization. (Continued on next page)

3

ARTICLE VII

Restrictions of Activities

No part of the net earnings of the corporation shall inure to the benefit of or be distributable to its members, trustees, officers or other private persons, except that the corporation shall be authorized and empowered to pay reasonable compensation for services rendered and to make payments and distributions in furtherance of the purposes set forth in Article III hereof. No substantial part of the activities of the corporation shall be the carrying on of propaganda, or otherwise attempting, to influence legislation, and the corporation shall not participate in, or intervene (including the publication and distribution of statements) in any political campaign on behalf of any candidate for public office. Notwithstanding any other provision of these Articles, the corporation shall not carry on any other activities not permitted to be carried on (a) by a corporation exempt from federal income tax under Section 501(c)(3) Internal Revenue Code, or (b) by a corporation contributions to which are deductible under Section 170(c)(2) Internal Revenue Code, or (c) by Section 508 (e) Internal Revenue Code.

ARTICLE VIII

Distribution on Dissolution

Upon the dissolution of this corporation, the Governing Board of Trustees shall, after paying or making the provision for the payment of all of the liabilities of the corporation, dispose of all of the assets of the corporation in such manner, or to such organization or organizations organized and operated exclusively for religious, charitable, scientific, literary or educational purposes as shall at that time qualify as an exempt organization or organizations under Section 501(c)(3) Internal Revenue Code; it being intended that such assets be first distributed to or conveyed as a gift to the Trustees-in-Trust of the Church of Jesus Christ of Latter-day Saints and/or the Genealogical Society of the Church of Jesus Christ of Latter-day Saints, Inc. as the Governing Board of Trustees shall determine.

ARTICLE IX

Governing Board of Trustees

The property, business, and affairs of the corporation shall be managed by a Governing Board of Trustees of no less than three (3) in number. Trustees must be members of the corporation but need not be residents of the state of incorporation. The initial Governing Board shall consist of three Trustees. The names and addresses of the initial Trustees of the Governing Board are:

Figure 202. Articles of Incorporation of the Gerald Alder Family Organization. (Continued on next page)

4

1. John N. Alder   627 East Elm, Orem, Utah 84057
2. Diane G. Haines   487 South State, Provo, Utah 84601
3. Harry D. Alder   372 East Nash, Orem, Utah 84057
4. David Haines   487 South State, Provo, Utah 84601

ARTICLE X

Initial Principal Office and Agent

The initial principal office of the corporation is 627 East Elm, Orem, Utah 84057, and the name of the initial registered agent at such address is John N. Alder.

ARTICLE XI

The Incorporators

The four officers, as incorporators, are as follows:

1. John N. Alder   President   627 East Elm, Orem, Utah 84057
2. Diane G. Haines   V. Pres.   487 South State, Provo, Utah 84601
3. Harry D. Alder   Secretary   372 East Nash, Orem, Utah 84057
4. David Haines   Treasurer   487 South State, Provo, Utah 84601

_____
President

_____
Vice President

_____
Secretary

_____
Treasurer

State of_____

County of_____

Subscribed and sworn to before me this _____ day of

_____, 19____.

My commission expires_____.

_____
Notary Public

Figure 202.   Articles of Incorporation of the Gerald Alder Family Organization. (Concluded)

7. Keep accurate records of all income and expenditures, including receipts, vouchers, and canceled checks. If requesting recognition as a public charity, the general public must contribute more than one-third of the income. (Spouses, ancestors, or descendants of the founders, officers, directors, trustees, or substantial contributors are not considered the general public, but are referred to as "disqualified persons.")

8. Complete Form 1023, "Application for Recognition of Exemption," and submit it to the District Internal Revenue Office in the district in which the principal office is located. Attach a copy of the approved articles of incorporation and by-laws or other rules of operation. If the organization has existed for less than one year, attach an up-to-date financial statement plus a projected two-year budget. If the organization is applying for exemption as a public charity, also attach a statement that the corporation is not a private foundation and provide reasons. (See Figure 203, "Statement Requesting Public Charity Status.")

9. Write to the State Tax Commission requesting a copy of "Application for State Sales Tax Exemption Number" if applicable.

10. Annually submit to the Internal Revenue Service a completed copy of Form 990 if a public charity, Form 990-PF if a private foundation. If the organization is a private foundation and the annual assets are over $5,000, a Form 990-AR must also be filed. The filing date conforms to the month in which the annual accounting period ends, and this month is established by the organization at the time the application for exempt status (Form 1023) is filed with the Internal Revenue Service.

11. Annually submit a report to the Secretary of State listing the names and addresses of the corporation officers and giving other information as required; this report is automatically mailed to the corporation each year.

The steps outlined in this chapter for forming a tax-exempt organization are general and do not include complete rules and regulations; Internal Revenue laws and rulings may change. Therefore, the applicant may desire to consult an attorney and/or a tax consultant for assistance in incorporating in the state of residence and in meeting the requirements of the Internal Revenue Code.

Current Date

TO: District Internal Revenue Service Center
     1160 West 1200 South Street
     Ogden, Utah 84201

FROM: John Alder, President
       Gerald Alder Family Organization
       627 East Elm
       Orem, Utah 84057

The Gerald Alder Family Organization hereby makes a
formal declaration and statement that it is a public charity and
not a private foundation. The purposes and objectives of the
organization are to provide resources and contribute information
to The Church of Jesus Christ of Latter-day Saints, Inc., for
certain religious ordinances performed in the temples of said
Church.

This objective is in keeping with the objective of a public
charity as outlined in Rev. Rul. 71-580, 71-2 C.B. 235, which
states "Section 1.101 (c) (3) - 1 (d) (2) of the Income Tax Regulations includes in its definition of the term 'charitable' the
advancement of religion... the subject organization is similarly
accomplishing a charitable purpose by engaging in an activity
that advances religion....Accordingly it is held that the organization is exempt from federal income tax under Section 501 (c) (3)
of the Code."

More than one-third of the contributions to this organization
are from the general public and not from spouses, descendants,
nor ancestors of the officers, trustees, directors, incorporators,
or other "disqualified persons."

Therefore, we request that the Gerald Alder Family
Organization be declared a public charity and not a public
foundation.

John N. Alder, President

Figure 203.   Statement requesting public charity status.

13
Research Services

Each person should complete his own research by searching records personally or by writing directly to the record custodian. Often this is impossible because of the location of the records or because the researcher lacks the technical knowledge to make a successful search, in which case it is necessary to obtain the services of a genealogical agent or a genealogical research specialist.

GENEALOGICAL AGENT

A genealogical agent is someone who searches records under the direction of another individual. When it is not possible to search the records personally and the information cannot be obtained by writing directly to the record repository, it becomes necessary to engage an agent to search the records. There should be an understanding concerning the agent's fees prior to his searching the records. An agent can be a friend or relative who might search for no fee or an individual who charges for his searches.

The researcher who engages an agent should supply the following information (see sample letter, Figure 204):

1. The exact name of the record to be searched
2. The name or names of persons for whom information is desired
3. The exact date of the event or a specific time period to search
4. The Genealogical Society call number, if known

An agent does not attempt to analyze the research problem, but follows specific instructions under the direction of the researcher. He makes the search, copies the information exactly and completely, and forwards it to the researcher. (See Figure 205.) If no restrictions are put on the search, the agent might repeat previous searches.

Your Name
Your Address
Current Date

Name of Agent
Address of Agent

Dear Sir:

Thank you for your willingness to act as my agent in
searching the records at the county courthouse in your town.
Would you please search the marriage records from 1862
to 1872 for the following marriages:

John H. Palmer to Anna Miller
Amos B. Richardson to Emily Stout

I would like to have the information copied exactly as it is
in the record or obtain a photocopy of the record. Enclosed
is an American Express Money Order for $5.00 as a deposit
for this search and for copies of any information found.

Thank you.

Sincerely yours,

Your Name (signed)

Encl: $5.00

Figure 204.   Letter to a genealogical research agent.

Name of Agent
Address of Agent
Current date

Name of Patron
Address of Patron

Dear Sir:

    I have searched the marriage records at the local
courthouse for the years 1862 to 1875 for the marriage of
John Palmer to Anna Miller and the marriage of Amos B.
Richardson to Emily Stout. The following is the only
information I could find:

        Married on 12 July 1867, John Palmer to
    Mrs. Anna Miller, widow. His age, 42; her age,
    37; both residents of Jackson County and the town
    of Albion. Minister, Rev. John R. Richards.
    Witnesses, Samuel H. Miller and George A.
    Richardson. License applied for 2 July 1867.

    The search required one hour of time, and the $5.00
deposit will be sufficient payment. If there are other
searches you would like in the courthouse or in local
cemeteries, I would be happy to do this for you.

Sincerely yours,

Name of Agent (signed)

Figure 205. Letter from a genealogical research agent to a patron.

GENEALOGICAL RESEARCH SPECIALIST

A genealogical research specialist is one who is skilled in research in a particular geographic area. When one lacks the technical knowledge necessary to search in person or to direct an agent, it may be necessary to obtain the advice of a genealogical research specialist. A genealogical research specialist may perform the following services:

1. Give technical advice.
2. Act as an agent in searching specific records.
3. Teach genealogical research classes.
4. Translate foreign languages.

Figure 206 is an example of a letter to a research specialist. To obtain names and addresses of individuals willing to do genealogical research for others, the following sources are recommended:

1. List of accredited researchers from the Genealogical Society. (See Chapter 9.)

2. *The Genealogical Helper* (Logan, Utah: Everton Publishers, published bimonthly) for names of individuals willing to search records in their locality.

Your Name
Your Address
Current Date

Name of Accredited Researcher
Address of Accredited Researcher

Dear Sir:

You have been recommended as being qualified to
teach genealogical research procedures of Switzerland.
There are several of us with Swiss ancestry who are
desirous of taking a class in Swiss research. Would you
be willing to teach such a class, and if so, could you furnish
us the following information:

    1.   Minimum or maximum number of students.
    2.   Fee, including travel expense.
    3.   Number of weeks required for class.
    4.   Day of week and time for class.

We look forward to hearing from you. Enclosed is a
stamped self-addressed envelope for your convenience.

Thank you.

Sincerely yours,

Your Name (signed)

Encl: Stamped self-addressed envelope

Figure 206.   Letter to a genealogical research specialist.

SECTION III

BASIC GENEALOGICAL RECORDS

14
Home Records

The goal in genealogical research is to identify each ancestral couple and their children by searching records that provide specific information:

1. Given name(s) and surname
2. Birth and/or christening date
3. Birthplace and/or christening place
4. Marriage date
5. Marriage place
6. Death and/or burial date
7. Death and/or burial place

In addition to identifying each individual on the ancestral family group records, members of The Church of Jesus Christ of Latter-day Saints have the goal of establishing complete and correct LDS ordinance dates for each individual:

1. Baptism date
2. Endowment date
3. Sealing to parents date
4. Sealing to spouse date

The best records for establishing correct identity are government birth, marriage, and death records, and church christening, marriage, and burial records. The only records for establishing correct ordinance dates are the membership and temple records of The Church of Jesus Christ of Latter-day Saints.

The following are representative of records that originate in the home and that could provide clues to vital records and temple records:

1. Family tradition
2. Bible records
3. Handwritten diaries and journals
4. Photographs
5. Letters
6. Announcements of vital events
7. Temple record books
8. Biographical records (see Chapter 15)
9. Family group records and pedigree charts (see Chapter 21)

10. Pedigree Referral Service
11. Research Department Files

FAMILY TRADITION

Tradition is oral testimony that has been passed from one generation to another. Family traditions are not always accurate, but provide clues which lead to valuable genealogical records. (See Figure 207.)

PETERSON, Andrew (1857)   tradition

Andrew left Sweden when about 17 years of age as a cabin boy on a freighter. The captain of the ship was very unkind to Andrew so he "jumped ship" in Australia and hid himself near the dock. Some Irishmen working on a railroad nearby protected Andrew until the captain gave up looking for him and set sail without him. Andrew stayed in Australia until he earned enough money to fulfill his boyhood dream to sail to America. The first thing he did when he landed in America was to declare his intention to become an American citizen. He married a Swedish girl and homesteaded a farm on the Columbia River.

Family Tradition as told by Agnes P. Christian, daughter.

Figure 207.   White surname note card for family tradition.

BIBLE RECORDS

Genealogical information found in Bibles usually consists of dates of birth, marriage, and death and often is recorded on the pages between the Old and New Testaments. (See Figure 208.) The place where the events occurred is often omitted. It is not always possible to determine who recorded the information or the date when the information was recorded. In examining a family Bible record, it is important to note whether the Bible was published before or after the dates recorded in the Bible. If the events occurred before the publication date, then there was a time lapse between the date of the event and the date of its recording and the information may have been recorded from memory. When events are recorded in the same handwriting and ink, it can be assumed that they were written on the same day and by the same person. The address of the publisher or other addresses may be clues to places of residence.

```
┌─────────────────────────────────────────────────────────────┐
│  SLOPER, Charles Abner                          Bible         │
│                                                               │
│     Charles Abner Sloper and Daisy Nell Lott                  │
│        were married October 14, 1901.                         │
│                                                               │
│                                                               │
│                                                               │
│                                                               │
│                                                               │
│  Bible of Olive Jane Doud Lott, printed 1849                  │
│     in possession of Laura Berdell Lott Farnum, Portland,     │
│     Oregon.                                                    │
└─────────────────────────────────────────────────────────────┘
```

Figure 208.   White surname note card for a Bible record.

HANDWRITTEN DIARIES AND JOURNALS

Genealogical information from diaries and journals is especially valuable, for the information was often recorded at or near the time of the event, and the informant or recorder was often a witness or participant to the recorded events. (See Figure 209.)

```
┌─────────────────────────────────────────────────────────────┐
│  HARRIS, John                                   diary         │
│                                                               │
│    Mother received a letter today from Aunt Martha            │
│    stating that Uncle John, mother's brother, had died        │
│    from consumption.  He was 50 years old and did not         │
│    emigrate from England with the rest of his family in       │
│    1850.  It was a very sad day for mother as she had not     │
│    seen her brother for 30 years.                             │
│                                                               │
│                                                               │
│                                                               │
│  Diary of Elizabeth Martin dated 15 August 1880 in posses-    │
│     sion of Lee James, 53 Liberty St., Adams, Ohio.           │
└─────────────────────────────────────────────────────────────┘
```

Figure 209.   White surname note card for a diary entry.

PHOTOGRAPHS

An inscription on a photograph and the name and address of the photographer often lead to the solution of genealogical problems, particularly concerning relationships and places of residence. (See Figure 210.)

```
┌─────────────────────────────────────────────────────────────┐
│  WHITMORE, Susannah (1820)                      photograph   │
│                                                               │
│    Susannah Whitmore Davis, grandmother, aged about 30        │
│    Photograph taken in Coventry, England.                     │
│                                                               │
│                                                               │
│                                                               │
│                                                               │
│                                                               │
│  Photograph in possession of Charlotte Woodbury               │
│    583 Condon Way, Johnsville, Colorado.                      │
└─────────────────────────────────────────────────────────────┘
```

Figure 210.   White surname note card for a photograph.

LETTERS

Family letters tell of circumstances at or near the time of an event, and the recorder often is associated with the event. (See Figure 211.) The following items should be noted when examining family letters:

1. Name and address of the writer
2. Name and address of the person to whom the letter was written
3. Relationship of the writer and the person to whom the letter was written
4. Date and place the letter was written or postmarked

ANNOUNCEMENTS OF VITAL EVENTS

Funeral announcements, baby annoucements, and marriage announcements contain valuable clues that could aid in obtaining government or church vital records. (See Figure 212.)

```
┌─────────────────────────────────────────────────────────────────┐
│  ANDREWS, Albert                                      letter      │
│                                                                   │
│      Albert Andrews born 9 July 1879                              │
│         in Parisville, Kansas                                     │
│      Firstborn to Thomas and Charlotte Andrews                    │
│                                                                   │
│      Letter dated 9 August 1879 from Charlotte Andrews            │
│         to her sister Asenath Bowers in St. George, Utah.         │
│                                                                   │
│                                                                   │
│                                                                   │
│                                                                   │
│                                                                   │
│      Letter in possession of Henry Bowers, 2350 Juniper          │
│         Circle, Springville, Utah.                                │
└─────────────────────────────────────────────────────────────────┘
```

Figure 211.   White surname note card for a letter.

```
┌─────────────────────────────────────────────────────────────────┐
│  SCHMIDT, Fritz                                     funeral       │
│                                                                   │
│      Fritz Schmidt, b. 23 January 1879, Barsinghousen,            │
│         Germany, to Karl and Wilhelmina Schmidt.                  │
│         d. 10 October 1949 in Salt Lake City, Utah.               │
│                                                                   │
│      Buried:  City Cemetery 14 October 1949                       │
│                                                                   │
│      Survivors:  Wife, Anna Schmidt                               │
│          Children:  John Schmidt, Fredrick Schmidt, Karl          │
│            Schmidt, Anna Jensen, Bertha Powers.                   │
│                                                                   │
│      Funeral Services at Deseret Mortuary, Salt Lake              │
│         City, Utah  14 October 1949.                              │
│                                                                   │
│  Funeral Service Announcement                                     │
└─────────────────────────────────────────────────────────────────┘
```

Figure 212.   White surname note card for a funeral announcement.

TEMPLE RECORD BOOKS

Records of temple ordinances performed by family members for their deceased relatives provide valuable clues that lead to obtaining vital records and to verifying the ordinance dates in the original temple records. (See Figure 213.)

```
WALKER, William  (1841)                    temple
                                           record book

   William Walker b. 6 July 1841, Maryhill, Dumbarton,
      Scotland; d. 2 Nov 1907

   Baptized:  24 Jan 1921 SL
   Endowed:   27 Jan 1921 SL




   Temple Record Book in possession of David Walker,
      5316 Conway Road, Salt Lake City, Utah
```

Figure 213.   White surname note card for a temple record book.

BIOGRAPHICAL RECORDS

Published information pertaining to an individual's life story such as biographies, family histories, locality histories, and obituaries provide valuable clues to vital records. (See Chapter 15.)

FAMILY GROUP RECORDS AND PEDIGREE CHARTS

Previously compiled family group records and pedigree charts provide valuable clues to vital records and temple ordinance records. (See Chapter 21.)

PEDIGREE REFERRAL SERVICE

The Pedigree Referral Service of the Genealogical Society provides names and addresses of relatives who have compiled genealogical records. (See Chapter 9.)

RESEARCH DEPARTMENT FILES

The original Research Department Files assembled as a result of individuals and family organizations hiring the Research Department of the Genealogical Society may be available in the home. These files may provide copies of original records and provide clues to further research. (See Chapter 9.)

AVAILABILITY

The researcher should begin his search for home records in his own home, then proceed to the homes of relatives.

Known Relatives

For the most effective means of obtaining names and addresses of known relatives, see Chapter 11, "Biographical Questionnaire," Figure 198. When the researcher obtains names and addresses of known relatives, an address note card is made for each relative (see Figure 214) to be filed in the address section of the file box. An additional surname note card is made indicating the type of genealogical information the relative could provide (see Figure 215), and the relative is contacted either in person or by correspondence. (See sample letter, Figure 216.)

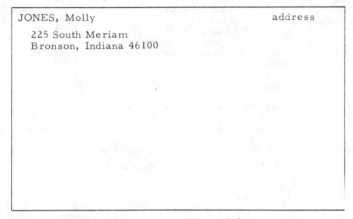

```
JONES, Molly                              address

    225 South Meriam
    Bronson, Indiana 46100
```

Figure 214.   White address note card for a relative.

```
COOMBS                            relative

    Mrs. Molly Jones
    225 South Merriam
    City, State, Zip

    Write to Aunt Molly about the family Bible of Great
        Grandfather Coombs.
```

Figure 215.   White surname note card for a relative.

Your Name
Your Address
Current Date

Mrs. Molly Jones
225 South Meriam
Bronson, Indiana 46100

Dear Aunt Molly,

    I am gathering information on our Coombs line of
ancestry and am wondering if you have Great Grandfather
Coombs' old family Bible. Mother remembers seeing
some births, marriages, and deaths recorded in it; but,
she doesn't remember where she saw it or whose names
were recorded.

    If you do not have it, can you tell me who has it?

    I am compiling a family history which will eventually
be made available to members of the family. Any information you can give me will be appreciated.

    I am enclosing a stamped self-addressed envelope
for your reply.

    Thank you.

Sincerely yours,

Your Name (signed)

Encl: Stamped self-addressed envelope

Figure 216.   Letter to a relative.

Unknown Relatives

The following are suggestions for obtaining names and addresses of unknown relatives:

1. Biographical questionnaire (see Chapter 11, Figure 198)

2. Newspaper offices (see Figure 217; see sample letter, Figure 220)

3. Postmasters (see Figure 218; see sample letter, Figure 221)

4. Telephone company (see Figure 219)

```
COOMBS                                      newspaper office

     Newspaper Office
     Town, State or Country

     Write and ask if they will run a news item or an ad
        to help locate relatives of the Coombs family.




```

Figure 217.   White surname note card for a newspaper office.

```
COOMBS                                        postmaster

     Postmaster
     Town, State or Country

     Write and ask if he will give letter to anyone with the
        surname Coombs.




```

Figure 218.   White surname note card for a postmaster.

COOMBS   telephone company

Call the local telephone business office and request
a copy of the telephone directory for Slippery Rock,
Pennsylvania; request billing through regular
monthly statement.

Figure 219.   White surname note card for a telephone company.

Your Name
Your Address
Current Date

Newspaper Office
Town, State or Country

Gentlemen:

I am compiling a family history of my relatives who settled in your town. I would like to contact descendants, relatives, or other persons who have any information about my second great grandfather and his family:

Cyrus P. Coombs
Had two brothers: Samuel and Levi
Married Elizabeth
Lived about thirty years in Bellevue
Died in Bellevue about 1849
Had the following children: Cyrus, Thomas
    John, Eliza, and Charlotte

If you would print this request for information in your newspaper, it will be appreciated. I will be happy to pay for this service.

Thank you.

Sincerely yours,

Your Name (signed)

Figure 220.   Letter to a newspaper office.

```
                                        Your Name
                                        Your Address
                                        Current Date




        Postmaster
        Town, State or Country

        Dear Sir:

              I am compiling a family history of my relatives who
        settled in your town.  I would like to contact descendants
        or other relatives of my second great grandfather, Cyrus
        P. Coombs.

              Would you be so kind as to refer this letter to anyone
        with the surname of Coombs or anyone whom you know to
        be a relative of the Coombs family?

              Enclosed is a stamped self-addressed envelope for
        their convenience.

              Thank you.

                                        Sincerely yours,




                                        Your Name (signed)

        Encl:  Stamped self-addressed envelope
```

Figure 221.   Letter to a postmaster.

15
Biographical Records

Information pertaining to an individual's life story is classified as a biographical record and may be available in the following forms:
1. Individual biographies
2. Family histories
3. Biographies in locality histories
4. Obituaries

Reference to individual biographies, family histories, locality histories, and obituaries is often included in library surname indexes. (See Chapters 8 and 9.)

GENEALOGICAL APPLICATION

1. General information is given on names, places, dates, and relationships, which adds to presently known information and provides clues to further research.

GENEALOGICAL LIMITATIONS

1. The name of the informant may not be given, making it impossible to evaluate the source of information.

2. Because it is impossible to determine whether the information was given by a witness or a participant and given at or near the time of the event, all birth, marriage, and death information must be verified.

INDIVIDUAL BIOGRAPHIES

Individual biographies are of two types:

1. Autobiography—the story of a person's life written by himself, including journals and diaries (see Figure 222)

2. Biography—the story of a person's life written by another (see Figure 223)

ALTON, Margaret (1872)   autobiography

   Margaret Alton was born in England in 1872 and came
to America in 1889 with her parents. She married
Harold Johnson in New York in 1897.

Personal journal of Margaret Alton Johnson in possession
of David Moore.

Figure 222.   White surname note card for an autobiography.

ADAMS, Harry (1814)   biography

   Harry Adams was born in Mantua, Portage Co., Ohio
3 April 1814.   His father was a native of Massachusetts, and his mother came from Connecticut.

The Life of Harry Adams by Dr. Thomas Adams, in
possession of David Williams.

Figure 223.   White surname note card for a biography.

    Individual biographies are available in the home and in li-
braries (see Figure 224):
    1. The home (see Chapter 14)
    2. Libraries in the locality of residence (see Chapter 8; see
also sample letter, Figure 225)

```
ADAMS, Harry (1814)                          biography

  Availability:
    Homes of relatives
    Local library, city, state, or country
    Genealogical Society Library or branch library
```

Figure 224.   White surname note card for availability of a biography.

3. Library of the Genealogical Society (see Chapter 9)

4. Branch libraries of the Genealogical Society (see Chapter 9, the Surname Section of the Genealogical Society Microfilmed Card Catalog; very incomplete for biographies)

FAMILY HISTORIES

A family history is a compilation of several individual biographies of persons who are related. (See Figure 226.) Family histories are available in the following places (see Figure 227):

1. The home (see Chapter 14)

2. Libraries in the locality of residence (see Chapter 8; see also sample letter, Figure 225)

3. Library of the Genealogical Society

4. Branch libraries of the Genealogical Society (see Chapter 9, the Surname Section of the Genealogical Society Microfilmed Card Catalog)

Your Name
Your Address
Current Date

Local Library
Town, State or Country

Gentlemen:

   Would you please search your index for [insert the
name of the applicable record: biographies, family histories,
locality histories, or obituaries] and if you find information
about Jonathan Bates, would you please send me a copy of the
information found? Jonathan Bates was born in 1810 in Pennsylvania and died 4 August 1882 in your town.

   If you do not provide these services in your library,
could you refer someone to me who would make the searches.
I will be happy to pay for the information.

   I am looking forward to hearing from you and am enclosing a stamped self-addressed envelope for your convenience. Any information you can send to me will be very
much appreciated.

   Thank you.

                                Sincerely yours,

                                Your Name (signed)

Encl: Stamped self-addressed envelope

Figure 225.   Letter to a local library.

```
┌─────────────────────────────────────────────────────────────┐
│  KNAPP, Byron McDonald (1896)              family history     │
│                                                               │
│    Byron McDonald Knapp, son of Herman and Mary               │
│    (McDonald) Knapp was born 15 Dec 1896                      │
│    in Ames, Iowa.  He married Helen Catherine                 │
│    Kegley in Los Angeles, California.                         │
│                                                               │
│                                                               │
│                                                               │
│                                                               │
│                                                               │
│  Nicholas Knapp Genealogy compiled by Alfred Averill          │
│    Knapp.  From Library at Ames, Iowa.                         │
└─────────────────────────────────────────────────────────────┘
```

Figure 226.   White surname note card for a family history.

```
┌─────────────────────────────────────────────────────────────┐
│  KNAPP, Byron McDonald (1896)              family history     │
│                                                               │
│    Availability:                                              │
│      Homes of relatives                                       │
│      Local library, city, state or country                    │
│      Genealogical Society Library or branch library            │
│                                                               │
│                                                               │
│                                                               │
│                                                               │
│                                                               │
│                                                               │
└─────────────────────────────────────────────────────────────┘
```

Figure 227.   White surname note card for availability of a family history.

BIOGRAPHIES IN LOCALITY HISTORIES

Locality histories of towns, counties, and states often include biographies of early settlers and/or prominent people. (See Figure 228.) Locality histories are available in the following places (see Figure 229):

1. The home (see Chapter 14)

2. Libraries in the locality of residence (see Chapter 8; see also sample letter, Figure 225)

3. Library of the Genealogical Society (see Chapter 9)

4. Branch libraries of the Genealogical Society (see Chapter 9, the Locality Section of the Genealogical Society Microfilmed Card Catalog)

```
┌─────────────────────────────────────────────────────────────┐
│ GARDNER, Abigail (1851)                    locality history   │
│                                     Penn, Cambria, Johnstown   │
│                                                               │
│   Abigail Gardner, b. 1851, Johnstown, Penn. to               │
│     Alexander Gardner and Martha Howland,                     │
│     married George Taylor.                                    │
│                                                               │
│   Children:  Abraham, b. about 1871                           │
│              Charity, b. about 1873                           │
│              Lawrence, b. about 1875                          │
│              George b. about 1877                             │
│         /    Charlotte, b. 1875                               │
│                                                               │
│                                                               │
│                                                               │
│ History of Johnstown, Pennsylvania--From library at           │
│   Johnstown, Pennsylvania                                     │
└─────────────────────────────────────────────────────────────┘
```

Figure 228.   White surname note card for a locality history.

```
┌─────────────────────────────────────────────────────────────┐
│ GARDNER, Abigail (1851)                    locality history   │
│                                     Penn, Cambria, Johnstown   │
│                                                               │
│   Availability:                                               │
│     Homes of relatives                                        │
│     Local Library, Johnstown, Pennsylvania                    │
│     Gennealogical Society Library or branch library           │
│                                                               │
│                                                               │
│                                                               │
│                                                               │
│                                                               │
│                                                               │
└─────────────────────────────────────────────────────────────┘
```

Figure 229.   White surname note card for availability of a locality history.

OBITUARIES

Obituaries are biographical sketches about individuals compiled and published in newspapers at the time of the individual's death. (See Figure 230.) Obituaries are available in the home, libraries, and newspaper offices (see Figure 231):

```
┌─────────────────────────────────────────────────────────┐
│  JOHNSON, Louis William (1875)              obituary      │
│                                                           │
│  Died on Tuesday [4 Aug 1882] Louis W. Johnson.           │
│  Born 8 Sept. 1810 in Lancaster County, Pennsylvania.     │
│  Survived by two sons, L. William Johnson and Carl        │
│     Johnson; and three daughters, Mrs. John (Amanda)      │
│     Carson, Mrs. Robert (Jane) Williams, and Mrs.         │
│     David (Caroline) Hicks; all of Slippery Rock.         │
│                                                           │
│                                                           │
│                                                           │
│                                                           │
│                                                           │
│  Slippery Rock Guardian, 7 Aug 1882--rec'd by corres.     │
└─────────────────────────────────────────────────────────┘
```

Figure 230.   White surname note card for an obituary.

```
┌─────────────────────────────────────────────────────────┐
│  JOHNSON, Louis William (1875)              obituary      │
│                                                           │
│  Died 4 Aug 1882                                          │
│                                                           │
│  Availability:                                            │
│     Homes of relatives                                    │
│     Local library, city, state or country                 │
│     Local newspaper office, city, state or country        │
│                                                           │
│                                                           │
│                                                           │
│                                                           │
│                                                           │
│                                                           │
└─────────────────────────────────────────────────────────┘
```

Figure 231.   White surname note card for availability of an obituary.

1. The home (see Chapter 14)

2. Libraries in the locality where the death occurred (see Chapter 9; see also sample letter, Figure 225)

3. Newspaper offices in the locality where the death occurred (see sample letter, Figure 232)

Your Name
Your Address
Current Date

Newspaper Office
Town, State or Country

Gentlemen:

    Would you please search your newspaper obituaries
for information about my grandfather:

        Louis William Johnson, died 10 February,
        1925, in your city.

    I understand he was very well known in the community
and lived most of his life there.

    I would be most grateful for any information which
you could send to me, and would be happy to pay you for
your services. A stamped self-addressed envelope is
enclosed for your convenience.

    Thank you.

                Sincerely yours,

                Your Name (signed)

Encl: Stamped self-addressed envelope

Figure 232. Letter to a newspaper office.

16
Vital Records

The most valuable records in genealogical research are vital records initiated by government (civil) jurisdiction and church (ecclesiastical) jurisdiction:

1. Government vital records:
   a. Birth
   b. Marriage
   c. Death
2. Church vital records:
   a. Christening (baptism)
   b. Marriage
   c. Burial

When birth, marriage, and death records are available for each member of each ancestral family, the necessity for searching other records is greatly reduced.

In countries where there is a state church, the church registration may be supervised by the government and the records may be the same. In countries where the information in the government records differs from the information in the church records, copies from both jurisdictions should be obtained.

The information presented in this chapter will provide the researcher with basic techniques for obtaining vital records. More detailed research in the vital records requires an understanding of the origin, content, time period, genealogical application, genealogical limitations, and availability of the vital records of the specific locality, and can be learned by studying a more detailed textbook on genealogical records of the locality or country.

GENEALOGICAL APPLICATION

1. Information from vital records is used to verify dates and places of birth/christening, marriage, and death/burial listed on the objective family group records.

2. General information is given on names, places, dates, and relationships that adds to presently known information and provides clues to further research.

GENEALOGICAL LIMITATIONS

1. Vital records may not be available for the time period and locality listed on the objective family group records, in which case the researcher must substitute other records that provide vital information.

2. Vital records may not be available to the public for a personal search.

CONTENTS

Information varies with each record within each government jurisdiction and within each church denomination. The following is representative of information that may be found in vital records.

Birth Records (See Figures 233 and 234)

A birth record may contain the following information:
  1. Name of the individual
  2. Sex of the individual
  3. Legitimate or illegitimate birth of the individual
  4. Birth date of the individual
  5. Birthplace of the individual
  6. Name of the father
  7. Maiden name of the mother
  8. Birthplace of the father
  9. Birthplace of the mother
  10. Age of the father
  11. Age of the mother
  12. Occupation of the father
  13. Occupation of the mother
  14. Marriage date of the parents
  15. Marriage place of the parents
  16. Name of the informant
  17. Address of the informant
  18. Relationship of the informant
  19. Date of registration

```
BURCH, Robert Applin (1856)                        birth

  Robert Applin, male
     Born: 16 February 1856, Alderney
     Father: Josiah Burch, labourer
     Mother: Susana Perkins

     Registered: 4 Mar 1856




  Government Birth Certificate rec'd from the Registrar's
     Office, Alderney, Channel Islands, by correspondence.
```

Figure 233.   Yellow surname note card for a government birth record.

```
WEINHEIMER, Herbert (1923)                    christening

  Herbert Weinheimer
     Born: 4 Nov 1923, Haniuniu, Tarnopolski, Poland
        [now Hanunin, Tarnopol, Ukraine]
     Christened: 1 Dec 1923, Augsburska Parish

     Father: Jakoba Weinheimer
     Mother: Wilhelminy Boos

  Certificate No. 392



  Church Christening Certificate issued by the Registrar's
     Office, Warsaw, Poland.  Rec'd. by correspondence.
```

Figure 234.   Yellow surname note card for a church christening record.

Marriage Records (See Figures 235 and 236)

A marriage record may contain the following information:
1. Name of the groom
2. Name of the bride
3. Place of the marriage
4. Date of the marriage
5. Age or birth year of the groom
6. Age or birth year of the bride
7. Birthplace of the groom
8. Birthplace of the bride
9. Current residence of the groom
10. Current residence of the bride

11. Marital status prior to marriage
12. Father of the groom
13. Father of the bride
14. Mother of the groom
15. Mother of the bride
16. If father is deceased
17. If mother is deceased
18. Names of witnesses
19. Church denomination and name of the minister
20. Date of registration
21. Date of license

```
WALKER, William (1841)                    marriage

  William Walker, 22, Grocer, Bachelor, of 369 Garscube
    Road, Glasgow
    Father: David Walker, Blacksmith, deceased
    Mother: Jane Walker, M.S. Durie

  Married 2 June 1863 at 2 Clifton Street, Glasgow, after
    banns according to the Forms of the Free Church of
    Scotland by the minister of Free St. Marks Church.

  Janet Atkinson, 21, Spinster, of 300 Garscube Road,
    Glasgow
    Father: Joseph Atkinson, Iron Forger, deceased
    Mother: Elizabeth Atkinson, M.S. Ford

  Witnesses: William Stein and Mary Atkinson

Marr Cert #138 from Dist. of Anderston, Glasgow, Scotland
```

Figure 235.   Pink surname note card for a government marriage record.

```
NIELSEN, Mathias (1740)                    marriage

  Mathias Nielsen, Church Caretaker of Lyngby

  Married 23 Sep 1762 in the Church

  Maren Pedersdatter of Lyngby




Parish Register of Kongens-Lyngby, Copenhagen, Den.
GS F 055,774
```

Figure 236.   Pink surname note card for a church marriage record.

Death Records (See Figures 237 and 238)

A death record may contain the following information:
1. Name of the individual
2. Sex of the individual
3. Age of the individual
4. Date of the death
5. Date of the burial
6. Place of death
7. Place of burial
8. Residence of the individual
9. Length of residence of the individual
10. Previous residence of the individual
11. Birthplace of the individual
12. Birth date of the individual
13. Marital status of the individual
14. Occupation of the individual
15. Name of the informant
16. Relationship of the informant
17. Address of the informant
18. Name of the father
19. Name of the mother
20. Birthplace of the father
21. Birthplace of the mother
22. Cause of death
23. Autopsy results
24. Name and address of the funeral home
25. Date of registration

```
DOUD, Jeremiah Osborne (1817)                    death

  J.O. Doud, died 12 Dec 1898 at St. Vincents Hospital
      White, male, age 82, farmer
      Birth:  Pennsylvania
      Death:  Portland, Oregon
      Residence in City:  About 10 years
      Previous Residence:  Kansas
      Nativity of Father:  U.S.A.
      Nativity of Mother:  U.S.A.
      Place of Interment:  Lone Fir Cemetery
      Date of Interment:  13 Dec 1898

  Date of Registration:  12 Dec 1898


  Death Cert Rec'd from City of Portland, Multonomah Co.,
      Oregon, by correspondence.
```

Figure 237.   Blue surname note card for a government death record.

```
TREPASS, Sarah (1768)                              burial
(Wife of Richard Ward)


#51  Sarah buried 24 August 1814 at age 46
     Wife of Richard Ward, a labourer from
     Westwood Heath




Parish Register of Stoneleigh, Warwickshire, England
GS F 554,728
```

Figure 238.   Blue surname note card for a church burial record.

AVAILABILITY—CIVIL VITAL RECORDS, UNITED STATES[1]

In the United States there is no nationwide index to civil (government) vital records, since there is no national registration of civil vital records. Civil vital registration in the United States is within the jurisdiction of the state, county or city.

In the United States one begins the search for vital records within the state jurisdiction because the records are indexed statewide, and one does not need to know the name of the county or town. City or county repositories may have vital records prior to the time period listed for state registration, and in some states, marriages are registered on a city or county basis only. If the beginning date of state registration is too recent and the name of the county is known, the county jurisdiction is searched, then the city jurisdiction if in a large city.

---

[1]Information for this section has been taken from the following sources: George B. Everton, Sr., *The Handy Book for Genealogists*, 6th ed. (Logan, Utah: Everton Publishers, 1971). U.S. Department of Health, Education, and Welfare, Public Health Service, *Where to Write for Birth and Death Records, United States and Outlying Areas*, No. 630 A-1 (Washington, D.C.: Superintendent of Documents, U.S. Government Printing Office, 1975). U.S. Department of Health, Education, and Welfare, Public Health Service, *Where to Write for Marriage Records*, No. 630-B (Washington, D.C.: Superintendent of Documents, U.S. Government Printing Office, 1974).

Records are available upon request at the record repository, by correspondence with the record custodian, and copies may be available at libraries. To obtain civil vital records, one may write to the jurisdictions in the order indicated in Figure 239. (See sample letter, Figure 240.)

Jurisdiction	Address
State	See "Availability of State Vital Records in the United States," Figure 241.
County	County Clerk County Courthouse County Seat, State
City	City Clerk City Hall City, State

Figure 239.   Availability of civil vital records, United States.

Your Name
Your Address
Current Date

County Clerk
County Courthouse
County Seat, State

Dear Sir:

Would you please search your marriage indexes from 1882 to 1902 for the marriage of Jacob Mulford Lott and Olive Jane Doud? If this record is found, I would appreciate a photocopy of the record or an exact typewritten or hand-written copy of the information.

Enclosed is an American Express Money Order for $2.00 to cover the cost of the search and the copy of the record. I will be happy to send more if necessary.

Thank you.

Sincerely yours,

Your Name (signed)

Encl: $2.00

Figure 240.   Letter to a county clerk.

State	Earliest Date	Address
Alabama	b,d -- 1 Jan 1908 m -- Aug 1936	Bureau of Vital Statistics State Health Department Montgomery, Ala. 36104
Alaska	b,m,d -- 1913	Bureau of Vital Statistics Dept. of Health & Welfare Pouch "H" Juneau, Alaska 99801
Arizona	b,d -- 1 July 1909	Division of Vital Records State Health Department P.O. Box 3887 Phoenix, Ariz. 85030
	m --	Clerk of Superior Court County Seat, Ariz.
Arkansas	b,d -- 1 Feb 1914 m -- 1917	Bureau of Vital Statistics State Health Department Little Rock, Ark. 72201
California	b,m,d -- 1 July 1905	Bureau of Vital Statistics State Health Department 744 "P" Street Sacramento, Calif. 95814
Colorado	b -- 1900 d -- 1910 m -- State-wide index, except 1940-1967	Records and Statistics State Health Department 4210 East 11th Avenue Denver, Colo. 80220
	m --	County Clerk County Seat, Colo.
Connecticut	b,m,d -- 1 July 1897	Public Health Statistics State Health Department 79 Elm Street Hartford, Conn. 06115
Delaware	b,d -- 1861-1863; 1881 m --	Bureau of Vital Statistics State Health Department Jesse S. Cooper Memorial Building Dover, Del. 19901
District of Columbia	b -- 1871 d -- 1855	D.C. Dept. of Public Health Vital Records Division Room 1022 300 Indiana Ave., N.W. Washington, D.C. 20001
	m -- 1811	Clerk, Superior Court of District of Columbia Washington, D.C. 20004

Figure 241.   Availability of state vital records, United States. (Continued on next page)

State	Earliest Date	Address
Florida	b -- Apr 1865 d -- 1877 m -- 6 June 1927	Bureau of Vital Statistics State Board of Health P.O. Box 210 Jacksonville, Fla. 32201
Georgia	b,d -- 1 Jan 1919 m -- 9 June 1952	Vital Records Service State Health Department 47 Trinity Ave., S.W. Atlanta, Ga. 30334
Hawaii	b,m,d -- 1853	Research and Statistics State Health Department P.O. Box 3378 Honolulu, Hawaii 96801
Idaho	b,d -- 1911 m -- 1947	Bureau of Vital Statistics State Health Department Statehouse Boise, Idaho 83707
Illinois	b,d -- 1 Jan 1916 m -- 1 Jan 1962	Office of Vital Records State Health Department 535 W. Jefferson Street Springfield, Ill. 62706
Indiana	b -- 1 Oct 1907 d -- 1900 m -- 1958	Division of Vital Records State Board of Health 1330 West Michigan St. Indianapolis, Ind. 46206
Iowa	b,m,d -- 1 July 1880	Division of Vital Statistics State Health Department Des Moines, Iowa 50319
Kansas	b,d -- 1 July 1911 m -- May 1913	Division of Vital Statistics 535 Kansas Avenue Topeka, Kans. 66603
Kentucky	b,d -- 1 Jan 1911 m -- 1 July 1958	Office of Vital Statistics State Health Department 275 East Main Street Frankfort, Ky. 40601
Louisiana	b,d -- 1 July 1914 m -- 1946	Division of Public Health State Board of Health P.O. Box 60630 New Orleans, La. 70160
Maine	b,m,d -- 1892	Office of Vital Statistics State Health Department State House Augusta, Maine 04330

Figure 241.   Availability of state vital records, United States. (Continued on next
page)

State	Earliest Date	Address
Maryland	b,d -- 1898 m -- 1 June 1951	Division of Vital Records State Health Department 201 West Preston Street P.O. Box 13146 Baltimore, Md. 21203
Massachusetts	b,m,d -- 1841	Registrar of Vital Stat. 272 State House Boston, Mass. 02133
Michigan	b,m,d -- 1867	Vital Records Section State Health Department 3500 North Logan Street Lansing, Mich. 48914
Minnesota	b,d -- Jan 1908 m -- Jan 1958	State Department of Health Section of Vital Stat. 717 Delaware Street, SE. Minneapolis, Minn. 55440
Mississippi	b,d -- 1 Nov 1912 m -- Jan 1926	Vital Recs. Reg. Unit State Board of Health P.O. Box 1700 Jackson, Miss. 39205
Missouri	b,d -- Jan 1910 m -- July 1948	Office of Vital Records State Health Department Jefferson City, Mo. 65101
Montana	b,d -- 1907 m -- July 1943	Division of Vital Records State Health Department Helena, Mont. 59601
Nebraska	b,d -- 1904 m -- Jan 1909	Bureau of Vital Statistics State Health Department Lincoln Building 1003 "O" Street Lincoln, Nebr. 68508
Nevada	b,d -- 1 July 1911	Department of Health Section of Vital Statistics Carson City, Nev. 89701
	m --	County Recorder County Seat, Nev.
New Hampshire	b,m,d -- 1640	Department of Health Office of Vital Statistics 61 South Spring Street Concord, N.H. 03301
New Jersey	b,m,d -- May 1848- May 1878	Archives and History State Library Division State Dept. of Education Trenton, N.J. 08625

Figure 241. Availability of state vital records, United States. (Continued on next page)

State	Earliest Date	Address
New Jersey (cont.)	b,m,d -- June 1878	Bureau of Vital Statistics Box 1540 Trenton, N.J. 08625
New Mexico	b,d --	Vital Records PERA Bldg., Room 118 Santa Fe, N. Mex. 87501
	m --	County Clerk County Seat, N. Mex.
New York	b,d -- 1880 m -- Jan 1880-Dec 1907; May 1915	Bureau of Vital Records State Health Department Albany, N.Y. 12208
North Carolina	b,d -- 1 Oct 1913 m -- 1 Jan 1962	Vital Records Section State Board of Health P.O. Box 2091 Raleigh, N.C. 27602
North Dakota	b,d -- 1 July 1893 m -- 1 July 1925	Division of Vital Statistics State Health Department Bismarck, N. Dak. 58501
Ohio	b,d -- 20 Dec 1908 m -- Sept 1949	Division of Vital Statistics G-20 State Dept. Bldg. Columbus, Ohio 43215
Oklahoma	b,d, -- Oct 1908	Division of Vital Statistics 3400 North Eastern Oklahoma City, Okla. 73105
	m --	County Clerk County Seat, Okla.
Oregon	b,d, -- July 1903 m -- Jan 1907	Vital Statistics Section State Board of Health P.O. Box 231 Portland, Oreg. 97207
Pennsylvania	b,d -- 1 Jan 1906	Division of Vital Statistics State Health Department 101 South Mercer Street P.O. Box 1528 Newcastle, Pa. 16103
	m -- 1941	Division of Vital Statistics State Health Department P.O. Box 90 Harrisburg, Pa. 17120
Rhode Island	b,m,d -- 1853	Division of Vital Statistics Room 101 Health Bldg. Davis Street Providence, R.I. 02908

Figure 241.   Availability of state vital records, United States. (Continued on next page)

State	Earliest Date	Address
South Carolina	b,d -- 1 Jan 1915 m -- 1 July 1950	Bureau of Vital Statistics Sims Building Columbia, S.C. 29201
South Dakota	b,m,d -- 1 July 1905	Division of Public Health State Health Department Pierre, S.Dak. 57501
Tennessee	b,d -- 1 Jan 1914 m -- July 1945	Division of Vital Records State Health Department Cordell Hull Building Nashville, Tenn. 37219
Texas	b,d -- 1903	Bureau of Vital Statistics State Health Department 410 East 5th Street Austin, Tex. 78701
	m --	County Clerk County Seat, Tex.
Utah	b,d, -- 1905	Division of Vital Statistics State Health Department 554 South Third East Salt Lake City, Utah 84113
	m --	County Clerk County Seat, Utah
Vermont	b,d -- 1760 m -- 1857	Vital Records Dept. State House Montpelier, Vt. 05602
Virginia	b,d -- Jan 1858-Dec 1896; June 1912 m -- Jan 1853	Bureau of Vital Records James Madison Building P.O. Box 1000 Richmond, Va. 23208
Washington	b,d -- 1 July 1907 m -- 1 Jan 1968	Bureau of Vital Records State Health Department P.O. Box 709 Olympia, Wash. 98504
West Virginia	b,d -- Jan 1917 m -- 1921	Division of Vital Statistics State Health Department Charleston, W. Va. 25305
Wisconsin	b,d -- 1814 m -- April 1835	Bureau of Vital Statistics P.O. Box 309 Madison, Wis. 53701
Wyoming	b,d -- July 1909 m -- May 1941	Division of Vital Statistics State Health Department State Office Building Cheyenne, Wyo. 82001

Figure 241.   Availability of state vital records, United States. (Concluded)

AVAILABILITY—CIVIL VITAL RECORDS, COUNTRIES OUTSIDE THE UNITED STATES[2]

The following availability list (Figure 242) contains the names of countries outside the United States arranged alphabetically and provides the date of civil vital registration, when known, and the address of the record repository. The date of registration is either the earliest date that records are available or the date that registration became mandatory by law. In either case, early records may be missing or incomplete.

In some countries, registration of civil (government) vital records is on a national basis, and a national index is available. In other countries, registration is on a district, state, or even a town basis, and no national index is available. The civil vital records are available upon request at the record repository by correspondence with the record custodian (see sample letter, Figure 243), and copies may be available at libraries.

For countries not included in the availability list, write to the national archives of the particular country and request information on civil registration (see sample letter, Figure 244):

National Archives
Capital City
Name of Country

---

[2]Information for this section is taken from the following sources: George B. Everton, Sr., ed., *The Handy Book for Genealogists* 6th ed. (Logan, Utah: Everton Publishers, 1971); L. G. Pine, *American Origins* (Garden City, New York: Doubleday and Co., 1960); correspondence with foreign embassies.

Albania	b, m, d - - 1929	Local Registrar's Office Town, Albania
Argentina	b, m, d - - 1886	Registrar, Vital Statistics Uruguay 753 Buenos Aires, Argentina
Australia Capital Territory	b, m, d - - 1 Jan 1930	Registrar, Vital Statistics P. O. Box 370 Canberra City, Canberra A. C. T., Australia
New South Wales	b, m, d - - 1 Mar 1856	Registrar General Prince Albert Road Sydney N. S. W., Australia
Northern Territory	b, m, d - - 1842-1870	See Southern Territory
	b, m, d - - 1870	Registrar, Vital Statistics Law Court Building Mitchell St. Box 1281 Darwin No. Territory, Australia
Queensland	b, m, d - - 1 Mar 1856	Registrar General Treasury Building Queen Street Brisbane B7 Queensland, Australia
Southern Territory	b, m, d - - July 1842	Principal Registrar Flinders Street G. P. O. Box 1351 H. Adelaide So. Australia, Australia
Tasmania	b, m, d - - 1 Dec 1838	Registrar General 59 Collins Street G. P. O. Box 875 J Hobart Tasmania, Australia
Victoria	b, m, d - - 1 July 1853	Government Statistics 295 Queen Street Melbourne Victoria, Australia
Western Territory	b, m, d - - 1841	Registrar General Cathedral Avenue Perth Western Australia Australia

Figure 242. Availability of civil vital records, countries other than the United States. (Continued on next page)

Austria	b, m, d--1938	Civil Registry Office Town, Austria
Belgium	b, m, d--1795	Civil Registrar Town, Belgium
Bolivia	b, m, d--	Civil Registrar Town, Bolivia
Brazil	b, m, d--1870	Civil Registrar Town, Brazil
Bulgaria	b, m, d--1 Jan 1893	Dist. Peoples' Council Town, Bulgaria
Burma *	b, m, d--	Director, Health Services Rangoon, Municipal Corp. Rangoon, Burma
Canada Alberta	b, m, d--1886	Bureau of Vital Statistics Department of Health Edmonton, Alberta, Can.
British Columbia	b, m, d--1 Sept 1872	Registrar, Vital Statistics Parliament Building Victoria British Columbia, Canada
Manitoba	b, m, d--1812	Recorder, Vital Statistics Health & Welfare Dept. Winnipeg, Canada
New Brunswick	m--1887-1919	Secretary Board of Health County, Canada
	b, m, d--1 Jan 1920	Registrar General Fredericton New Brunswick, Canada
Newfoundland	b--15 Mar 1891 m--2 June 1891 d--1 May 1891	Registrar, Vital Statistics Health & Welfare Dept. St. John's Newfoundland, Canada
Nova Scotia	b, d--1864-1876; 1908 m--1763	Registrar, Vital Statistics Halifax Nova Scotia, Canada
Ontario	b, m, d--1 July 1869	Registrar General Parliament Building Toronto Ontario, Canada

Figure 242. Availability of civil vital records, countries other than the United States. (Continued on next page)

Canada (cont.)		
Prince Edward Island	b, d--June 1906 m--1831	Registrar General Provincial Building Charlottetown, Prince Edward Island, Canada
Quebec	b, d--1894 m--1642	Director, Health Dept. Quebec, Canada
Saskatchewan	b--1854 m--1878 d--1882	Registrar, Vital Statistics Parliament Building Regina, Saskatchewan Canada
Yukon Territory	b, m--1899 d--1898	Registrar, Vital Statistics Territorial Treas. Office Whitehorse, Yukon, Can.
Canal Zone (See also Panama)	b, d--4 May 1904	Vital Statistics Health Bureau Balboa Heights Canal Zone
	m--Sept 1905	Clerk, U. S. Dist. Court Ancon, Canal Zone
Ceylon	b, m, d--	The Registrar General Colombo 1, Ceylon
Channel Islands Alderney	b--3 Aug 1850 m--1 July 1891 d--2 Aug 1850	Registrar General Greffe, Guernsey Channel Islands
Guernsey	b, m, d--1840	"
Jersey	b, m, d--1842	Superintendant Registrar States' Building St. Helier, Jersey Channel Islands
Chile	b, m, d--1885	National Archives Santiago, Chile
China (Taiwan)	b, m, d--	Census Administration Ministry of Interior 107 Roosevelt Road Section 4, Taipei Taiwan
Columbia	b, m, d--1853	National Administration of Statistics (CAN Bogoto, D. E. Columbia

Figure 242.   Availability of civil vital records, countries other than the United
States. (Continued on next page)

Costa Rica	b, m, d -- 1 Jan 1888	Civil Registrar San Jose, Costa Rica
Cuba	b, m, d -- 1 Jan 1885	Civil Registrar Town, Cuba
Czechoslovakia	b, m, d -- 1921	Ministry, Foreign Affairs Prague, Czechoslovakia
Denmark	b, m, d -- 1645	Danish State Archives Copenhagen, Denmark
Dominican Republic	b, m, d -- 1828	Registrar, Vital Statistics Santo Domingo Dominican Republic
Ecuador	b, m, d -- 1901	Registrar, Vital Statistics Quito, Ecuador
Egypt	b, m, d --	Registrar, Vital Statistics Cairo, Egypt
El Salvador	b, m, d -- 1879	Registrar, Vital Statistics San Salvador, El Salvador
England	b, m, d -- 1 July 1837	Registrar General General Register Office Somerset House London, W. C. 2, England
Estonia	b, m, d -- 29 June 1920	Civil Registrar Town, Estonia
Finland	b, m, d -- 1918 (civil) b, m, d -- 1680 (church)	Registrar, Vital Statistics Rauhankatu 17 Helsinki, Finland
France	b, m, d -- 1792	Office of the Mayor Town, France
Germany	b, m, d -- 1 Jan 1876; 1798 West of Rhine	Civil Registrar Town Germany
Greece	b, m, d -- 1925	The Mayor Town, Greece
Guam	b, m, d -- Oct 1901	Office of Vital Statistics Dept. of Medical Service Government of Guam Agana, Guam
Guatemala	b, m, d -- 1877	Civil Registrar Town, Guatemala

Figure 242. Availability of civil vital records, countries other than the United States. (Continued on next page)

Haiti	b, m, d--	Registrar, Vital Statistics Port-au-Prince, Haiti
Honduras	b, m, d--1821	Civil Registrar Town, Honduras
Hungary	b, m, d--1 Oct 1895	Leveltarak Orszagos Kozpontja Budapest I Uri Utoa 54-56 Hungary
Iceland	b, m, d--1 July 1746	The National Archives Reykjavik, Iceland
Ireland Northern	b, m, d--Prior to 1921	See Republic of Ireland
	b, m, d--1921	The Registrar General General Register Office Fermanagh House Ormean Avenue Belfast, Ireland
Republic of	b, d--1 Jan 1864 m--1845	Registrar General Customs House Dublin, Ireland
Isle of Man	b, d--1878 m--1849	Registrar General Government Office Douglas, Isle of Man
Israel	b, d--1948	Consulate Gen. of Israel 659 S. Highland Drive Los Angeles, Calif. 90036
	m--	Local Rabbinical Office Town, Israel
Italy	b, m, d--1869 North Italy--1803-1815	Municipal Town Govt. Town, Italy
Japan	b, m, d--645 A.D.	Ministry of Law 1-1-1, Kasumigaseki Chiyoda-ku, Tokyo Japan
Jordan	b, m, d--	Ministry of Health Amman, Jordan
Latvia	b, m, d--1919	Soviet Embassy Washington, D.C.
Lebanon	b, m, d--1 Dec 1924	Ministry of Interior Beirut, Lebanon

Figure 242.   Availability of civil vital records, countries other than the United
States. (Continued on next page)

Liechtenstein	b, m, d -- 1878	Regierungskanzlei Vaduz, Liechtenstein
	b, m, d -- 1640	Catholic Priest Town, Liechtenstein
Lithuania	b, m, d -- 1918	State Central Archives Kaunas, Lithuania
Luxembourg	b, m, d -- 1796	Archiviste, Hotel Ville Guillaume, Luxembourg
Mexico	b, m, d -- 1859	Civil Registrar Town, Mexico
Monaco	b, m, d -- 1600	Mairie de Monaco Monte Carlo, Monaco
Morocco	b, m, d --	Civil Registrar Town, Morocco
Netherlands	b, m, d -- 1811	Algemeen Ryksarchief 7 Bleyenburg The Hague, Netherlands
New Zealand	b, m, d --	Registrar General Private Bag Wellington, New Zealand
Nicaragua	b, m, d -- 1879	Civil Registrar Town, Nicaragua
Norway	b, m, d -- 1870	Demographic Section Statistisk Sentralbyra Dronningens Gate 16 Oslo, Norway
Paraguay	b, m, d -- 1899	Registrar, Vital Statistics Asunción, Paraguay
Panama (See also Canal Zone)	b, m, d -- 1904	Registrar, Vital Statistics Panama City, Panama
Peru	b, m, d -- 1852	Office of Vital Statistics Lima, Peru
Philippine Islands	b, d -- 1903 m -- 1898	Division of Archives National Library Manila Philippine Islands
Baguio	b, m -- July 1906 d -- Jan 1905	Local Civil Registrar Baguio Philippine Islands

Figure 242.   Availability of civil vital records, countries other than the United States. (Continued on next page)

Philippine Islands (cont.) Manila	b--Mar 1900 m--12 Jan 1900 d--Oct 1899	Local Civil Registrar Manila Philippine Islands
Poland	b, m, d--1946 German area--1876	The Peoples' Council Town, Poland
Portugal	b, m, d--16 May 1832	Civil Registrar Minister of Justice Lisbon, Portugal
Puerto Rico	b, m, d--Prior to 21 July 1931	Municipal Secretary Town, Puerto Rico
	b, m, d--21 July 1931	Bureau of Vital Statistics Department of Health Town, Puerto Rico
Romania	b, m, d--1895	United States Embassy Strada Tudor Arghezi No. 7-9 Bucharest, Romania
Russia	b, m, d--1913	Ministry, Internal Affairs Civic Status Records Moscow, Russia
Samoa American	b, m, d--1900	Registrar, Vital Statistics Pago Pago American Samoa
British or Western	b, m, d--	Civil Registrar Island of Savaii Western Samoa
	b, m, d--	Civil Registrar Island of Upolu Apia, Western Samoa
Scotland	b, m, d--1855	General Registry Office New Register House Edinburgh 2, Scotland
South Africa Cape Province	b, m, d--1895	Registrar, Vital Statistics Interior Building Pretoria, South Africa
Natal	b, m, d--1868	"
Orange Free State	b, m, d--1902	"
Transvaal	b, m, d--1902	"

Figure 242. Availability of civil vital records, countries other than the United States. (Continued on next page)

Spain	b, m, d--17 June 1870	Central Registry Madrid, Spain
Sweden	b, m, d--1686	The National Archives Stockholm, Sweden
Switzerland	b, m, d--1876	Civil Registrar Town, Switzerland
Syria	b, m, d--	Ministry of the Interior Damascus Syrian Arab Republic
Thailand	b, m, d--	Registrar, Vital Statistics Bangkok, Thailand
Tunisia	b, m, d--	Embassy of Tunisia 2408 Massachusetts Ave. Washington, D.C.
Turkey	b, m, d--	Registrar, Vital Statistics Ankara, Turkey
Uruguay	b, m, d--1879	Registrar General Canelones 968 Montevideo, Uruguay
Venezuela	b, m, d--1873	Registrar General Caracas, Venezuela
Virgin Islands Christiansted and Frederiksted Dists.	b, d--1 July 1906 m--1887	Custodian Judge of Police Court St. Croix, Virgin Islands
St. Thomas and St. John	b, d--1 July 1906 m--1918	Custodian Judge of Police Court St. Thomas, Virgin Islands
Wales	b, m, d--1 July 1837	Registrar General General Register Office Somerset House London, W.C. 2, England
Yugoslavia	b, m, d--9 May 1946	People's Committee of the Commune Town, Yugoslavia

Figure 242.   Availability of civil vital records, countries other than the United
States. (Concluded)

Your Name
Your Address
Current Date

Office of the Mayor
Town, Country

Dear Sir:

 Would you please search your birth records from 1795
to 1799 for the following:

  Birth of Hans Peter Jaussi, August 1796 in
  your town; parents, Peter Jaussi and Benedicta
  Dousse.

 If this information is found, I would appreciate receiving an exact copy of the entry. If you do not have this information in your possession, would you please refer this
letter to the proper record custodian?

 Enclosed is an American Express Money Order for
$2.00 to cover the cost of the search, copy of the information
found, and return postage by air mail. I will be happy to
pay any balance due.

 Thank you.

        Sincerely yours,

        Your Name (signed)

Encl: $2.00

Figure 243. Letter to a foreign government.

Your Name
Your Address
Current Date

National Archives
Capital City
Country

Gentlemen:

Could you please tell me on which date your government
began registration of births, marriages, and deaths, and the
address to which I would write to request the birth, marriage,
and death information?

I am looking forward to hearing from you and am enclosing a stamped self-addressed envelope for your convenience.

Thank you.

Sincerely yours,

Your Name (signed)

Encl: Stamped self-addressed envelope

Figure 244.   Letter to a national archives.

AVAILABILITY—CHURCH VITAL RECORDS

Church vital records of christening (baptism), marriage, and burial often are available for an earlier time period than civil vital records. There are numerous religious denominations, and the availability of church vital records varies with each denomination and each minister or clerk. In countries where there is a state church, the government supervises the recording of church vital records for that particular denomination. Religious denominations other than the state church are referred to as non-parochial or non-conformist. The availability of church vital records in the United States is often difficult to determine because there is no state church nor a predominate religion.

Church vital records are available upon request at the record repository by correspondence with the minister (see sample letter, Figure 245), and copies may be available at libraries. To search church vital records by correspondence, the name of the denomination and the name of the town must be known. The exact address of the record repository or the record custodian is not necessary; a general address is acceptable:

Minister
Name of Church
Town
State or Country

Your Name
Your Address
Current Date

Minister
Name of Church
Town, State or Country

Reverend and Dear Sir:

     Would you please be so kind as to search your church records from 1850 to 1854 for the christening of Henry John Lott, son of Jacob S. Lott and Eliza Lowers? If the information is found, I would appreciate an exact copy of the entry.

     If you do not have this information in your possession, would you please refer this letter to the proper record custodian?

     Enclosed is an American Express Money Order for $2.00 as a deposit for this search. I will be happy to send any balance due.

     Thank you.

Sincerely yours,

Your Name (signed)

Encl: $2.00

Figure 245.   Letter to a minister.

17
Genealogical Society Temple Processing Records

The Temple Services Division of the Genealogical Department of The Church of Jesus Christ of Latter-day Saints (see Chapter 9) processes names of individuals for LDS temple ordinances. As a result, several types of temple processing records are available to the genealogical researcher through the Genealogical Society Library:

1. Temple Records Index Bureau (see chapter 18)
2. Computer File Index (see Chapter 20)
3. Main Record Section family group records (see Chapter 21)
4. Temple recorders records (see Chapter 22)

GENEALOGICAL APPLICATION

1. Genealogical Society temple processing records prevent duplication of research activity.

2. Genealogical Society temple processing records prevent duplication of LDS temple ordinances.

3. Genealogical Society temple processing records provide names of other individuals interested in genealogical research on the particular pedigree line.

4. Genealogical Society temple processing records provide verification of LDS temple ordinance dates.

5. Genealogical Society temple processing records include names of ancestors of non-LDS individuals.

6. Genealogical Society temple processing records are available to both non-LDS and LDS genealogical researchers.

7. Genealogical Society temple processing records provide clues that lead to further research in other genealogical records.

GENEALOGICAL LIMITATIONS

1. The Genealogical Society is not concerned about duplication of genealogical research; the genealogical researcher must assume this responsibility.

2. There is much duplication of baptisms and endowments prior to 1927.

3. There is much duplication of sealings of couples and sealings of children prior to 1942.

4. The Genealogical Society does not assume responsibility for the accuracy of the information submitted, and some genealogical information is incorrect.

HISTORY

It is important that one understand the history of processing names for temple ordinances so that he can properly interpret the genealogical information. The following explains the various methods used for processing names for temple ordinances from 1840 to the present. (See also Figure 246.)

1840-1927

1. Ordinances were performed individually, and it was not necessary to identify complete family groups.

2. Copies of the forms submitted for temple ordinances were not retained by the Genealogical Society.

3. There was no Churchwide file or index of baptism, endowment, and sealing records used in processing names for temple ordinances; therefore, some temple ordinances were repeated or duplicated.

4. Temple recorders records for this time period are available in the temples or on microfilm at the Genealogical Society. (See Chapter 22.)

1927-1941

1. Ordinances were performed individually, and it was not necessary to identify complete family groups.

2. Copies of the forms submitted for temple ordinances were not retained by the Genealogical Society.

3. A Churchwide file of endowment records (Temple Records Index Bureau) was prepared from temple records of endowments and used in processing names for temple ordinances. (See Chapter 18.)

4. There was no Churchwide file of baptism records or sealing records used in processing names for temple ordinances; therefore, some of these ordinances were repeated or duplicated.

Time Period	Submission Form	Copy of Form Available at Genealogical Society	Central Processing File		
			Baptisms	Endowments	Sealings
1840-1927	Separate list of names for: Baptisms and endowments Sealing to husband Sealing to parents	None	None	None	None
1927-1941	Separate list of names for: Baptisms and endowments Sealing to husband Sealing to parents	None	None	Temple Records Index Bureau	Temple Records Index Bureau (few)
1942-1969	Family group record for all temple ordinances	Main Records Section with ordinance dates added	None	Temple Records Index Bureau	Temple Records Index Bureau (few) Main Records Section
1970-	Entry Form – for baptism, endowment, sealing to parents Marriage Entry – for sealing to husband Family group record – for baptism, endowment, sealing to parents	Microfilm copy	Name Tabulation Computer Manual Processing	Name Tabulation Computer Temple Records Index Bureau Manual Processing	Name Tabulation Computer Main Records Section Manual Processing

Figure 246.   History of processing names for temple ordinances.

5. Temple recorders records for this time period are available at the temple where the ordinance was performed or on microfilm at the Genealogical Society. (See Chapter 22.)

1942-1969

1. Baptisms and endowments were performed individually, but sealings were performed as family groups, making it necessary to identify complete family groups prior to submitting names for temple ordinances.

2. Copies of the family group records submitted for temple ordinances with temple dates added were filed at the Library of the Genealogical Society. These family group records are known as the Main Records Section. (See Chapter 21.)

3. The Churchwide file of endowment records (Temple Records Index Bureau) continued to be used in processing names for temple ordinances. The cards in the Temple Records Index Bureau were cross-referenced to the family group records in the Main Records Section. (See Chapters 18 and 21.)

4. The Main Records Section provided a Churchwide file of dates of sealing ordinances performed from 1942 to 1969 and prevented duplications of sealings during this time, but not prior to 1942.

5. Temple recorders records for this time period are available at the temple where the ordinance was performed or on microfilm at the Genealogical Society. (See Chapter 22.)

1970-

1. The Name Tabulation Program was established in 1970 to process names for temple ordinances and to avoid duplication of baptism, endowment, and sealing ordinances. (See Chapter 19.)

2. After 1970, ordinances were performed individually, and it was not necessary to identify complete family groups in order to submit names for temple ordinances.

3. Copies of the forms submitted for processing for temple ordinances were microfilmed and are available at the Genealogical Society.

4. The Churchwide file of endowment records (Temple Records Index Bureau) continued to be used in processing names for temple ordinances to avoid duplications, but no TIB cards have been added since 1969.

5. The family group records in the Main Records Section continue to be used to avoid duplication of sealings of children

performed between 1942 and 1969, but no new family group records have been added since 1969.

6. Most ordinance information for this time period is available through the Computer File Index. (See Chapter 20.)

7. Names of individuals from a few geographic areas and ethnic groups continue to be processed through the Manual Processing Department with the family group record as a submission form. A copy of these family group records is filed in the Patrons Section, Family Group Records Archive, 1962 to present. The Manual Processing Department retains a copy of each family group record and maintains a separate endowment file (Temple Records Index Bureau). (See Chapter 18.)

Future

1. The Name Tabulation Program will continue to be used to process names of individuals for temple ordinances and to avoid duplication of baptisms, endowments, and sealings. (See Chapter 19.)

2. The Family Entry System will be established to process names of individuals that do not meet minimum identification standards for the Name Tabulation Program, but which do provide identification as members of an ancestral family group.

3. The Temple Records Index Bureau will continue to be used in processing names for temple ordinances until a substantial portion of the file is converted to the Name Tabulation Program.

4. The Main Records Section will continue to be used as a Churchwide file to avoid duplications of sealings of children to parents performed between 1942 and 1969.

5. Manual processing will continue to be used for processing names of individuals from certain geographic areas and for certain ethnic groups.

RESEARCH STEPS TO VERIFY ORDINANCE DATES

The researcher should search the Genealogical Society temple processing records in a specific order to most efficiently verify ordinance dates; records that are most easily accessible and most easily interpreted should be searched first. (See Figure 247.) Each record searched provides information necessary to efficiently search the next record until the information necessary to search the original temple recorders records is obtained. Not only is information obtained for verifying temple ordinance dates, but information is obtained that provides clues to further research.

Time Period of Ordinance	Living Baptisms	Proxy Baptisms	Endowments	Sealing of Couples Sealing of Families
1840-1941	1. TIB for clues 2. CFI for clues 3. Family group records for clues 4. LDS Church membership records to verify*	1. TIB for clues 2. CFI for clues 3. Family group records for clues 4. Temple recorders records to verify (See Chapter 22)	1. TIB for date 2. CFI for clues 3. Family group records for clues 4. Temple recorders records to verify if error or omission suspected (See Chapter 22)	1. TIB for clues 2. CFI for clues 3. Family group records for clues 4. Temple recorders records to verify (See Chapter 22)
1942-1969	1. TIB for clues 2. CFI for clues 3. Family group records for clues 4. LDS Church membership records to verify*	1. TIB for clues 2. CFI for clues 3. Family group records for clues 4. Temple recorders records to verify (See Chapter 22)	1. TIB for date 2. CFI for clues 3. Family group records for clues 4. Temple recorders records to verify if error or omission suspected (See Chapter 22)	1. TIB for clues 2. CFI for clues 3. Main Records Section for dates 4. Family group records for clues 5. Earlier temple recorders records if repeat sealing suspected
1970-	1. Ward clerk 2. Memberships, PBO	1. CFI 2. Manual Processing	Proxy: 1. CFI 2. Manual Processing Living: 1. Ward clerk 2. Memberships, PBO	Proxy: 1. CFI 2. Manual Processing Living: 1. Ward clerk 2. Memberships, PBO

*Laureen R. Jaussi and Gloria D. Chaston, *Genealogical Records of Utah* (Salt Lake City, Utah: Deseret Book Co., 1974), Chapter 6.

Figure 247.   Research steps to verify ordinance dates.

18
The Temple Records Index Bureau

The Temple Records Index Bureau[1] (Temple Index Bureau—TIB) is a Churchwide index to temple endowments performed for both the living and the dead and was established for the purpose of preventing duplication of temple ordinances. Information on 38 million temple endowments performed from the Nauvoo period through 1969 have been entered on TIB cards. (See Figure 248.) Baptism and sealing dates have been included on some TIB cards, but *the TIB does not contain a record of all baptisms nor of all sealings.*

```
FORSSLING, Lars Fredrik (1803)        endowment (TIB)
      PC    TEMPLE      Salt Lake
   NO.                NO.  9094     BOOK   B      PAGE   257

   NAME Forsling-  Lars Fredric
   BORN       10 Aug 1803
   WHERE Sundsvall, Westmanland, Swed.
   DIED       22 Aug 1862
   F.    Lars Forsling (1772)
   M.    Marta Stina Roberg
   MD.   2 Aug 1836    TO  Magdalena Sundman
   F.R.  Knut A. Elg                        son il
   BAPT. 19 Jun 1894     PROXY
   END.  21 Jun 1894     PROXY
   SLD. H.                        TO
        W.                        PARENTS
                          Corrected from Lars
                          Frederick Torsling
```

Figure 248.   Orange surname note card for an LDS endowment (TIB) record.

ENDOWMENT TIME PERIOD
1842-1969

---

[1]Information for this chapter was taken from Laureen R. Jaussi and Gloria D. Chaston, *Fundamentals of Genealogical Research*, 1st ed. (Salt Lake City: Deseret Book Co., 1966); *A Brief Guide to the Temple Records Index Bureau*, Series F, No. 2 (Salt Lake City: Genealogical Society, no date—after May 1970); and *Supplement to A Brief Guide to the Temple Records Index Bureau*, Series F, No. 2 (Salt Lake City: The Genealogical Society, 1 February 1971).

ORIGIN

The program of indexing the original temple endowment records began in 1922 and took nearly five years to complete. The TIB was first used to process names for temple ordinances in January 1927. After 1927, cards were made as endowments were performed, and the file was kept current until January 1970, when the Name Tabulation Program was initiated as a central file for processing baptisms, endowments, and sealings. (See Chapter 19.)

FILE ARRANGEMENT

The Temple Records Index Bureau is grouped by geographic locality, and cards are filed for each individual according to his country of birth. The "Place Name Catalog," an alphabetical listing of the countries, islands, kingdoms, etc., is used as a guide to indicate the geographic group in which the locality is filed. The "Place Name Catalog" is available to those who have direct access to the TIB file.

Some TIB cards are not filed in the regular geographic groups but are filed in the Manual Processing Department, which contains the following:

1. Records of the Special Information Service (SIS), which contain information of a confidential nature, such as adoptions, cancellation of sealings, excommunications, special sealings, etc., and which is available to direct descendants upon request (formerly Supplementary Information Service)

2. Records of countries where the language cannot be converted to the Roman alphabet easily, such as the Asian countries

3. Records of Polynesia

4. Records of American Indians

5. Records of Iceland

The geographical groups in the TIB are as follows:

1. African—an alphabetical grouping of the countries of Africa

2. American—an alphabetical grouping of the countries of North America, South America, and Central America

3. Asian—Records of Asian countries, located in the Manual Processing Department

4. Australian—the country of Australia only

5. European—an alphabetical grouping of the countries of Europe within geographic sub-groups:

    a. British—an alphabetical grouping of the countries of England, Ireland, Scotland, and Wales
    b. Scandinavia—an alphabetical grouping of the countries of Denmark, Finland, Norway, and Sweden (Iceland is located in the Manual Processing Department)
    c. Central Europe—an alphabetical grouping of the countries of Austria, Czechoslovakia, Germany, Hungary, and Lichtenstein
    d. Continental Europe—an alphabetical grouping of all other countries of Europe

  6. Islands—an alphabetical grouping of the independent islands. (The Polynesian islands are located in the Manual Processing Department)

  7. Medieval—an alphabetical grouping of cards for individuals born in Europe prior to 1501

  8. Miscellaneous—an alphabetical grouping of cards for individuals for which no birthplace or place of residence is listed on the card

  9. Ships at Sea—an alphabetical grouping of cards for persons born "at sea"

Temple Records Index Bureau cards within each geographic group are filed alphabetically by surname and given name by two systems: "System A" and "System B." In "System A" double letters are filed as one letter:

    Abbott is filed as Abot
    Abott is filed as Abot
    Aaron is filed as Aron
    Arron is filed as Aron

In "System B" cards are filed by actual spelling:

    Abbott is filed as Abbott
    Abott is filed as Abott
    Aaron is filed as Aaron
    Arron is filed as Arron

All files not marked "System B" are filed as "System A."

Standard spellings of surnames have been established and blue surname combination divider cards with the standard spelling are filed in alphabetical order. This blue surname combination card contains a list of all other spellings that are assumed to be the same surname or that are phonetically the same. (See Figure 249.) All spellings listed on the blue card are filed together behind the blue card as if they were the same surname.

```
BRYAN                                    UNITED STATES
_____ALSO_____

BRIAN            BRIANT
BRIEN            BRIENT
BRION            BRYAND
BRYEN            BRYANT
BRYON            BRYANTT
BREYANDT         BRYENT
BREYANT
BRIAND
```

Figure 249.   Blue surname combination divider card.

A white cross-reference card is made for each surname spelling that is *not* a standard spelling used in the TIB. This card is filed in proper alphabetical location in the file and refers to the standard spelling where the cards for the particular surname are filed. (See Figures 250 and 251.)

```
                                         UNITED STATES
BRIAN———————————SEE——————————— BRYAN
```

Figure 250.   White cross-reference card.

```
                                         UNITED STATES
BRIEN———————————SEE——————————— BRYAN
```

Figure 251.   White cross-reference card.

Certain given names are standardized, and all spellings for the particular name are filed together. The "Catalog of Combined Given Names," a compilation prepared by employees of the TIB for their use, is an aid in determining which given names are standardized and which given name is used as the standard. For example, Eliza and Elizabeth are considered two different names. (See Figures 252 and 253.)

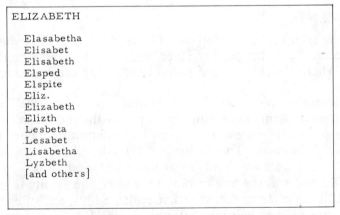

ELIZA

Eliese	Elize	Lise	Elysa
Elisa	Eliza	Liza	Elizae
Elisah	Elyza	Lize	Elieza
Elise	Lisa	Lysa	Elizsa
Elizah	Lissa	Lyse	

Figure 252.   Names filed by the standard given name, Eliza.

ELIZABETH

Elasabetha
Elisabet
Elisabeth
Elsped
Elspite
Eliz.
Elizabeth
Elizth
Lesbeta
Lesabet
Lisabetha
Lyzbeth
[and others]

Figure 253.   Names filed by the standard given name, Elizabeth.

Cards for individuals with the same standard surname and given name are filed chronologically with the card for the earliest birth year filed first. Some cards contain no birth or christening date, but in this space is written a marriage date, death date, or other dated event, and the card is filed chronologically by this event as if it were the birth or christening date. (See Figure 254.)

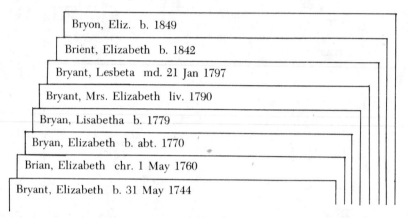

Figure 254.   Names filed by the standard surname, Bryan, and the given name, Elizabeth.

CONTENTS

The reference at the top of a TIB card refers to the temple, the record book, the page number, and the specific line on that page where the information is recorded in the original temple record.

"Instance of," "heir," and "family representative" are synonymous terms indicating the name of the individual who was assigned to represent the family in submitting names for temple ordinances. This individual's relationship to the deceased individual was recorded on the submission form.

The heir was the first or oldest member of a family to join The Church of Jesus Christ of Latter-day Saints, and often his name was used as heir long after his death. A "d" was used to indicate the heir was deceased. Sometimes, when the heir died, the eldest son or daughter became the heir and his or her name was used for processing names for temple ordinances. (See Figure 255.)

```
┌──────────────────────────────────────────────────────────┐
│                                                            │
│   P    INDEX CARD TO   Salt Lake    TEMPLE RECORDS         │
│  No.              No.  5659    Book  6 P    Page  252       │
│                                                            │
│  Name in full    Forsling- Lars                            │
│  When born        1772                                     │
│  Where born    Sundsvall, Vesternorreland, Sweden          │
│  When died        1812                                     │
│  Father                                                    │
│  Mother                                                    │
│  When married       1799          to  Marta Stina Roberg   │
│  Instance of   Albert F. Elg, d.     Rel.   gg son         │
│  When baptized   6 May 1939       When    31 May 1940       │
│                                   Endowed                  │
│          Husband                  To                       │
│  Sealed  Wife                     Parents                  │
│  References                                                │
│                                                            │
└──────────────────────────────────────────────────────────┘
```

Figure 255.   TIB card indicating the heir is deceased.

With the expanded growth of the Church, it became apparent that the blood heir was difficult to determine; and if the heir could be determined, often he was not interested in genealogical research nor active in the Church. In 1952 the term "family representative" was substituted for "heir." The "family representative" was a living individual, a baptized member of The Church of Jesus Christ of Latter-day Saints, and was selected by the family because of his interest in genealogical research.

In 1970, with the introduction of the Name Tabulation Program, the term "family representative" was discontinued, and the relationship of the patron (individual submitting the form) to the deceased individual is recorded on the processing form.

When the person referred to on the TIB card performed his own endowment, the term "self" is recorded in the space for "instance of," "heir," or "family representative." These endowments are referred to as "self endowments." (From 1927 to 1975 some early sealing of couples records and one book of sealing of children records were available in the TIB on orange cards.)

These sealing cards have been removed from the endowment file and placed in a separate section of the TIB available only to accredited researchers and Genealogical Society employees.

Figures 256 and 257 are examples of Temple Records Index Bureau cards with an explanation of the information and symbols that could appear on the cards. Buff-colored cards are used for male endowments, living (self) or deceased. (See Figure 256.) White cards are used for female endowments, living (self) or deceased. (See Figure 257.)

```
    PC      TEMPLE        Manti
   NO. 37492MT      NO.              BOOK  29372     PAGE  0047

   NAME    Campbell- Adam
   BORN        14 Dec 1791
   WHERE   Dunoon, Argyll, Scotland
   DIED
   F.      John Campbell
   M.      Joan
   MD.                  TO  Elizabeth
   F.R.    Alexander Cromwell                          7c 4r
   BAPT.   26 Jun 1962   PROXY  Henry I. McIntosh
   END.    14 Aug 1962   PROXY  Aaron M. Dugdale
   SLD.H.                        TO.
       W.                        PARENTS
```

Figure 256.   Buff TIB card for male endowment.

```
         INDEX CARD TO   Salt Lake    TEMPLE RECORDS
   No.                No.  9340    Book  H      Page  445

   Name in full   Sabin- Wynona Marie
   When born          23 Jul 1914
   Where born     Durant, Greer, Oklahoma
   When died
   Father         Lee Roy Sabin
   Mother         Rozella Mae Mixon
   When married   5 Nov 1933              to  Hillard Mortensen
   Instance of    self                    Rel.
   When baptized  1 Nov 1942     When     10 Nov 1944
                                 Endowed
   Sealed Husband 10 Nov 1944     To
          Wife                    Parents
   References
```

Figure 257.   White TIB card for female endowment.

Buff and white cards were made for potential endowments for living individuals whose names appeared on family group records submitted for temple ordinances between 1941 and 1969. (See Figure 258.) One hundred and ten years after the birth of the individual, the information on the potential endowment card is transferred to the Name Tabulation Program (110-year file) for completion of temple ordinances. (See Chapters 19 and 20.)

```
  C          TEMPLE
 NO.              NO.              BOOK              PAGE

NAME    LE DOUX- Marc Edward
BORN          4 Mar 1912
WHERE   Biddeford, York, Mn
DIED                                               L
 F.     Antoine LeDoux (1868)
 M.     Valerie Cabana
MD.               TO   Rollande Gagnon
FR.     Yvonne LeDoux
BAPT.             PROXY
END.              PROXY
SLD. H.                      TO
     W.                      PARENTS
```

Figure 258.   TIB card for potential endowment for a living individual.

When information on an individual is submitted to the Name Tabulation Program, it is processed through the TIB to determine if an endowment has previously been performed for the individual. When information in the TIB matches information in the Name Tabulation entry, the ordinance dates in the TIB are transferred to the Name Tabulation computer and the TIB card is punched with a "G" to indicate the transfer of information. (See Figure 259.)

```
  P    INDEX CARD TO   End. House   TEMPLE RECORDS
 No.                   No. 4606     Book  D      Page  228

Name in full    Trepess- Sarah                    ( G )
When born           20 Mar. 1839
Where born      Coventry, Warwick, Eng.
When died           31 May 1916             (lvg.)
Father          John Trepess
Mother          Susannah
When married    11 Jul 1863         to  Homer Duncan (1815)
Instance of     Self                Rel.
When baptized   4 Mar. 1861    When Endowed  11 July 1863
Sealed  Husband                To
        Wife                   Parents
References
```

Figure 259.   TIB card indicating information transferred to the
             Name Tabulation computer.

All of the information on a TIB card may not have been recorded at the same time. The data recorded in red is an addition and usually was supplied by a person other than the one giving the original information. The information added in red is considered a "correction," but it cannot be considered reliable unless a reliable source for the information is established. The red information appears in light type when photocopied. (See Figure 260.)

C **INDEX CARD TO** Salt Lake **TEMPLE RECORDS**				
No.	No. 23522	Book 4Y	Page 1028	
Name in full	Forsling- Anna Marta			
When born	22 July 1837			
Where born	Sundsvall,	Sweden		
When died	10 Oct. 1921			
Father	Lars /Frederie Forsling (1803) /Fredric			
Mother	Magdalnea---Sunman Magdalena Sundman			
When married				
Instance of	France Albert Elg. d.	Rel. nep.		
When baptized	11 Oct. 1932	When Endowed 13 Apr. 1933		
Sealed Husband/Wife		To Parents		
References				

Figure 260.   TIB card with correction in red.

A "P" in the upper left-hand corner of a TIB card indicates that the individual appears as a parent on a family group record in the Main Records Section. (See Figure 261. See also Chapter 21.)

P	TEMPLE		
NO.	NO.	BOOK	PAGE
NAME			
BORN			
WHERE			
DIED			
F.			
M.			
MD.	TO		
F.R.			
BAPT.	PROXY		
END.	PROXY		
SLD. H./W.		TO PARENTS	

Figure 261.   TIB card with a P.

A "C" in the upper left-hand corner of a TIB card indicates that the individual appears as a child on a family group record in the Main Records Section. (See Figure 262. See also Chapter 21.)

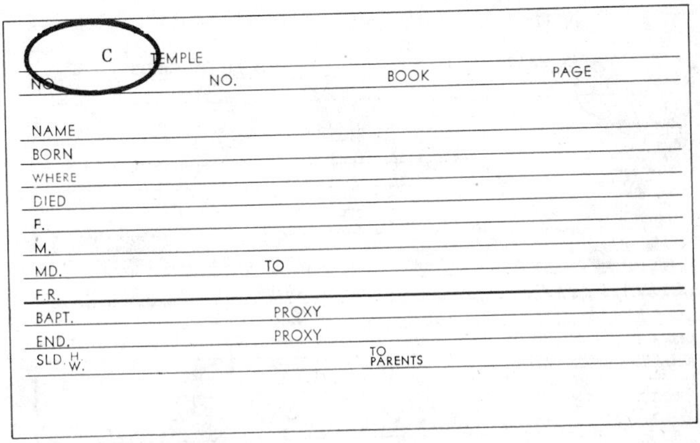

Figure 262.   TIB card with a C.

A "PC" in the upper left-hand corner of a TIB card indicates that the individual appears as a parent on one family group record and as a child on another family group record in the Main Records Section. (See Figure 263. See also Chapter 21.)

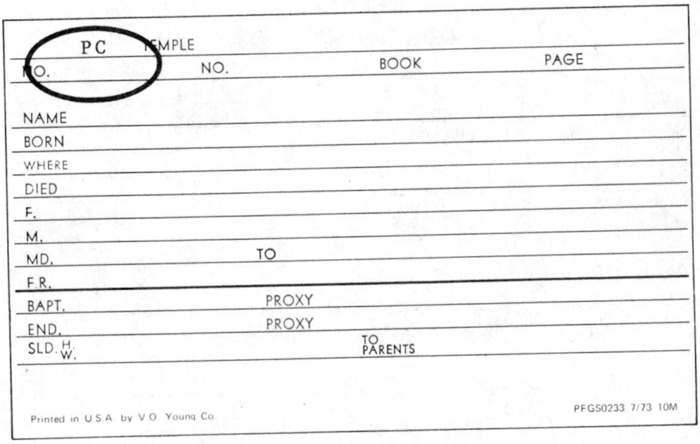

Figure 263.   TIB card with a PC.

A "P," "C," or "PC" on the No. line of the TIB card, rather than in the upper left-hand corner, indicates the individual appears on a family group record in the Patrons Section. (See Figure 264; see also Chapter 21.)

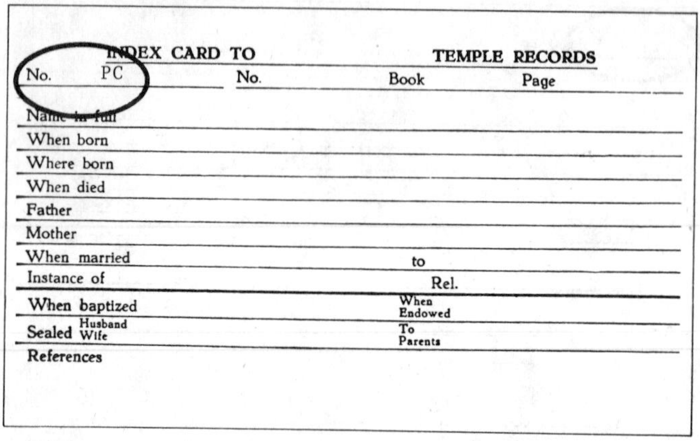
INDEX CARD TO TEMPLE RECORDS

No. PC No. Book Page

Name in full
When born
Where born
When died
Father
Mother
When married to
Instance of Rel.
When baptized | When Endowed
Sealed Husband Wife | To Parents
References

Figure 264. TIB card with a PC on the No. line.

A Special Information Service (SIS) card with "Q" and "SIS" indicates there is another card on file for the individual. (See Figure 265.)

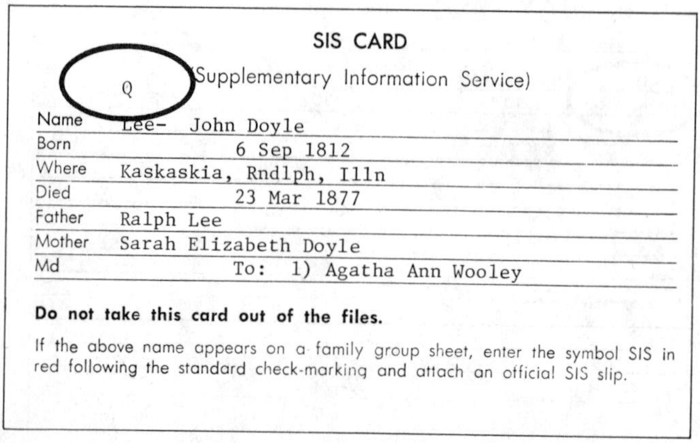
SIS CARD

Q (Supplementary Information Service)

Name Lee- John Doyle
Born 6 Sep 1812
Where Kaskaskia, Rndlph, Illn
Died 23 Mar 1877
Father Ralph Lee
Mother Sarah Elizabeth Doyle
Md To: 1) Agatha Ann Wooley

Do not take this card out of the files.

If the above name appears on a family group sheet, enter the symbol SIS in red following the standard check-marking and attach an official SIS slip.

Figure 265. Special Information Service (SIS) card.

"SIS" in red on a TIB card indicates that there is information in the Special Information Service. (See Figure 266.)

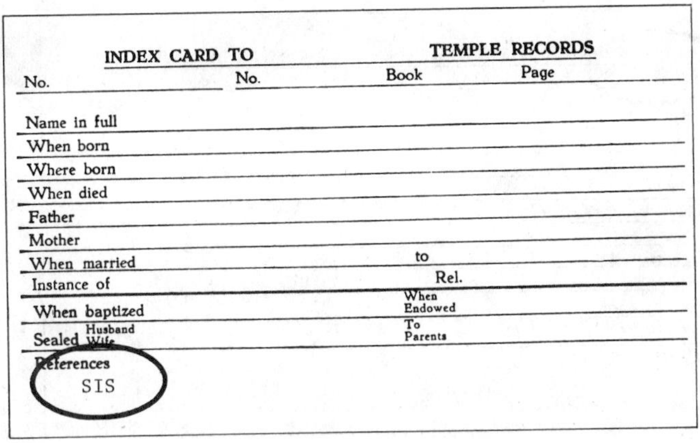

INDEX CARD TO TEMPLE RECORDS

No. No. Book Page

Name in full

When born

Where born

When died

Father

Mother

When married to

Instance of Rel.

When baptized When Endowed

Sealed Husband Wife To Parents

References

SIS

Figure 266. TIB card with SIS.

Two red dots preceding a "P," "C," or "PC" with "SIS" in the lower left-hand corner of the card indicates that the individual appears on a family group record in the Special Information Service rather than the Main Records Section. (See Figure 267.)

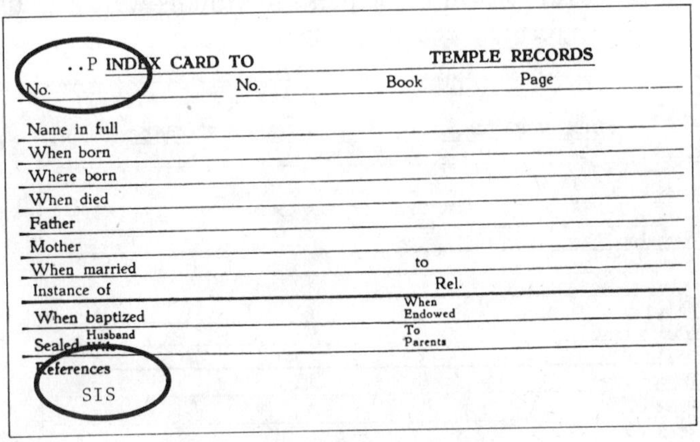

..P INDEX CARD TO TEMPLE RECORDS

No. No. Book Page

Name in full

When born

Where born

When died

Father

Mother

When married to

Instance of Rel.

When baptized When Endowed

Sealed Husband Wife To Parents

References

SIS

Figure 267. TIB card with P and SIS.

Parentheses around a "P," "C," or "PC" indicates that the name was submitted on a family group record just prior to 1 July 1969. (See Figure 268.) Because of the large volume of family group records (300,000) submitted just prior to this processing deadline, the Genealogical Society did not retype the family group record on an archive family group record, but

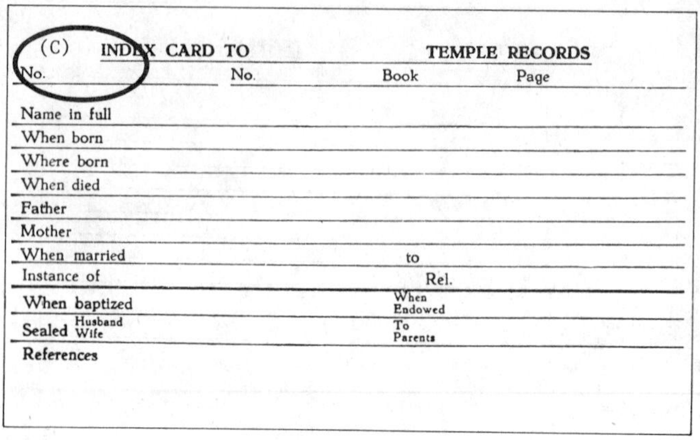
(C) INDEX CARD TO TEMPLE RECORDS
No. No. Book Page
Name in full
When born
Where born
When died
Father
Mother
When married to
Instance of Rel.
When baptized When Endowed
Sealed Husband Wife To Parents
References

Figure 268. TIB card with (C).

used the original. The ordinance dates were stamped on the original family group record, and it was returned to the patron. A photocopy of the family group record was placed in the Main Records Section.

One asterisk [*] indicates that the card was typed from an old-style processing form on which individuals were not listed in family group form. (See Figure 269.)

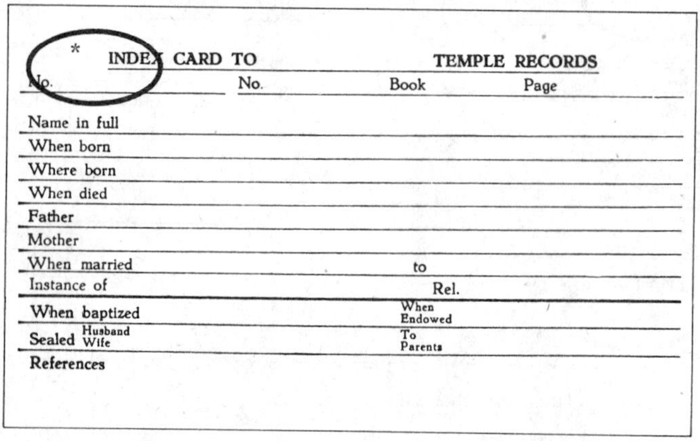
* INDEX CARD TO TEMPLE RECORDS
No. No. Book Page
Name in full
When born
Where born
When died
Father
Mother
When married to
Instance of Rel.
When baptized When Endowed
Sealed Husband Wife To Parents
References

Figure 269. TIB card with one asterisk, *.

Two asterisks [**] indicate that the name does not appear on a family group record in the Main Records Section, although the proxy ordinances were performed after 1942. (See Figure 270.)

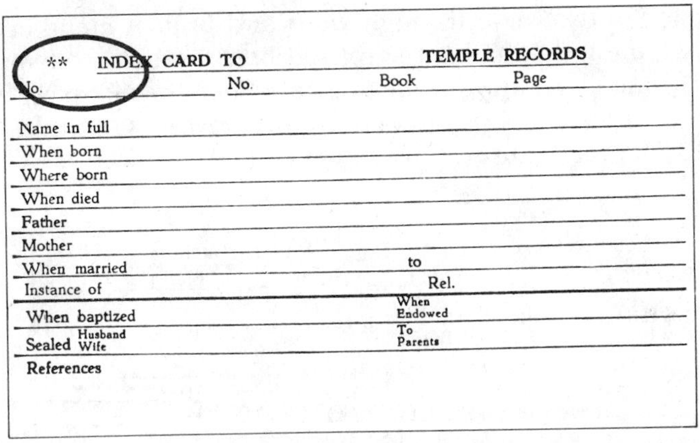

Figure 270.   TIB card with two asterisks, **.

Three asterisks [***] indicate there is uncertainty as to the parentage of the individual. (See Figure 271.)

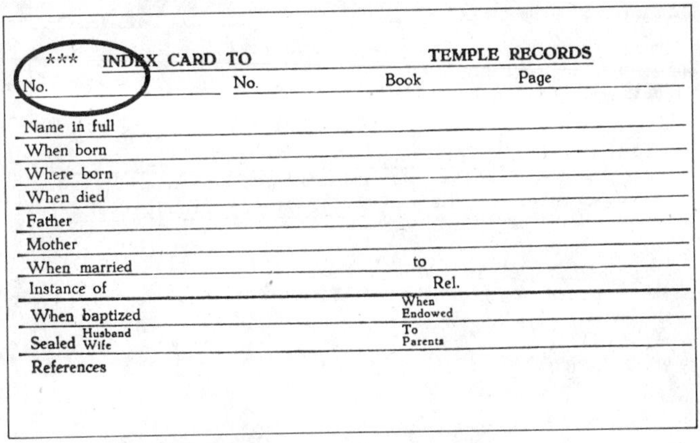

Figure 271.   TIB card with three asterisks, ***.

Some TIB cards show recent proxy baptism dates with earlier endowment dates; an asterisk [*] in place of a complete baptism date refers to a rebaptism and reconfirmation of the endowment recorded on the back of the card. This most often pertains to early members of The Church of Jesus Christ of Latter-day Saints who did not know or did not give a complete baptism date at the time of the endowment. Ordinance dates are not considered valid unless they are complete with day, month, and year. Therefore, when it is impossible to find the complete baptism date through ward and branch membership records,[1] the individual is rebaptized by proxy. This rebaptism is performed as the Genealogical Society discovers the omission, or it can be initiated by the patron submitting an entry form. (See Figure 272.)

PC No.	**INDEX CARD TO** End. House **TEMPLE RECORDS** No. 4050 Book I Page 174

Name in full   Cheshire- William
When born   30-~~29~~-Dec. 1852
Where born   Barton, Bedford, Eng.
When died   12 Feb. 1927   ~~liv.~~
Father   ~~Geo~~/Cheshire (George) (Sr.) 1822
Mother   ~~Betsey~~/Keyes (Elizabeth)
When married   10 Feb. 1881   to Ella Silver Rogers
Instance of   Self   Rel.
When baptized   ?   *   When Endowed 10 Feb. 1881
Sealed Husband Wife 10 Feb. 1881   To Parents
References   (over)

Info on Archive Sheet:
Mother: Elizabeth Keys

    Baptized   21 Sep 1967   Proxy Deloy C. Densley
    All prev. Ch. blessings reconfirmed & ratified in the
    confirmation ordinances.   Salt Lake Temple

Figure 272.   TIB card indicating rebaptism.

Much ordinance work was performed in the early days of The Church of Jesus Christ of Latter-day Saints when research standards were not established. The proxy ordinances were often performed with little identifying information, such as Great-Grandfather Hancock, Uncle Ivey, etc. Often just the

---

[1] See Laureen R. Jaussi and Gloria D. Chaston, *Genealogical Records of Utah* (Salt Lake City: Deseret Book Company, 1974).

surname is given, preceded by a Miss, Mr., or Mrs. These cards are filed at the beginning of each surname section. (See Figure 273.)

INDEX CARD TO St. George TEMPLE RECORDS			
No.	No. 2617	Book C	Page ½40
Name in full	Smith- 3d. G. G. Father		
When born	?		
Where born	U.S.		
When died	?		
Father			
Mother			
When married		to	
Instance of	Allen J. Stout	Rel. 3d. G.G.son	
When baptized	29 Jan. 1878	When Endowed 13 Feb. 1878	
Sealed Husband Wife		To Parents	
References			

Figure 273.   TIB card with little identifying information.

"DUP" indicates that there is another card in the TIB for the same person, but with an earlier endowment date. A "P," "C," or "PC" crossed through on the card with "DUP" indicates that these symbols are no longer applicable. (See Figure 274.)

DUP ¢ INDEX CARD TO		TEMPLE RECORDS	
No.	No.	Book	Page
Name in full			
When born			
Where born			
When died			
Father			
Mother			
When married		to	
Instance of		Rel.	
When baptized		When Endowed	
Sealed Husband Wife		To Parents	
References			

Figure 274.   TIB card with DUP.

"WAC" in the lower left-hand corner indicates the date and name of proxy for the initiatory ordinances. When the date and proxy for the initiatory ordinances differs from the date and proxy for the endowment, this information is recorded on the TIB card. (See Figure 275.)

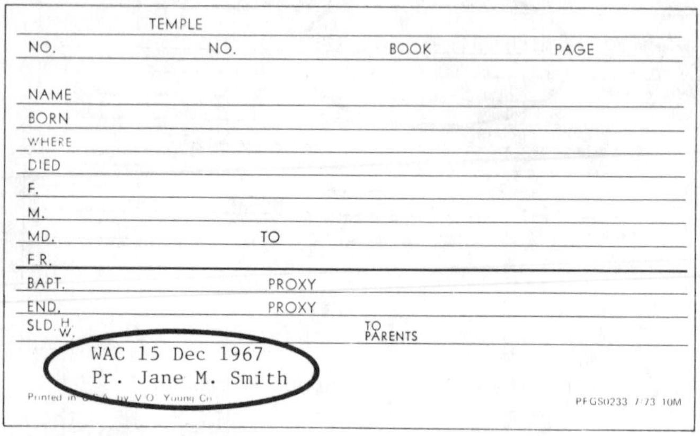
TEMPLE
NO. NO. BOOK PAGE
NAME
BORN
WHERE
DIED
F.
M.
MD. TO
F.R.
BAPT. PROXY
END. PROXY
SLD. H. W. TO PARENTS
WAC 15 Dec 1967
Pr. Jane M. Smith
Printed in U.S.A. by V.O. Young Co.
PFGS0233 7/73 10M

Figure 275. TIB card with WAC.

GENEALOGICAL APPLICATION

A search of the TIB should be made for the name of each individual on the objective family group record. As research progresses and new names are found, the researcher should continue to check each new name in the TIB for the following reasons:

1. A search of the TIB may prevent duplication of research.

2. A search of the TIB may prevent duplication of temple ordinances performed between the Nauvoo period and 1970. (For ordinance work performed after 1970, see Name Tabulation Program, Chapter 19, and Computer File Index, Chapter 20.)

3. Endowment dates are given. The information recorded on the endowment card is the same as that in the original temple endowment record, and it is not necessary to search the original temple endowment record unless one suspects an error in copying or unless a TIB card is missing. The TIB cards showing endowment dates prior to 1927 were copied from the original temple records. Since 1927, the processing system has

varied, and endowment dates have been recorded on the majority of the cards at the time of the endowment.

4. Baptism dates may be given. Temple recorders baptism records were not used in compiling the TIB cards. Some baptism dates on TIB cards were copied from the endowment record, and other baptism dates were recorded on the cards at the time of the proxy baptism. Often these baptism dates in the endowment records were supplied from memory. Temple recorders baptism records should be searched to verify each proxy baptism date. (See Chapter 22.) LDS Membership Records should be searched to verify each baptism performed in life.[2]

5. Sealing dates may be given. Sealing dates recorded on a TIB card should be verified in the temple recorders sealing records unless the date is stamped after 1942.

6. Clues are given concerning proxy baptism. The name of the temple, date of proxy baptism, and name of the heir aid in finding the original proxy baptism record for the particular individual as well as other relatives who may have been baptized on that date.

7. Clues are given concerning sealings. The name of the temple, date of endowments, and name of the heir (if by proxy) aid in finding the original sealing records for the particular individual(s) as well as other relatives who may have been sealed on the same date. Endowments and sealings frequently were performed on or near the same date and in the same temple. Temple recorders sealing records should be searched for the temple where the endowment was performed, on or near the date of the endowment. (See Chapter 22.) A proxy sealing date many years after the proxy endowment date could indicate there is an earlier sealing date.

8. Cross-reference is made to family group records in the Main Records Section. A "P" and/or "C" in the extreme upper left-hand corner of a TIB card indicates that the individual appears as a parent and/or child on a family group record(s) in the Main Records Section. (See Chapter 21.)

9. The TIB is an aid in establishing the spelling of names recorded on family group records in the Main Records Section. (See Chapter 21.)

---

[2]Laureen R. Jaussi and Gloria D. Chaston, *Genealogical Records of Utah* (Salt Lake City: Deseret Book Company, 1974.)

10. There may be information on TIB cards that has not been recorded on the family group records at the Genealogical Society. (See Chapter 21.)

11. The TIB includes information on individuals for whom endowment work was performed prior to the establishment (1942) of the Main Records Section. (See Chapter 21.)

12. The information given in the TIB may be from a primary source where the individual gave information about himself or close relatives: brothers, sisters, aunts, uncles, cousins, parents, and grandparents.

13. General information is given on names, places, dates, and relationships that may verify, or add to, presently known information and provides clues that lead to additional records to search.

14. Reference is sometimes given to Card-Indexed Pedigree Charts. (See Chapter 21.)

15. The TIB may be used as a finding tool to establish a possible place of residence for individuals with uncommon surnames.

16. Relationships may be established to previously unknown relatives. When the name of the heir or family representative is known and the relationship to the heir or family representative is known, one can search a particular surname section for all cards submitted by that particular heir or family representative and obtain information on other relatives.

GENEALOGICAL LIMITATIONS

1. The public does not have direct access to the TIB.

2. Only a small portion of the TIB has been microfilmed.

3. The information may be inaccurate and incomplete.

4. The baptism date may be incorrect.

5. The informant or source of the information is often undetermined.

6. There are no TIB cards for children who die under the age of eight, because they are not baptized and endowed.

7. Original baptism records are not indexed in the TIB.

8. Original temple recorders records are not indexed in the TIB.

9. Some TIB cards are missing.

10. Self-endowment cards for individuals other than the patron will not be copied unless the individuals were born over 110 years ago, or a death date is supplied, or there is a "P" and/or "C" on the card.

11. The information submitted by the patron must match the information in the TIB as to name, birth date, and birthplace (at least a country), or the TIB card may not be found.

12. The relationship of the patron to the individual must be provided when the individual was born within the last 95 years.

13. Only information on direct-line ancestral families will be provided through the correspondence service.

AVAILABILITY

The following chart (Figure 276) illustrates the availability of the Temple Records Index Bureau.

Record	Genealogical Society Patrons	Genealogical* Society Correspondence Request Form	Branch Libraries	Accredited*** Researchers
Original Temple Records Index Bureau	No	Yes	No	Yes
Microfilmed** Temple Records Index Bureau	Yes	–	No	Yes

*TIB request forms available for a small fee at the Church Distribution Center, 1999 West 1700 South, Salt Lake City, Utah 84104. There is a charge for TIB searches made by the Genealogical Society.

**Very small portion microfilmed; restricted to LDS Church members with current recommends.

***See sample letter, Figure 277.

Figure 276.   Availability of the Temple Records Index Bureau.

Your Name
Your Address
Current Date

Name of Accredited Researcher
Address of Accredited Researcher

Dear Sir:

    Enclosed is a family group record. Please search
the Temple Records Index Bureau for TIB cards pertaining
to individuals on the family group record.

    Enclosed is an American Express Money Order for
$5.00 as a deposit for this research.

    Thank you.

                    Sincerely yours,

                    Your Name (signed)

Encls: 1 family group record
        $5.00

Figure 277.   Letter to an accredited researcher.

19
The Name Tabulation Program

The Name Tabulation Program of the Genealogical Department of The Church of Jesus Christ of Latter-day Saints refers to the system through which LDS ordinance information is processed and stored by computer. Computer processing was adopted in October 1969 because it was determined to be more efficient and economical than manual processing. A program is entered in the Name Tabulation Program because of one of the following reasons:

1. To perform baptism, endowment, and sealing ordinances by proxy for deceased individuals who were not affiliated with the LDS Church in life and to store this information to prevent future duplication of these ordinances.

2. To complete endowment and sealing ordinances by proxy for individuals who were members of the LDS Church and to store this information to prevent future duplication of ordinances.

3. To store information concerning ordinances performed prior to the Name Tabulation Program to prevent future duplication of these ordinances.

When the name of an individual is entered in the Name Tabulation computer, it is either "cleared" for temple ordinances, "rejected" for temple ordinances, or "stored" to prevent future duplication.

To control and minimize duplication, the computer is programmed to clear only names of individuals who meet minimum identification standards.[1] Minimum identification for *individual* ordinances (baptism, endowment, and sealing to parents) is defined as follows:

---

[1]Names of some individuals are processed manually. The alphabet and language of certain geographic areas (Asian and Arabic countries and Greece) are not adaptable to the Name Tabulation Program. Records of certain ethnic groups (American Indians and Polynesians) whose records do not meet minimum identification standards are not processed by computer. (See Chapter 20.)

1. Name of the individual or at least a surname and sex
2. Birth date of individual (the year only is acceptable, if the name of one parent is included)
3. Birthplace of the individual (at least a county in the United States, or a town or parish in a foreign country)
4. Name of father (for sealing to parents)

Minimum identification for the *marriage* ordinance (sealing of wife to husband) is defined as follows:
1. Name of groom
2. Name of bride
3. Date of marriage (at least a year)
4. Place of marriage (at least a county in the United States, or a town or parish in a foreign country)

TIME PERIOD

October 1969-present.

CONTENTS

Nine major input programs provide information for the Name Tabulation Program:
1. Patron Input
2. Controlled Input
3. Temple Records Index Bureau Conversion
4. Sealing of Couples Records Conversion
5. Ward/Branch Membership Records Conversion
6. Deceased Members Files
7. 110-Year Files
8. Temple Originated Family Group Records
9. Royalty and Special Problems

Patron Input

Patron Input (Records Submission, Genealogical Information and Name Tabulation, GIANT, and Name Tabulation) refers to the system initiated in October 1969 to process names of deceased individuals for temple ordinances where names are submitted by members of The Church of Jesus Christ of Latter-day Saints. (For standards for submitting this information, see the current edition of the *Records Submission Manual.*[2] Various editions may have varying titles.)

---

[2]The Genealogical Society of The Church of Jesus Christ of Latter-day Saints, *Records Submission Manual, How to Submit Names for Temple Ordinance Work,* 4th ed., 1973.

In addition to requiring minimum identification, Patron Input is a program of record priorities; that is, certain records are preferred over others.[3] Record priority has been established on the basis of the best record that provides the required minimum identification. If the preferred record that provides minimum identification is available, it must be searched and used as the basis for submitting names for temple ordinances.

The record priorities for the *United States* and *Canada* for individual ordinances (baptism, endowment, and sealing of child to parents) are as follows:

1. Government birth record
2. Church christening record
3. A single source other than a government birth or church christening that provides minimum identification for birth
4. Multiple sources (a combination of two or three single sources) that provide minimum identification for birth
5. 1850, 1860 United States census[4] and 1851, 1861 Canadian census[4] (date and place of census substituted for date and place of birth)
6. Probate of the father[4] (date and place of probate substituted for date and place of birth)

The record priorities for *other countries* for individual ordinances (baptism, endowment, sealing of child to parents) are as follows:

1. Government birth record
2. Church christening (baptism) record
3. Probate of the father[4] (date and place of probate substituted for date and place of birth)

Only rarely will a census record, or other single source, or multiple sources qualify the entry for individual ordinances because of early registration of government vital records and/or state church vital records.

The record priorities for all countries for the marriage ordinance (sealing of wife to husband) are as follows:

1. Government marriage record
2. Church marriage record
3. A single source other than a government marriage or church marriage record that gives minimum identification for marriage

---

[3] Laureen R. Jaussi and Gloria D. Chaston, "A Simplification of The Records Submission Manual," 1976.

[4] Census and probate entries will eventually be processed through the Family Entry System and census and probate entries presently in the Name Tabulation Program will be transferred to the Family Entry System Computer.

4. Multiple sources (a combination of two single sources) that provide minimum identification for marriage

Only rarely will another single source or multiple source qualify the entry for the marriage ordinance because of early registration of government and/or church marriages.

Controlled Input

Controlled Input includes two programs:
1. Record Tabulation
2. Controlled Extraction

Record Tabulation (R-Tab) was initiated in 1961 as a pilot project for developing the Patron Input system and for maintaining a supply of names for temple ordinances. (Patron Input does not maintain an adequate supply of names at the temples.) Approximately eight million names of individuals were processed between December 1961 and July 1969. Parish registers from England were used in the pilot project because language translation was not necessary and because English parish registers were available at the Library of the Genealogical Society. Christening entries for individuals who were born more than 110 years ago were extracted and processed for baptism, endowment, and sealing to parents. Burial entries were also extracted and compared with christening entries, and when it was determined that an individual died under the age of eight, no baptism and endowment was performed. No marriage records were extracted.

Controlled Extraction is a continuation of the Record Tabulation Program and was initiated in 1970 concurrently with Patron Input. This program includes marriage entries (sealing of wife to husband) as well as christening entries (baptism, endowment, and sealing to parents). Parish records of England were the major record source for Record Tabulation; however, vital records from many different localities are included in the Controlled Extraction (other localities may be added):

Atlantic Islands	Iceland	Nova Scotia
Australia	Illinois	Pennsylvania
Baden	Indonesia	Poland
Bavaria	Ireland	Portugal
Belgium	Italy	Prussia
Brazil	Luxembourg	Rhode Island
Channel Islands	Maine	Saxony
China	Malaysia	Scotland
Connecticut	Maryland	Singapore
Delaware	Massachusetts	South Africa
Denmark	Mexico	South Carolina
Egypt	Netherlands	Sweden
England	New Hampshire	Switzerland
Finland	New Mexico	USSR
Florida	New Jersey	Vermont
France	New York	Virginia
Georgia	North Carolina	Wales
Gibraltar	Norway	

Temple Records Index Bureau Conversion

Names of individuals in the Temple Records Index Bureau (TIB) (see Chapter 18) that meet minimum identification standards are gradually being converted to the Name Tabulation Program. When this program is completed, the TIB will no longer be used as a temple record processing tool. There are three separate programs that convert TIB information to the Name Tabulation Program:

1. Patron Input
2. Controlled Input
3. Temple Services Division Conversion Program

When the name of an individual is submitted for temple ordinances, either through Patron Input or through Controlled Input, and it is determined that the name is not in the Name Tabulation Program (computer check), the name is processed through the Temple Records Index Bureau to determine if an endowment has previously been performed for the individual. When information (minimum identification) in the TIB matches information from the entry, the ordinance dates in the TIB are transferred to the computer, and the TIB card is punched with a "G" to indicate the transfer of information. (See Chapter 18, Figure 259.) (The "G" was initiated when the Name Tabulation Program was referred to as "GIANT.")

The Temple Services Division of the Genealogical Department is gradually converting names of individuals in the TIB to the Name Tabulation Program. This program began with the Medieval Section and the South and Central America Section and will eventually include the conversion of all TIB information that meets minimum identification standards. As each section of the TIB is converted to the computer, that section is no longer used in temple records processing. The section is microfilmed and made available to Genealogical Society Library patrons on a restricted basis. The restriction is necessary because the TIB contains information on living persons.

Sealing of Couples Records Conversion

Genealogical Society employees have extracted names of individuals from the records of sealings of couples (wife to husband) (see Chapter 22) and entered this information in the Name Tabulation Program. The purpose of this program is to prevent duplication of sealings of couples when marriage information is submitted through Patron Input and Controlled Extraction. Only entries that provided minimum identification for marriage were extracted except for a few from the early Utah period (1855-1889). The latter records were entered with the name of the temple and the date of the temple sealing substituted for the place of the civil marriage and the date of the civil marriage.

Ward/Branch Membership Records Conversion

Genealogical Society employees are extracting names of individuals from the ward and branch membership records of the LDS Church and are entering them in the Name Tabulation Program. The purpose of this program is to provide an opportunity for all members of the Church to have all temple ordinances completed. Where identifying information does not meet minimum identification standards for birthplace and birth date, the name of the ward/branch and the date of baptism are substituted. The records extracted in this program along with inclusive dates are as follows:[5]
  1. Ward/Branch Records of Membership, 1830s to 1941
  2. Membership Card Index, 1840s to early 1900s
  3. Deaths in Missions, 1919 to 1940.

---

[5]Laureen R. Jaussi and Gloria D. Chaston, *Genealogical Records of Utah* (Salt Lake City: Deseret Book Company, 1974), Chapters 2 and 6.

Ward/branch records included in the Membership Card Index are entered from the index rather than from the original ward/branch record. For localities included in the Membership Card Index see *Register of LDS Church Records.*[6]

Deceased Members Files

Names of deceased members of the LDS Church are entered in the Name Tabulation Program from two different deceased members files:[7]

1. Deceased Members Card File, 1941-1972/73
2. Deceased Members Computer File, 1972/73-present

The purpose of this program is to provide an opportunity for deceased members of the Church to have all temple ordinances completed.

The Deceased Members Card File is a Churchwide file of membership records of members who have died since 1941, the year the individual card system for membership was initiated. The names of these deceased individuals are entered in the Name Tabulation Program for completion of all temple ordinances, and the ordinance information is stored to avoid future duplication. When identifying information does not meet minimum identification standards, the baptism date and place is substituted for the birth date and birthplace.

Church membership records are now maintained through a computer program. When a member dies, his record is placed in an "inactive-deceased" file where it is stored for five years, giving relatives time to complete all temple ordinances. After five years, the name of the individual is entered in the Name Tabulation Program, any remaining ordinances are completed, and the ordinance information is stored to avoid future duplication.

110-Year Files

Names of individuals submitted for temple ordinances with no death date and who were born within the last 110 years, are not processed for temple ordinances because of the possibility that they could be living. Names are entered in the Name

---

[6]Laureen R. Jaussi and Gloria D. Chaston, *Register of LDS Church Records* (Salt Lake City: Deseret Book Company, 1968), pages 67 to 72.

[7]Laureen R. Jaussi and Gloria D. Chaston, *Genealogical Records of Utah* (Salt Lake City: Deseret Book Company, 1974), Chapters 2 and 6.

Tabulation Program from two separate files 110 years after the birth of the individuals:

1. 110-Year Card File
2. 110/95-Year Computer File

The 110-Year Card File originated between 1941 and 1969 when family group records were used as temple processing forms. All family members were included on each family group record submitted, although some individuals could still be living and not be eligible for proxy temple ordinances. Names of individuals born within 110 years for whom no death date was provided were recorded on cards and filed in the TIB; another copy was maintained in a "110-year file." Names of individuals in this file are entered in the Name Tabulation Program 110 years after the birth of the individuals and then processed for temple ordinances. (If minimum identification standards are not met, the name of the individual is processed manually.) The 110-Year Card File will gradually be phased out.

The 110/95-Year Computer File originated with the Name Tabulation Program in October 1969. Names of some individuals for whom no death date of parents is provided are submitted for temple ordinances; no sealing to parents is performed, and the name is placed in the 110/95-Year Computer File until the individual would have been 95 years of age. Ninety-five years after the birth of the individual, the name of the individual is entered in the Name Tabulation Program, and the individual is sealed to his parents. Between 1969 and 1975, names of some individuals born within the last 110 years for whom no death date was provided were submitted for temple ordinances; no temple ordinances were performed, and the names were placed in the 110/95-Year Computer File until the individual would have been 110 years of age. The name of the individual is entered in the Name Tabulation Program and the temple ordinances completed 110 years after the birth of the individual. Since 1975, names of individuals born within 110 years for whom no death date is provided are rejected for temple ordinances.

Temple Originated Family Group Records

If a patron desires to perform temple ordinances for a deceased member of his immediate family, he does not need to submit the information through Patron Input, but can take the information on a completed family group record directly to the temple. The patron must be shown on the family group record as either a parent or a child. These family group records are referred to as "temple originated." The identifying data for the individual(s) for whom temple ordinances are performed are entered in the Name Tabulation Program.

Royalty and Special Problems

Names of deceased individuals from royal lines are entered in the Name Tabulation Program by the Genealogical Department, which assumes the responsibility for the genealogical research; royal lines are not submitted through Patron Input. Special problems (adoptions, divorce, illegitimacy) resulting from other Name Tabulation Programs are also considered by the Genealogical Society. Names of individuals from royal families, or where special problems are involved, are usually compiled on family group records and then entered in the Name Tabulation Program.

AVAILABILITY

The index to the Name Tabulation Program with clues to the original reference sources is available through the Computer File Index. (See Chapter 20.)

20
The Computer File Index

The Computer File Index is a geographically arranged file of microfiche cards printed from information in the Name Tabulation Program. The 1975 edition of the Computer File Index contains 2,689 microfiche cards with 270 pages printed on each card; each page contains approximately 60 names. As additional names are entered in the Name Tabulation Program, new editions of the Computer File Index are printed.

FILE ARRANGEMENT

The Computer File Index is arranged by geographic region, and each region is assigned a code letter. (See Figure 278.) To use the Computer File Index, one must determine the code letter for the region in which the country of interest is located. (See Figure 279.) (Code letters may change with each edition of the Computer File Index; see the instructions provided with each edition.)

Code Letter	Name of Region	Code Letter	Name of Region	Code Letter	Name of Region
A . . .	England	F . . .	Denmark	K . . .	Central Europe
B . . .	England	G . . .	Finland	L . . .	Southern Europe
C . . .	England	H . . .	Iceland	M . . .	North America
D . . .	England	I . . .	Norway	N . . .	Central and South America
E . . .	England	J . . .	Sweden	O . . .	Miscellaneous

Figure 278. Code letters for geographic regions.

Country	Code Letter	Country	Code Letter	Country	Code Letter
Afghanistan	O	Germany	K	Persian Gulf States	O
Albania	L	Gibraltar	L	Peru	N
Algeria	O	Greece	L	Philippines	O
Andorra	L	Guatemala	N	Poland	K
Argentina	N	Guiana	N	Portugal	L
At sea	O	Guyana	N	Rhodesia	O
Atlantic Islands	O	Honduras	N	Rumania	L
Australia	O	Hong Kong	O	San Marino	L
Austria	K	Hungary	K	Scotland	E
Bangladesh	O	Iceland	H	Senegal	O
Belgium	K	India	O	Sierra Leone	O
Bolivia	N	Indian Ocean		Singapore	O
Botswana	O	Islands	O	South Africa	O
Brazil	N	Indonesia	O	Southwest Africa	O
British Honduras	N	Iran	O	Spain	L
Bulgaria	L	Ireland	E	Sudan	O
Burma	O	Isle of Man	B	Surinam	N
Canada	M	Israel	O	Sweden	J
Caribbean	N	Italy	L	Switzerland	K
Ceylon	O	Japan	O	Syria	O
Channel Islands	E	Korea	O	Thailand	O
Chile	N	Lebanon	O	Tunisia	O
China	O	Libya (Libia)	O	Turkey	O
Colombia	N	Liechtenstein	K	United Arab	
Costa Rica	N	Luxembourg	K	Republic	O
Cyprus	L	Malaysia (Malay		United States of	
Czechoslovakia	K	Archipelago)	O	America	M
Denmark	F	Malta	L	Uruguay	N
Dist. of Columbia	M	Mexico	N	USSR	O
Ecuador	N	Monaco	L	Vatican City State	L
El Salvador	N	Morocco	O	Venezuela	N
England		Netherlands	K	Vietnam	O
Counties B-E	A	New Zealand	O	Wales	E
Counties G-Le	B	Nicaragua	N	Yugoslavia	L
Counties Li-Nor	C	Nigeria	O	Zambia	O
Counties Not-Y	D	Norway	I		
Channel Islands	E	Pacific Islands	O		
Ethiopia	O	Pakistan	O		
Finland	G	Panama	N		
France	L	Paraguay	N		

Figure 279.   Countries with code letters.

The heading at the top of each microfiche card (see Figure 280) provides the region code letter, the sequential number of the particular card within the region, the name of the region and the name of the country or subdivision of the country, the date of the Computer File Index printout, and the name of the first individual listed on the first page of the card. (The heading of the first card in each country or subdivision of a country does not include a beginning name; instead, the name of the country or subdivision is repeated.)

CONTENTS

The 270 pages printed on each microfiche card are enlarged for reading through the use of a special microfiche reading machine. The headings at the top of each page vary slightly for different geographic areas (see Figure 281), but in general the

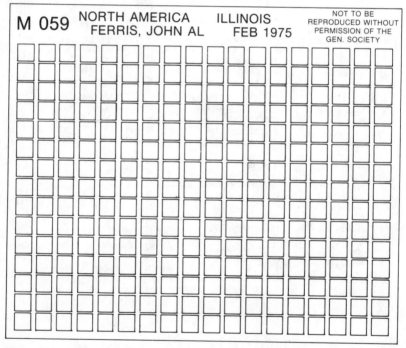

Figure 280.   Microfiche card from the Computer File Index.

COUNTRY: ENGLAND   COUNTY: WARWICKSHIRE   AS OF FEB. 1975   PAGE 8,138

NAME / FATHER-MOTHER OR SPOUSE	SEX (M MALE/ F FEMALE/ H HUSBAND/ W WIFE)	TYPE	EVENT DATE	TOWN, PARISH	BAPTISM DATE/TEMPLE	ENDOWMENT DATE/TEMPLE	SEALING DATE/TEMPLE	BATCH	SERIAL SHEET
HARRIS, HANNAH									
HARRIS, HANNAH — DAVID GILLINGHAM	W	M	21NOV1801	FOLESHILL			CLEARED	7325207	16
HARRIS, HANNAH — WILLIAM BARR	W	M	13FEB1845	FOLESHILL			CLEARED	7325228	28
HARRIS, HARRY — ANN PILE	H	M	11DEC1796	FOLESHILL			29MAR1948LG	A178128	3058
HARRIS, HARRY MEREDITH	M	C	19OCT1828	STONELEIGH	CLEARED	CLEARED	CLEARED	7424611	88
HARRIS, HENRY — JOSEPH HARRIS/HARRIET JONES / JOANNA BALLARD	H	M	06MAY1548				12FEB1946LG	A178120	1296
HARRIS, HENRY — ANNE PILE	H	M	09DEC1796	FOLESHILL			30APR1952SL	A456698	0404
HARRIS, HENRY — ELIZABETH AIRRIS	H	M	12NOV1812	STONELEIGH			13APR1971LG	7009808	63
HARRIS, HENRY — BARNABAS/HARRIOTT	M	C	11JUL1819	STONELEIGH	09JAN1973OG	06FEB1973OG	03MAY1973OG	7222201	17
HARRIS, HENRY — HUMPHREY/ELIZABETH	M	B	05OCT1861	COVENTRY	CLEARED	CLEARED	CLEARED	6940007	0
HARRIS, HESTER — MATHEW HARRIS/EDITH	F	F	13JAN1737	FOLESHILL	CLEARED	CLEARED	CLEARED	7424612	2
HARRIS, HUMFREY — THOMAS HARRIS/	M	C	28NOV1824	FOLESHILL	CLEARED	CLEARED	CLEARED	7424611	83
HARRIS, HUMPHREY — HUMPHREY HARRIS/	M	C	30JAN1862	FOLESHILL	CLEARED	CLEARED	CLEARED	7424611	90
HARRIS, JAMES — HUMPHREY HARRIS/	M	C	15APR1864	FOLESHILL	CLEARED	CLEARED	CLEARED	7424611	70
HARRIS, JAMES — THOMAS HARRIS/	M	C	30MAR1826	FOLESHILL	CLEARED	CLEARED	CLEARED	7424611	75
HARRIS, JAMES — WILLIAM HARRIS/	M	C	15APR1831	FOLESHILL	CLEARED	CLEARED	CLEARED	7424611	80
HARRIS, JAMES — JOSEPH HARRIS/	M	C	15MAY1832	FOLESHILL	CLEARED	CLEARED	CLEARED	7424611	79
HARRIS, JEREMY — WILLIAM HARRIS/	M	C	10FEB1833	FOLESHILL	CLEARED	CLEARED	CLEARED	7424611	83
HARRIS, JOAN — PETER/ELIZABETH	F	C	05OCT1796	FOLESHILL	09JAN1973OG	06FEB1973OG	03MAY1973OG	7222201	14
HARRIS, JOAN — DAVID HARRIS/SARAH BARR	F	B	17APR1840	COVENTRY	28FEB1935SL	29MAR1935SL	19MAY1936SL	7155302	50
HARRIS, JOANN	F	C	15JUN1841	COVENTRY	28FEB1935SL	15MAY1935SL	19MAY1936SL	7155302	51
HARRIS, JOANNA — JOSEPH HARRIS/ELIZABETH ELLIOTTE / THOMAS HARRIS/ESTER	F	C	30SEP1820	FOLESHILL	CLEARED	CLEARED	CLEARED	7424611	74
HARRIS, JOHN — JOHN HARRIS/HEPZIBAH DAVIDSONN	M	C	13FEB1840	COVENTRY	28FEB1935SL	17MAY1935SL	19MAY1936SL	7155302	53

Figure 281. Page from the microfiche printout of the Computer File Index.

CFI printout pages include the following headings (words in brackets are not included in the actual headings, but are added for clarification):

1. Region or Country—Region or country in which the event occurred

2. Country or County—Country within the region, or subdivision (county, state, or province) within the country, in which the event occurred

3. [Printout date]—Date or edition of the Computer File Index; a new printout is issued periodically

4. Page [number]—Page number within the country or subdivision of the country

The headings for the name of each individual are as follows:

1. Name [of Individual] (see Figure 282). The actual spelling (spelling from the submission record) of the name of each individual appears in the Computer File Index. If the actual spelling differs from the standard spelling (spelling designated by the Genealogical Department), the actual spelling is filed as if it were the standard spelling. The standard spelling is indicated by an asterisk (*) preceding the name. The actual spelling is listed in proper alphabetical order with a reference to the standard spelling. When reference is made from an actual spelling to a standard spelling, the actual spelling is preceded with an equal (=) sign and the standard spelling is preceded with two asterisks (**).

Names are arranged alphabetically by surname (last name) in all localities except Monmouthshire, England prior to 1813, Wales prior to 1813, and Norway. Names are arranged alphabetically by given name (first name) in Monmouthshire, England; in Wales; and in Norway. (For events after 1813 in Monmouthshire, England and for Wales, there are two alphabetically arranged sets of names, one by given name and one by surname. There is only one set of names for Norway, and it is arranged alphabetically by given name.)

When the names are filed by surname (last name), surnames with similar sounds and/or translations are filed together under a standard spelling; the given name is not standardized, but is alphabetized as entered in the computer. (See Figure 283.)

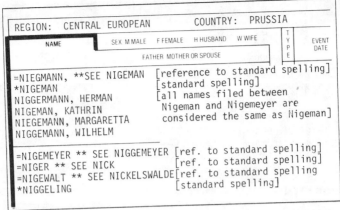

Figure 282. Standard and actual spellings of names of individuals in the CFI.

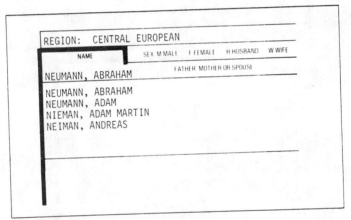

Figure 283. Names of individuals filed by standard surname.

When the names are filed by given (first) name, the given names with similar sounds and/or translations are filed together under a standard spelling; the surname is not standardized, but is alphabetized as entered in the computer. (See Figure 284.)

2. [Name of] Father/Mother or Spouse (see Figure 285). The name of the father, mother, or spouse is listed after the name of the individual if it was provided in the information submitted.

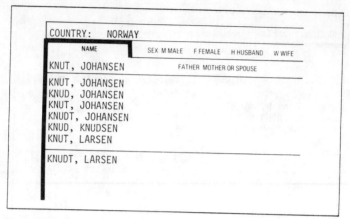

Figure 284.   Names of individuals filed by standard given names.

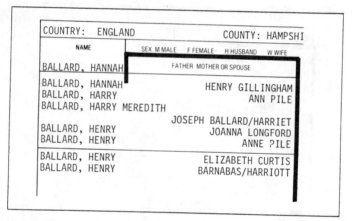

Figure 285.   Name of father/mother or spouse, CFI.

3. Sex [designation] (see Figure 286). The sex of the individual is designated as follows:

M   Male (individual ordinances)
F   Female (individual ordinances)
H   Husband (marriage ordinance)
W   Wife (marriage ordinance)

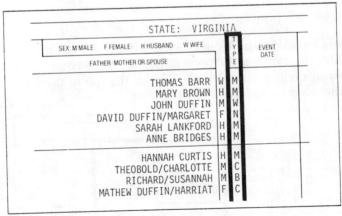

Figure 286.   Sex designation, CFI.

4. Type [of Record] (see Figure 287). The type of record used as the submission source is designated as follows:

C   Christening
B   Birth
M   Marriage
N   Census[1]
W   Probate (Will)[1]

Figure 287.   Type of record, CFI.

No letter designation indicates other source or other combination of sources.

---

[1]When the Family Entry System is initiated, the census and probate entries presently in the Name Tabulation Program will be transferred to the Family Entry System Computer.

5. Event Date (see Figure 288). This date refers to the minimum identification date in the record used as the submission source:

Birth date
Christening date
Marriage date
Census document date
Probate document date
LDS baptism date
Temple sealing date

SHIRE — AS OF FEB. 1975

	TYPE	EVENT DATE	TOWN, PARISH	BAPTISM DATE TEMPLE
W	M	21NOV1801	MILFORD ON SEA	
H	M	11DEC1796	BOLDRE BY LYMINGTON	
M	C	19OCT1828	ROMSEY	CLEARED
H	M	06MAY1548		
H	M	09DEC1796	BROCKENHURST	
H	M	12NOV1812	IBSLEY	

Figure 288. Event date, CFI.

6. Town, Parish, County (see Figure 289). This column provides the name of the town or parish. If the county is not included in the main locality heading at the top of the card, it is also included in this column.

AS OF FEB. 1975

W WIFE	TYPE	EVENT DATE	TOWN, PARISH	BAPTISM DATE TEMPLE
		21NOV1801	MILFORD ON SEA	
		11DEC1796	BOLDRE BY LYMINGTON	
		19OCT1828	ROMSEY	CLEARED
		06MAY1548		
		09DEC1796	BROCKENHURST	
		12NOV1812	IBSLEY	
		11JUL1819	ROMSEY	09JAN1973OG
		05OCT1861	HARTLEY ROW	CLEARED
		13JAN1737	ROMSEY	
		28NOV1624	ROMSEY	

Figure 289. County, town, parish, CFI.

7. Baptism Date/Temple (see Figure 290). This column provides the date of the LDS Church baptism. If the event was performed by proxy in an LDS temple, the abbreviation of the name of the temple may be included. (See temple abbreviations, Figure 291.) The term "cleared" indicates that the name of the individual has been cleared by the computer for baptism (does not match an entry in the computer) and is either at the TIB to be checked or is at the temple waiting for the baptism to be performed. The word "infant" indicates that the individual may have died under the age of eight, and no baptism is necessary. "Not in proc" (process) refers to an entry from Ward/Branch Membership Conversion where the individual has been deceased less than five years. For interpretation of other terms, consult the Temple Services Department of the Genealogical Department.

AS OF FEB. 1975			
COUNTY, TOWN, PARISH		BAPTISM DATE/TEMPLE	ENDOWMENT DATE/TEMPLE
WEBER,	OGDEN	09JAN1973OG	13FEB1973OG
SALT LAKE	MIDVALE	CLEARED	CLEARED
SALT LAKE	MIDVALE	CLEARED	CLEARED
SALT LAKE	MIDVALE	06FEB1973LG	12MAR1973LG
PROVO	UTAH	15JUN1934SL	19JUN1973LG
PROVO	UTAH	INFANT	INFANT
PRICE	CARBON	17APR1899	14JUN1920MT

Figure 290.   Baptism date/temple, CFI.

AL .. Alberta (Cardston)	NV .. Nauvoo
AZ .. Arizona (Mesa)	NZ .. New Zealand
EH .. Endowment House	OG .. Ogden
HA .. Hawaii	OK .. Oakland
HO .. Historian's Office	PO .. President's Office
IF .. Idaho Falls	PV .. Provo
LA .. Los Angeles	SG .. St. George
LD .. London	SL .. Salt Lake
LG .. Logan	SW .. Swiss
MT .. Manti	WA .. Washington

Figure 291.   Temple abbreviations.

8. Endowment Date/Temple (see Figure 292). This column provides the date of the LDS temple endowment, and the abbreviation of the name of the temple where the endowment was performed. (See temple abbreviations, Figure 291.) The term "cleared" indicates that the name has been cleared by the computer for the endowment (does not match an entry in the computer), and the name of the individual is either at the TIB to be checked for duplication or is at the temple where the endowment will be performed. The word "infant" indicates that the individual may have died under the age of eight, and no endowment is necessary. "Not in proc" (process) refers to an entry from Ward/Branch Membership Conversion where the individual has been deceased less than five years. "Uncleared" indicates that no endowment will be performed. For interpretation of other terms, consult the Temple Services Department of the Genealogical Department.

975			PAGE
	BAPTISM DATE/TEMPLE	ENDOWMENT DATE/TEMPLE	SEALING DATE/TEMPLE
	01FEB19730G	06FEB19730G	BIC
	CLEARED	CLEARED	CLEARED
	CLEARED	CLEARED	CLEARED
	10JAN1930LG	06FEB1930LG	15MAR1932LG
	INFANT	INFANT	CLEARED
	28APR1935SL	13JUN1935SL	PARENTS LVG
	10NOV1942	13DEC1942MT	DO NOT SEAL

Figure 292.   Endowment date/temple, CFI.

9. Sealing Date/Temple (see Figure 293). This column provides the date of the LDS temple sealing to parents or sealing to spouse and the abbreviation of the name of the temple where the sealing was performed. (See temple abbreviations, Figure 291.) The term "cleared" indicates that the name of the individual has been cleared by the computer for the sealing ordinance (does not match an entry in the computer) and is at the temple where the sealing will be performed. "Not in proc" (process) refers to an entry from Ward/Branch Membership Conversion where the individual has been deceased less than five years. "BIC" indicates "Born in Covenant" (parents sealed

prior to the birth of a child, no sealing of child to parents re-quired). "Parents Lvg" (living) indicates a proxy sealing of child to parents will not be performed because the parents are living. "Do not seal" and "uncleared" indicate that no sealing will be performed. For interpretation of other terms, consult the Temple Services Department of the Genealogical Department.

PAGE 271			
ENDOWMENT DATE/TEMPLE	SEALING DATE/TEMPLE	SOURCE	
		BATCH	SERIAL SHEET
06FEB19730G	BIC	7132627	35
CLEARED	CLEARED	7138426	42
15MAY1951SL	30APR1952SL	7138426	43
10NOV1969LA	04JAN1970LA	7138426	60
CLEARED	CLEARED	7138425	61
13JUN1935SL	PARENTS LVG	6940313	0
10NOV1942MT	DO NOT SEAL	7143291	66
UNCLEARED	UNCLEARED	7112237	27

Figure 293.   Sealing date/temple, CFI.

10. Source, Batch, [and] Serial [or] Sheet (see Figure 294). These columns refer to the number of the processing batch and the individual serial number or patron sheet number. The batch number in combination with the serial or sheet number is known as the source reference number. The source reference number is used to obtain access to the original source used for submission.

PAGE 986			
ENDOWMENT DATE/TEMPLE	SEALING DATE/TEMPLE	SOURCE	
		BATCH	SERIAL SHEET
05DEC1972LG	03JAN1973LG	7132627	35
	19DEC1957SL	A457253	1694
15MAY1971LG	09JUN1971LG	P020275	7152
13NOV1971SL	19NOV1971SL	7126707	41
12JAN1971MT	02FEB1971MT	C999971	3790
06DEC1971MT	14JAN1971MT	C999971	7332
	03OCT1973SL	M024052	0951
12AUG1972SL	15AUG1972SL	7318618	72
	19DEC1957SL	A186207	6277
	10FEB1854EH	M183393	1930

Figure 294.   Source batch and serial or sheet, CFI.

GENEALOGICAL APPLICATION

The following list represents the genealogical application of the entire Computer File Index; additional genealogical application of specific input programs is included under the discussion of the particular program:

1. Provides a worldwide file of vital events

2. Provides an efficient means for searching several localities for the same surname

3. Provides verification of LDS baptism, endowment, and sealing dates after 1969

4. Provides clues to LDS baptism, endowment, and sealing dates prior to 1970

5. Provides minimal duplication of temple ordinances after 1969

6. Provides clues to further research

7. Refers to the original source, which may provide additional genealogical information

8. Names are entered individually and not as family groups; therefore, it is not necessary to identify parentage prior to using the CFI.

GENEALOGICAL LIMITATIONS

The following list represents the genealogical limitations of the entire Computer File Index; additional genealogical limitations of specific input programs are included under the discussion of the particular program:

1. The Computer File Index is never current, for names are continually added to the Name Tabulation Program and are printed only periodically in the CFI.

2. The locality of the event must be determined prior to using the Computer File Index.

3. The LDS ordinance date may not be the first ordinance date. It may be necessary to do further research to obtain the earliest ordinance date as well as to verify each ordinance date. (See Chapters 18 and 22. See also *Genealogical Records of Utah*,[2] Chapter 6.)

4. Duplication of temple ordinances performed prior to 1970 will temporarily increase; if an entry does not match with

---

[2]Laureen R. Jaussi and Gloria D. Chaston, *Genealogical Records of Utah* (Salt Lake City: Deseret Book Company, 1974).

minimum identification in the Temple Records Index Bureau, the ordinances will be repeated.

5. Individuals who were adopted may be entered under either the blood line or the adopted line.

6. There are few records in the United States and Canada which provide minimum identification; and therefore, the Computer File Index contains a smaller proportion of names from these countries.

7. Names of individuals are entered individually; therefore, it is difficult to reconstruct family groups from the Computer File Index.

PATRON INPUT

Patron Input is the program through which names of deceased individuals are submitted by members of the LDS Church to the Genealogical Department for temple ordinances.

Interpreting the Source Reference Number

When a patron input form is submitted for temple ordinances, it is assigned a nine-digit reference number composed of a seven-digit batch number and a two-digit sheet number. (See Figure 295.) The name of each individual submitted on the same form (maximum of three names) has the same reference number. The reference number is assigned according to the following information:

Source
Batch
(71)—The last two digits of the current year, 1971.
(326)—The number of the day of the current year, 326th day.
(27)—The number of the processing batch[3] started that day, 27th batch. (There may be as many as 99 batches each day.)

Sheet
(35)—The number of the submission form (sheet) within the batch, 35th sheet. (There are 99 forms or sheets in each batch.)

---

[3]The source batch number includes the processing batch number.

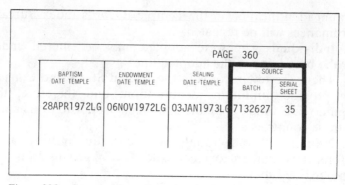

			SOURCE	
		PAGE 360		
BAPTISM DATE TEMPLE	ENDOWMENT DATE TEMPLE	SEALING DATE TEMPLE	BATCH	SERIAL SHEET
28APR1972LG	06NOV1972LG	03JAN1973LG	7132627	35

Figure 295.   Source reference number for Patron Input.

Obtaining the Original Source

Step 1. Obtain the reference number (batch number plus sheet number) from the patron notification printout or from the Computer File Index.

Step 2. Refer to the "Microfilm Index, Patron Sheets and Ordinance Lists,"[4] (see Figure 296), where the batch numbers are listed chronologically in the first column with the corresponding call numbers for the microfilmed patron entry form in the second column. (The last three columns are a reference to the temple recorders records, which contain the same ordinance dates as those in the CFI.)

Step 3. Obtain the appropriate microfilm, and use the year, day, processing batch number, and sheet number to find the chronologically arranged patron entry form.

Additional Genealogical Application

1. Through use of the microfilmed copies of the input (entry) forms, individuals can determine the exact record source used in submitting the information and can then search the original source.

2. Through use of the microfilmed copies of the input forms, individuals can obtain the name and address of the patron who submitted the entry and who may have additional genealogical information.

---

[4]A more appropriate title would be "Register of Call Numbers, Microfilmed Patron Entry Forms, and Microfilmed Temple Recorders Records."

Additional Genealogical Limitations

1. Typing, copying, and omission errors may occur if the patron does not carefully proofread all entries.

2. The place of residence may appear incorrectly as the name of the parish if the patron recorded the place of residence as the place of birth.

```
                        MICROFILM INDEX
               PATRON SHEETS AND ORDINANCE LISTS        PAGE 334
                         05 JAN 1976
```

BATCH NUMBER	PATRON SHEETS	BAPTISM-END ORD	SEALING TO PARENTS ORD	SEALING OF SPOUSES ORD
7132629	539,008	821,363*	821,363*	821,363*
7132630	820,053	821,286*	821,286*	821,286*
7132701	539,008	821,278	821,278	821,278
7132702	539,030	821,278	821,278	821,278
7132703	820,053	821,302	821,302	821,302
7132704	539,008	821,278	821,278	821,278
7132705	539,008	821,278	821,278	821,278
7132706	539,008	821,278	821,278	821,278
7132707	539,008	821,279	821,279	NONE
7132708	539,008	821,279	821,279	821,279
7132709	820,053	821,284	821,284	NONE
7132710	539,009	821,279	821,279	NONE
7132711	539,030	822,195	822,195	822,195
7132712	539,009	821,279	821,279	821,279
7132713	820,053	821,302	821,302	821,302
7132714	820,053	821,286	821,286	NONE
7132715	539,009	822,195	822,195	822,195
7132716	539,009	822,195	822,195	822,195
7132717	539,009	822,195	822,195	822,195
7132718	539,009	822,195	822,195	822,195
7132719	539,009	821,280	821,280	821,280
7132720	820,053	821,302	821,302	821,302
7132721	539,009	821,322	821,322	821,322
7132722	539,009	821,280	821,280	821,280
7132723	539,030	821,280	821,280	821,280
7132724	539,009	821,343	821,343	821,343
7132725	539,030	821,280	821,280	821,280
7132726	NA	821,286	821,286	NONE
7132727	539,030	821,280	821,280	NONE
7132728	539,030	521,280	821,280*	821,280
7132729	539,030	821,280	821,280	NONE
7132730	820,053	822,195*	822,195*	822,195*
7132731	539,009	821,280*	821,280*	821,280*
7132801	539,009	821,342	821,342	821,342
7132802	539,030	821,280	821,280	821,280
7132803	539,038	821,168	821,168	821,168
7132804	820,053	821,302	821,302	821,302
7132805	820,053	934,056	934,056	934,056
7132806	820,053	821,302	821,302	821,302
7132807	539,009	821,343	821,343	821,343
7132808	539,009	821,343	821,343	821,343

*, NA, or NONE - SEE INSTRUCTION PAGE

Figure 296.   Page from Microfilm Index, Patron Sheets, and Ordinance Lists.

CONTROLLED INPUT

Controlled Input includes the Record Tabulation Program and the Controlled Extraction Program, in which names of individuals are submitted by the Genealogical Department for temple ordinances.

Interpreting the Source Reference Number

Record Tabulation reference numbers are prefixed with the letter "P" followed by a six-digit batch number and a serial number. (See Figure 297.)

BAPTISM DATE TEMPLE	ENDOWMENT DATE TEMPLE	SEALING DATE TEMPLE	SOURCE	
			BATCH	SERIAL SHEET
22NOV1969SW	14FEB1970SW	09JUN1971LC	P020275	7152

PAGE 27,756

Figure 297. Source reference number for Controlled Input, Record Tabulation.

Controlled Extraction reference numbers are prefixed with the letter "C" for christening entries and the letter "M" for marriage entries, followed by a six-digit batch number and a serial number. (See Figure 298.) (The "M" prefix is also used in

BAPTISM DATE TEMPLE	ENDOWMENT DATE TEMPLE	SEALING DATE TEMPLE	SOURCE	
			BATCH	SERIAL SHEET
INFANT	INFANT	02FEB1971MT	C006331	8662
		03OCT1973SL	M024052	0951

PAGE 36,312

Figure 298. Source reference numbers for Controlled Input, Controlled Extraction.

the Sealings of Couples Records Conversion.) Extraction programs involving indexes may not be assigned a "P," "C," or "M" prefix. The indexed record may be assigned a seven-digit batch number and each name assigned a consecutive serial number. For example, see Figure 299 for an entry from the Gibson Marriage Index, Oxford, England.

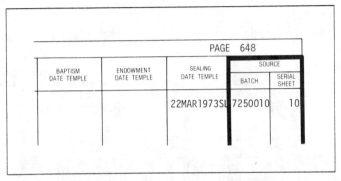

Figure 299.   Source reference number for Controlled Input, Controlled Extraction Index.

A reference number for Controlled Input indexes should not be confused with a reference number for Patron Input. The first two digits of the reference number for Controlled Input indexes appear to represent a year; however, the next three digits for Controlled Input indexes are too large to be a day of the year (larger or higher than 365/66), and therefore, could not be a Patron Input number. Eventually indexes will be assigned reference numbers with letter prefixes similar to other Controlled Input programs.

Parish and Vital Records Listings

The *Parish and Vital Records Listings*[5] contains a list of records from which names of individuals have been extracted and entered in the Controlled Input programs and must be used to obtain the original input source. This reference book is arranged alphabetically by locality: states in the United States, provinces in Canada, and names of other countries. It contains the following information arranged in columns (see Figure 300):

---

[5]*Parish and Vital Records Listings,* The Genealogical Society of The Church of Jesus Christ of Latter-day Saints, Inc., prepared in Salt Lake City, Utah, July 1975.

ENGLAND

PARISH AND VITAL RECORDS LISTINGS   JULY 1975   PAGE 115

1. COUNTY	2. TOWN AND/OR PARISH	3. PERIOD FROM TO	4. RECD TYPE	5. PAR PRINT CALL NO.	6. PROJECT NO.	7. SOURCE CALL NO.	8. SOURCE TYPE	9. BAP-END CALL NO.	10. SEALING CALL NO.
WARWS	SECKINGTON	1612-1813	CHR	0472882	C 2260-1	229125	MO	0820961	0820961
WARWS	SECKINGTON	1813-1845	CHR	* 0933453	C 2260-2	502301	MO		
WARWS	SHELDON	1700-1875	CHR	0820788	P 1978-1	229146	MF	***	***
WARWS	SHERBORNE	1737-1812	CHR	* 0933442	C 4384-1	549656	MO		
		1813-1875	CHR			555352	MO		
WARWS	SHILTON	1750-1812	CHR	* 0933435	C 4385-1	548400	MO		
WARWS	SHIPSTON ON STOUR	1813-1871	CHR	0933448	C 4386-1	560729	MO		
WARWS	SHIRLEY	1227-1876	CHR	* 0933449	C 4386-1	559239	MO		
WARWS	SHOTTESWELL	1833-1867	CHR		C 4387-1	198752	MO		
WARWS	SHUSTOKE	1813-1875	CHR	* 0933435	C 4388-1	554776	MO		
WARWS	SHUTTINGTON	1813-1875	CHR	0472836	C 2286-1	229175	MO	0821177	0821177
WARWS	SMETHWICK PR*	1715-1875	CHR	0820756	P 1599-1	198760 PLUS	MO	***	***
		SEE: BURMINGHAM, SMETHWICK PR*							
WARWS	SNITTERFIELD	1561-1688	CHR	* 0933426	C 4262-1	504460	MO		
		1813-1874	CHR			554763	MO		
WARWS	SOLIHULL	1539-1668	CHR	0472574	P 1075-1	599893	MF	***	M820555 F820051
WARWS	SOLIHULL	1813-1875	CHR	* 0933237	C 1075-3	234507-08	MO	0935610	0935610
WARWS	SOUTHAM	1539-1809	CHR	0472207	P 1081-1	942.48/S1 V2S	MS	***	M472555 M472645 F472641
WARWS	SPERNALL	1701-1812	CHR	* 0933426	C 4264-1	554766	MO		F472552
WARWS	STIVICHALL OR STYVECHALE	1757-1875	CHR	* 0933441	C 4270-1	557275	MO		
WARWS	STOCKINGFORD	1813-1844	CHR			502305	MO		
WARWS	STOCKTON	1824-1876	CHR	* 0933417	C 4271-1	555374	MO		
WARWS		1810-1870	CHR	* 0933426	C 4272-1	557148	MO		
WARWS	STOKE	1813-1876	CHR	* 0933417	C 4273-1	560716	MO		
WARWS	STRATFORD ON AVON, HOLY TRIN.	1558-1652	CHR	0472210	P 1079-1	599889	MF	***	M472575 M472825 F472576 F472827
WARWS	STRATFORD ON AVON, ST. JAMES	1856-1873	CHR	* 0933426	C 4274-1	560724	MO		
WARWS	STRETTON ON DUNSMORE	1742-1783	CHR	* 0933434	C 4276-1	548392	MO		
		1786-1842	CHR						
WARWS	STYVECHALE	SEE STIVICHALL OR STYVECHALE							

Figure 300.   Page from *Parish and Vital Records Listings* (Genealogical Society of The Church of Jesus Christ of Latter-day Saints, Inc., prepared in Salt Lake City, Utah, July 1975, page 115.)

Column 1. COUNTY. This column provides the abbreviated names of the counties within each state, province, or country, arranged alphabetically.

Column 2. TOWN AND/OR PARISH. This column provides the names of the towns and/or parishes within each county, arranged alphabetically. Non-conformist churches in England, Ireland, Scotland, and Wales are indicated by abbreviations after the name of the town.

Column 3. PERIOD FROM/TO. This column indicates the time period included in the record from the earliest to the latest entry. Records for some years within this time period may be missing; refer to the computer printout of the extraction program (Columns 5 and 6) or to the original record (Column 7). The Record Tabulation Program printouts, 1961-1969, Projects 1-3000, do not include notes on missing years. This information is available at the Genealogical Society in a Computer Parish Printout "Supplement" (Ref 942. V2ge Supp or GS film no. 845, 117).

Column 4. RECD TYPE. This column is referred to as the "record type"; however, it indicates the type of event recorded in the record: birth, christening, or marriage.

Column 5. PAR PRINT CALL NO. This column refers to the Genealogical Society Library call number for the microfilmed copy of the alphabetical computer printout for the particular record. (See Figure 301.) If there is only a microfilmed copy available and not a paperback copy available, an asterick (*) is placed prior to the microfilm call number. If there is no alphabetical printout as in the case of indexes, the word "NONE" appears in this column.

Column 6. PROJECT NO. This column provides the number of the Controlled Extraction project, which is also the Genealogical Society Library call number for the paperback printout if one is available. (See Figure 301.) The project number is also the first part of the source reference number (batch number) in the Computer File Index.

Column 7. SOURCE CALL NO. This column refers to the Genealogical Society call number for the record from which names were extracted. This is either a book number or microfilm number; the majority of the records are on microfilm. "No book or film" indicates a record from a private collection.

CHRISTENINGS SURNAME	DATES	GIVEN NAMES	REL	PARENTS AND OTHER DATA	SERIAL NO.	LDS BAPT.	ENDOWMENT
				SOUTHAM PARISH, WARKS, ENG 1539-1809 PAGE 230			
TREEN	CHR 30 SEP 1723	WM	S	WM TREEN AND MY SEE BURIAL ON 5 OCT 1723	P1081-002819-8		
TREEN	CHR 3 OCT 1725	WM	S	WM TREEN (F MISC) SEX ASSUMED	P1081-002878-9	18 MAY 1967	26 JUL 1967
*TREPASS							
TREPASS	CHR 20 JAN 1712	ANNE	D	SAM TREPASS AND ANNE	P1081-002530-0	4 MAY 1967	15 JUN 1967
TREPASS	CHR 15 OCT 1678	MY	D	WM TREPASS AND MY	P1081-001997-1	4 MAY 1967	15 JUN 1967
TREPASS	CHR 26 DEC 1705	RIC	S	SAM TREPASS AND ELIZ (F OCCUP) LAB	P1081-002394-4	18 MAY 1967	26 JUL 1967
TREPASS	CHR 30 JAN 1704	SAM	S	RIC TREPASS AND ELIZ (F OCCUP) LAB SEE BURIAL ON 5 FEB 1704	P1081-002340-0		
TREPASS	CHR 16 MAY 1704	SAR	S	SAM TREPASS (F OCCUP) LAB (F MISC) SEX ASSUMED	P1081-002348-8	4 MAY 1967	15 JUN 1967
TREPASS	CHR 22 JAN 1709	SAM	S	SAM TREPASS AND ANNE	P1081-002462-7	18 MAY 1967	26 JUL 1967
TREPASS	CHR 19 MAY 1719	SAR	D	SAM TREPASS AND ANNE	P1081-002713-1	5 MAY 1967	16 JUN 1967
TREPASS	CHR 26 APR 1702	THO	S	SAM TREPASS AND ELIZ (F OCCUP) LAB	P1081-002293-2	18 MAY 1967	25 JUL 1967
TREPASS	CHR 12 JAN 1674	WM	S	THO TREPASS AND SAR	P1081-001974-4	11 MAY 1967	25 JUL 1967
*TRIDWEL							
TRIDWELL	CHR 6 MAY 1800	CHAS		ELIZ TRIDWELL (PRIN) ILLEGITIMATE	P1081-004578-0	22 MAY 1967	28 JUL 1967

Figure 301.   Page from computer printout for parish and vital records.

Column 8. SOURCE TYPE. This column refers to the form in which the record source is found at the Genealogical Society Library:

    MO—Microfilm of original
    MF—Microfilm of other than original
    MS—Manuscript
    PR—Printed record
    VR—Vital records

Column 9. BAPTISM AND ENDOWMENT CALL NUMBER. This column refers to the Genealogical Society Library call number for the microfilmed temple recorders record of baptisms and endowments (ordinance lists) received from the temples at the completion of the ordinance work. Three asterisks (***) indicate that the ordinance dates are included in the computer printout (Columns 5 and 6) as well as on separate temple recorders ordinance lists. If this column is blank, the ordinances are not completed; the call number will appear in the next edition.

Column 10. SEALING CALL NUMBER. This column refers to the Genealogical Society Library call number for the microfilmed temple recorders record of sealings (ordinance lists) received from the temple at the completion of the ordinance work (sealing of child to parents and sealing of wife to husband). The letter "M" preceding the call number indicates sealings of male children to parents; an "F" indicates sealings of female children to parents. When no letter precedes the call number, the male and female names appear on the same roll of microfilm. Three asterisks (***) indicate that the ordinance dates are included in the computer printout (Columns 5 and 6) as well as on separate temple recorders ordinance lists. If this column is blank, the ordinances are not completed; the call number will appear in the next edition.

Obtaining the Original Source

Step 1. When it is determined, through use of the reference number, that a particular name in the Computer File Index was entered as a result of Controlled Input, refer to the *Parish and Vital Records Listings* (Figure 300) to obtain the Genealogical Society Library call number to the original input record.

Step 2. When the Genealogical Society Library call number to the original input record is obtained, locate the original extraction source and search the record. The original extraction source contains more detailed information than does the alphabetical computer printout (Columns 5 and 6); however, the alphabetical computer printout contains more information than does the Computer File Index.

Additional Genealogical Application

1. Computer File Index entries from Controlled Input provide an efficient means for searching vital records within several localities without searching the record of each locality separately, page by page.

2. The paperback and/or computer printout microfilm provides an alphabetical index to the original record.

3. Some computer printouts (paperback and/or microfilmed) provide notes on missing years, entries that are difficult to read, damaged pages, etc.

4. All burial entries were extracted and entered in the computer for possible determination of children who died under the age of eight (no baptism and endowment necessary, but the child is sealed to his parents). Burial dates that establish this fact appear in the paperback and/or microfilmed printout, but do not appear in the Computer File Index.

5. Paperback printouts contain entries that do not appear in the CFI because they do not meet minimum identification standards.

Additional Genealogical Limitations

1. Patrons may submit only names of direct-line families from records included in Controlled Input.

2. Not all names of all individuals in each submission source are included, for some names of individuals did not meet minimum identification standards or some entries were difficult to read.

3. Not all burial entries appear in the paperback and/or microfilmed printout; no burial entries appear in the Computer File Index.

4. A few names in the paperback printout did not meet the standards of the Record Tabulation Program, but later met the standards of the Name Tabulation Program and were processed as part of the Controlled Extraction Program; these dates are not in the CFI, but may be obtained through a special file in the Temple Services Division, Manager's Office.

TEMPLE RECORDS INDEX BUREAU CONVERSION

Names of individuals in the Temple Records Index Bureau (TIB) that meet minimum identification standards for baptism and endowment are gradually being converted to the Name Tabulation Program and appear in the Computer File Index. This conversion is accomplished in two ways:

1. Input Programs for Individual Ordinances
2. Temple Services Division Conversion

Interpreting the Source Reference Number

Computer File entries as a result of the Temple Services Division Conversion are assigned a six-digit batch number prefixed with a "T" and followed by a serial number. These batch numbers begin with T000011. (See Figure 302.)

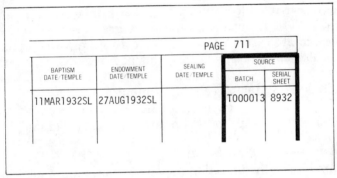

| | | | SOURCE | |
BAPTISM DATE/TEMPLE	ENDOWMENT DATE/TEMPLE	SEALING DATE/TEMPLE	BATCH	SERIAL SHEET
11MAR1932SL	27AUG1932SL		T000013	8932

PAGE 711

Figure 302.   Source reference number for TIB Conversion, Temple Services Division.

TIB conversions as a result of matching minimum identification in the TIB with that from an individual ordinance input program will have the same reference number as the particular input program, i.e., Patron Input, Controlled Input, Ward/Branch Membership Conversion, Deceased Members Files Conversion, etc. A TIB Conversion as a result of one of these programs is determined by noting if the baptism and endowment date is prior to the date the particular input program was initiated. (See Figure 303.)

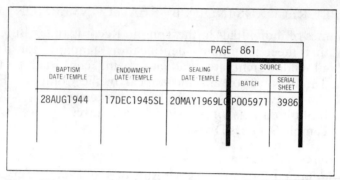

BAPTISM DATE TEMPLE	ENDOWMENT DATE TEMPLE	SEALING DATE TEMPLE	SOURCE	
			BATCH	SERIAL SHEET
28AUG1944	17DEC1945SL	20MAY1969LC	P005971	3986

PAGE 861

Figure 303.   Source reference number for TIB Conversion, Record Tabulation.

Obtaining the Original Source

Step 1. If it is determined that the ordinance dates are a result of a TIB Conversion, and the entry is for a direct-line ancestral family, send for a copy of the TIB card by completing a Genealogical Society correspondence request form. (See Chapter 18.)

Step 2. To obtain access to an input entry that initiated a TIB Conversion, obtain the reference number and follow the "original source" steps for that particular input program.

Additional Genealogical Limitation

Names of individuals that do not meet minimum identification standards are not converted.

SEALING OF COUPLES RECORDS CONVERSION

Names of individuals from the Sealings of Couples Records (wife to husband) have been entered in the Name Tabulation Program by employees of the Genealogical Department.

Interpreting the Source Reference Number

Reference numbers from the Sealing of Couples Records are prefixed with either the letter "A" or "M" followed by a six-digit batch number and then a serial number. The six-digit batch number is a Genealogical Society Library call number for a microfilmed temple sealing record, but it may not be the exact call number, since several rolls of microfilm may have been combined into one batch number. The "A" prefix indicates a sealing record where the civil marriage date and place were provided. (See Figure 304.)

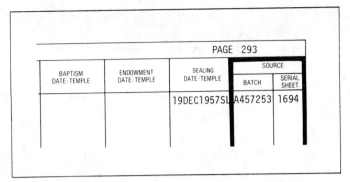

Figure 304.   Source reference number for Sealing of Couples
             Records Conversion.

The "M" prefix indicates a sealing record where the civil
marriage date and place were not provided; in these entries the
temple sealing date was substituted for the civil marriage date,
and the name of the temple was substituted for the civil marriage place. (See Figure 305.) The "M" prefix is always
followed by a serial number that begins with the number "1,"
and some individuals refer to this as an "M1" prefix. The "M"
prefix is also used in Controlled Extraction, but these serial
numbers do not begin with a "1."

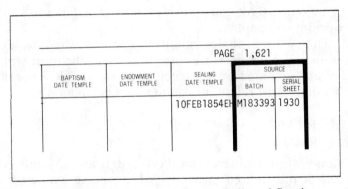

Figure 305.   Source reference number for Sealing of Couples
             Records Conversion.

Obtaining the Original Source

Step 1. Obtain the six-digit batch number from the Computer File Index.

Step 2. Assume that the batch number is also the Genealogical Society Library microfilm number for the temple sealing of couples record.

Step 3. Obtain the record in Special Collections, the Genealogical Society Library.

Step 4. Search the record in chronological order for the date of the sealing and then find the corresponding entry on that date.

Step 5. If the entry is not found, search sealing records on microfilms of the succeeding call numbers.

Additional Genealogical Application

1. Computer File Index entries from Sealing of Couples Records provide a partial index to the Temple Recorders Sealing of Couples Records. Previously there was no Churchwide index to the Temple Sealing of Couples Records other than the Main Records Section of the Family Group Records, 1941-1969.

2. Computer File Index entries from Sealing of Couples Records include a few names of individuals from temple recorders records that are not on microfilm at the Genealogical Society.

Additional Genealogical Limitations

1. Only entries that provide civil marriage date and place are included except for Utah 1855-1889; therefore, many names are omitted for couples who were married in a civil ceremony prior to a temple sealing.

2. The six-digit batch number may not be the exact microfilm call number, since three and four rolls of microfilm were often combined in one batch and assigned the microfilm number of the first roll of microfilm as the batch number.

WARD/BRANCH MEMBERSHIP RECORDS CONVERSION

Names of individuals from the Ward/Branch Membership Records of the Church through 1941 are being extracted and entered in the Name Tabulation Program by the Genealogical Department.

Interpreting the Source Reference Number

The reference number is a seven-digit batch number with the first three digits "694." (See Figure 306.)

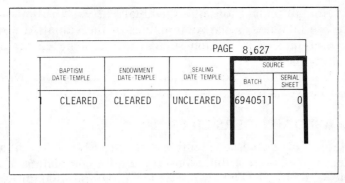

Figure 306.   Source reference number for Ward/Branch Membership Records
              Conversion.

Obtaining the Original Source

1. Obtain the reference number from the Computer File Index.

2. Refer to the "Microfilm Index, Patron Sheets and Ordinance Lists," where the batch numbers are listed chronologically with the corresponding call number for the microfilmed ward/branch record. (This is not always the exact call number, since more than one roll of microfilm may have been combined to form a batch.)

3. The easiest method for obtaining information on a specific individual from LDS Church membership records is to follow the research steps outlined in *Genealogical Records of Utah*, Chapter 6, "LDS Membership Records."

Additional Genealogical Limitations

1. The reference number does not refer to the name of the ward/branch membership record; it refers to the call number of the microfilm that contains several ward/branch records.

2. It is difficult to determine the name of the branch record from which the information was extracted because the birthplace or baptism place is provided rather than the name of the branch.

3. If the birth date and/or birthplace is not provided in the original membership record, the baptism date and/or baptism place is substituted; therefore, the name will appear in a later chronology in the Computer File Index than would a birth date and birthplace.

4. Not all names of all individuals in each submission source are included, since some names of individuals did not meet minimum identification standards and some entries are difficult to read.

5. Information is not included on individuals born within the last 110 years for whom death dates are not available.

DECEASED MEMBERS FILES

Names of deceased members of the LDS Church are entered in the Name Tabulation Program for completion of all temple ordinances. The two separate programs that provide names of deceased individuals are:

1. Deceased Members Card File—names of individuals entered in the program by the Genealogical Department.

2. Deceased Members Computer File—names of individuals entered in the program by the Membership Department.

Interpreting the Source Reference Number

If the information was extracted from one of the Deceased Members Files, the reference number is a six-digit batch number preceded by an "H" and followed by a serial number. (See Figure 307.)

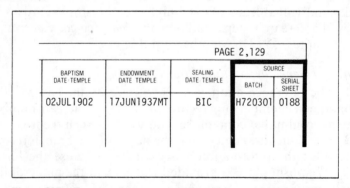

Figure 307.   Source reference number for Deceased Members File.

Obtaining the Original Source

1. Obtain the reference number from the Computer File Index.

2. If the reference number is prefixed by an "H," search the Deceased Members Card File. (See *Genealogical Records of Utah,* Chapter 2.)

3. If it is suspected that the entry was converted from the Deceased Members Computer File (death after 1972/73), check with the Church Historical Department for the entry.

Additional Genealogical Limitations

1. Not all names of all individuals in each submission source are included, since some names of individuals do not meet minimum identification standards.

2. If the birth date and birthplace are not provided in the Deceased Members File, the baptism date and baptism place are substituted for the birth date and birthplace.

110-YEAR FILES

There are two separate files that store names of individuals born within 110 years that were submitted for temple ordinances without a death date:

1. 110-Year Card File
2. 110/95-Year Computer File

The 110/95-Year Computer File also stores names of individuals born within 95 years that were submitted for sealing to parents without a death date for the parents.

Interpreting the Source Reference Number

If the entry was submitted from the 110-Year Card File (1941-1969), the reference number is a six-digit batch number prefixed by the letter "T" and followed by a serial number. (See Figure 308.) If the entry was submitted from the 110/95-Year Computer File (1969-present) as a result of Patron Input, the reference number is prefixed by the letter "D." (See Figure 309.)

| | | | SOURCE | |
BAPTISM DATE TEMPLE	ENDOWMENT DATE TEMPLE	SEALING DATE TEMPLE	BATCH	SERIAL SHEET
10MAR1971	03APR1971	22JUL1971	T000001	6821

PAGE 350

Figure 308.   Source reference number for 110-Year File.

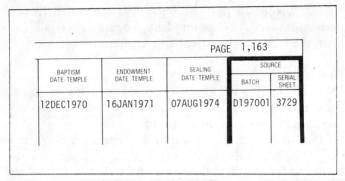

Figure 309.   Source reference number for 100/95-Year Computer File.

Obtaining the Original Source

Step 1. Obtain the reference number from the Computer File Index.

Step 2. If the reference number is prefixed by the letter "T," the entry was submitted on a family group record, a copy of which is available in the Main Records Section. (See Chapter 21.)

Step 3. If the reference number is prefixed by the letter "D," the entry was submitted as a Patron Entry, and there is no way to obtain the original Patron Input reference number and obtain access to the patron's submission form.

Additional Genealogical Application

1. The Computer File Index provides clues to copies of family group records in the Main Records Section.

Additional Genealogical Limitations

1. When identifying information from the 110-Year Card File does not meet minimum identification, the baptism date and baptism place are substituted for the birth date and birthplace.

2. It is not possible to obtain the original Patron Input reference number for entries processed from the 110/95-Year Computer File.

3. Not all names of all individuals in each submission source are included, since some names of individuals do not meet minimum identification standards.

TEMPLE ORIGINATED FAMILY GROUP RECORDS

Family group records that include names of deceased members of the immediate family can be taken directly to the temple for completion of ordinances, and the information is not submitted through Patron Input.

Interpreting the Source Reference Number

The reference number is a six-digit batch number with the first digit "9," the batch number is prefixed with the letter "T," and followed by a serial number. (See Figure 310.)

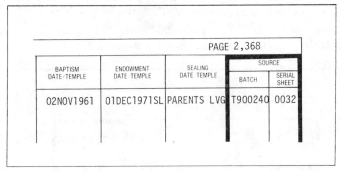

			SOURCE	
BAPTISM DATE/TEMPLE	ENDOWMENT DATE/TEMPLE	SEALING DATE TEMPLE	BATCH	SERIAL SHEET
02NOV1961	01DEC1971SL	PARENTS LVG	T900240	0032

PAGE 2,368

Figure 310. Source reference number for Temple Originated Family Group Records.

Obtaining the Original Source

Step 1. Obtain the date of the ordinance and the name of the temple from the Computer File Index.

Step 2. With the date of the ordinance and the name of the temple, obtain the microfilmed copy of the family group record through the temple recorders records, Special Collections, Genealogical Society Library.

Additional Genealogical Application

1. The name and address of the patron is provided.

2. Names and genealogical information for additional family members may be included.

Additional Genealogical Limitations

1. The source(s) of information is generally incomplete.

2. Family group records may be omitted in the chronological filming of the temple recorders records and appear at the beginning of the microfilm roll for a succeeding month.

ROYALTY AND SPECIAL PROBLEMS

Names of individuals from royal lines are not submitted through Patron Input, but are processed and submitted by the Genealogical Department. Some names of individuals with special situations, such as adoption, divorce, and illegitimacy, are not processed through Patron Input, but are processed by the Genealogical Department.

Interpreting the Source Reference Number

Prior to 1975 these entries were assigned a patron-type reference number. (See Figure 311.) From 1975 to the present, these entries are assigned a six-digit batch number beginning with the number "99," prefixed with the letter "T," and followed by a serial number. (See Figure 312.)

			SOURCE	
BAPTISM DATE TEMPLE	ENDOWMENT DATE TEMPLE	SEALING DATE TEMPLE	BATCH	SERIAL SHEET
22JUN1915	22DEC1915SL	19NOV1971SL	7108821	14

PAGE 52,687

Figure 311.   Source reference number for Royalty and Special Problems, prior to 1975.

			SOURCE	
BAPTISM DATE TEMPLE	ENDOWMENT DATE TEMPLE	SEALING DATE TEMPLE	BATCH	SERIAL SHEET
24MAY1914	06SEP1940SL	CLEARED	T990015	0117

PAGE 1,344

Figure 312.   Source reference number for Royalty and Special Problems, after 1975.

Obtaining the Original Source

Step 1. If the reference number is prefixed with a "T99" and the entry is for a royal line, search the Patrons Section, 1969-present, and/or the Main Records Section. (See Chapter 21.)

Step 2. If the reference number is prefixed with a "T99" and the entry is not for a royal line, contact the Special Information Service for further information. (See Chapter 18.)

Step 3. If the reference number is a Patron Input number, obtain the call number to the microfilm of the submission form through the "Microfilm Index, Patron Sheets, and Ordinance Lists."

Additional Genealogical Application

1. Additional information on special problems may be available in the SIS File. (See Chapter 18.)

Additional Genealogical Limitations

1. Prior to 1975, it is difficult to determine whether the reference number refers to a Royal Line and Special Problem entry or to a patron entry.

2. Individuals may be entered by name of royal title and not by surname.

3. The majority of names of individuals processed as Special Problems do not appear in the Computer File Index.

AVAILABILITY

Figure 313 illustrates the availability of the Computer File Index.

	Genealogical Society Patrons	Genealogical Society Correspondence Request Form*	Branch Libraries	Accredited Researchers**
Microfiche Computer File Index	Yes	Yes	Yes	Yes

*Computer File request forms are available for a small fee at the Church Distribution Center. 1999 West 1700 South. Salt Lake City. Utah 84104. There is a charge for Computer File searches made by the Genealogical Society.

**See sample letter. Figure 314.

Figure 313.   Availability of the Computer File Index.

SUMMARY

The researcher should use the "Guide to the Computer File Index" (Figure 315) as an aid when searching for names of individuals in the Computer File Index. This guide provides a summary of the items of information for each input program that must be understood in order to properly use and interpret the Computer File Index:

1. Examples of source reference numbers
2. Ordinance time period
3. Computer program time period
4. Organization or individual submitting names
5. Purpose of the program

> Your Name
> Your Address
> Current Date
>
> Name of Accredited Researcher
> Address of Accredited Researcher
>
> Dear Sir:
>
> Enclosed is a family group record with photocopies of some Temple Records Index Bureau (TIB) cards. Please search the Computer File Index (CFI) for the names of the parents and children listed on the family group record:
>
> Parents:
> Harry Martin born 1822 in Ohio--individual ordinances
> Jane Evans born 1832 in Penn. --individual ordinances
> Harry Martin and Jane Evans married 1850 in Ohio--marriage ordinance
>
> Children:
> Henry Martin born 1851 in Ohio--individual ordinances
> Margaret Martin born 1854 in Ohio--individual ordinances
> Esther Martin born 1856 in Ohio--individual ordinances
> Martha Martin born 1859 in Ohio--individual ordinances
>
> Enclosed is an American Express Money Order for $5.00 as a deposit for this research.
>
> Thank you.
>
> Sincerely yours,
>
>
>
> Your Name (signed)
>
> Encls: 1 family group record
>   TIB cards
> $5.00

Figure 314.   Letter to an accredited researcher.

Input Program	Examples of Source Reference Numbers	Ordinance Time Period	Computer Program Time Period	Organization or Individual Submitting Name	Purpose of Program
Patron Input	7132627-35	1969-present	1969-present	Patron	1. Ordinances — Non-LDS 2. Store ord. information
Controlled Input: Record Tabulation . . . . . . Controlled Extraction: Christening . . . . . Marriage . . . . Index	P020275-7152 C999971-7332 M024052-0951 72509I0-10	1961-1969 1970-present " "	1961-1969 1970-present " "	Genealogical Dept. Genealogical Dept. " "	1. Ordinances — Non-LDS 2. Store ord. information
TIB Conversion: Patron Input . . . . . . Record Tabulation . . . . . Controlled Extraction . . . Temple Services Division . .	7025322-33 P005971-3986 C033241-0638 T000013-8932	1830s-1969 " " "	1970-present " " "	Patron Genealogical Dept. " "	1. Store ord. information 2. Prevent duplication of previous ordinances
Sealing of Couples Conversion: Civil date and place . . . Temple date and place . . .	A457253-1694 M183393-1930	1846-1969 1855-1889	1968-1972 "	Genealogical Dept. "	1. Store ord. information 2. Prevent duplication of previous ordinances
Membership Conversion: Membership Records . . . Membership Card Index . . Deaths in Missions . . .	6940511-0 6942139-0 6941326-0	1836-1941 " "	1972-present " "	Genealogical Dept. " "	1. Ordinances — LDS 2. Store ord. information
Deceased Members Files: Card File . . . . Computer File	H720301-0188 H721369-1436	1880s-1973 1880s-present	1970-present "	Genealogical Dept. Membership Dept.	1. Ordinances — LDS 2. Store ord. information
110-Year Files: Card File . . . . Computer File	T000001-6821 D197001-3729	1970-present "	1970-present "	Genealogical Dept. or Patron	1. Ordinances — Non-LDS 2. Store ord. information
Temple Originated Family Group Records	T900240-0032	1970-present	1970-present	Patron	1. Ordinances — Non-LDS 2. Store ord. information
Royalty, Special Problems 1970-1975 . . . . 1975-present	7108821-14 T990015-0117	1970-1975 1975-present	1970-1975 1975-present	Genealogical Dept. "	1. Ordinances — Non-LDS 2. Store ord. information

Figure 315.   Guide to the Computer File Index.

The researcher should obtain a copy of the information available in the CFI for each individual listed on the objective family group record for each individual ordinance (see Figure 316) and for the marriage ordinance where applicable (see Figure 317).

```
AUSTIN, Henry (1825)          CFI (baptism, endowment,
                                   sealing to parents)

Henry Austin, Male
Born:  28 Dec 1825, Romsey, Hampshire, England
Parents:  William Austin and Eliza

Baptism:  9 Jan 1971  LA
Endowment:  1 June 1971 LA
Sealing to parents:  5 Nov 1971  LA
Reference Number:  6933520-23
```

Figure 316.   Orange surname note card for individual ordinances.

```
AUSTIN, Henry (1825)              CFI (sealing to spouse)

Henry Austin, husband
Married:  19 May 1850, Portsmouth, Hampshire,
     England
Wife:  Martha Ballard

Sealed:  20 Aug 1971  LA [Los Angeles]
Reference:  69335070-17
```

Figure 317.   Orange surname note card for a marriage ordinance.

21
Family Group Records and Pedigree Charts

Family group records and pedigree charts are filed at the Library of the Genealogical Society in the Family Group Records Archive, formerly known as the Church Records Archives. Some family group records were submitted for processing for temple ordinances and then filed; some family group records were submitted for filing only; and pedigree charts were submitted for filing only.

GENEALOGICAL APPLICATION

1. General information is given on names, places, dates, and relationships that may verify, or add to, presently known information and provide clues to further research.

2. The address of the patron or compiler is valuable for contacting other individuals doing research on the same pedigree problem. The patron or compiler may have hired research through the Research Department of the Genealogical Society where there may be a file. (See Chapter 9.)

3. Direct reference may be given to files in the Research Department of the Genealogical Society. This is indicated near the address of the patron by the initials (LMT) of the employee of the Research Department or by the abbreviation "GEN SOC." (See Chapter 9.)

4. Family group records are valuable for listing names of children not known to the researcher.

5. Family group records may contain ordinance dates not in the TIB.

6. The name of the heir or family representative is given, which is necessary for using indexes to temple ordinance records. (See Chapter 22.)

7. Through use of asterisks (*) in the Main Records Section, one frequently can trace a pedigree for several generations.

8. Ordinance dates stamped on family group records in the Main Records Section are the official temple ordinance dates.

9. The Main Records Section is cross-referenced in the TIB (see Chapter 18); therefore, the TIB always should be searched first.

GENEALOGICAL LIMITATIONS

1. Information is often inaccurate and incomplete.
2. Some family group records are misfiled or missing.
3. Family group records are filed alphabetically and one must know the exact spelling of the name.
4. Frequently an ordinance is repeated, and the recorded ordinance date may not be the first ordinance date.

FAMILY GROUP RECORDS

Family group records at the Genealogical Society are filed alphabetically by the surname of the husband. If there is more than one family group record for individuals with the same name, the family group record for the individual with the earliest birth date is filed first.

Main Records Section, 1942-1969

The Main Records Section refers to family group records submitted to the Genealogical Society for processing for temple ordinances between 1942 and 1969. There is only one record for each family. These family group records are available in pink-labeled binders, and can be identified by the words "Archive Record" on the left-hand side of the family group record. Each family group record in the Main Records Section will include at least one individual for whom ordinance work was performed between 1942 and 1969. Figure 318 is an example of a family group record from the Main Records Section.

For an explanation of special notations that may be found on family group records from the Main Records Section, see Figure 319.

Patrons Section, 1924 - Present

The Patrons Section refers to family group records submitted to the Genealogical Society since 1924 for filing. Those submitted from 1924 to 1962 are available on microfilm, and those submitted since 1962 are microfilmed and also available in yellow-labeled binders. There may be more than one record for the same family, and information on the family group

HUSBAND SAMUEL PUTNAM *
Birth 30 Sept 1707 Place Salem, Essex, Mass
Chr. Place
Death 15 Dec 1787 Place
Burial Place
Father Eleazer Putnam * Mother Hannah Boardman
Married 29 Dec 1736 Place

WIFE ELIZABETH PUTNAM *
Birth 20 May 1718 Place Salem, Essex, Mass
Chr. Place
Death 21 May 1784 Place
Burial Place
Father Tarrant Putnam * Mother Elizabeth Bacon

Where was information shown on this family record obtained?
Putnam fam. rec., books kept by Savannah Clarke Putnam see corrections under Putnam Leaflets

Family Representative:
Mona Putnam Leavitt
Beryl Putnam Duffin
1522 No. Washington
Stillwater, Okla.

HUSBAND'S Name (in full) Samuel Putnam 1707
Wife: Elizabeth Putnam

TEMPLE ORDINANCE DATA
HUSBAND Baptized 6 May 1930 Endowed 14 Mar 1934 2c 6r
WIFE 963318 Baptized 6 June 1931 Endowed 21 Jan 1932 Sealed to Husband 14 June 1960 1c 5r

CHILDREN	Sex	WHEN BORN Day Mo. Yr.	WHERE BORN Town	County	State or Country	DIED Day Mo. Yr.	MARRIED To	BAPTIZED	ENDOWED	SEALED To Parents
1 Elizabeth Putnam	F	1738	Salem,	Essex	Mass	13 Apr 1791	Daniel Putnam	14 Oct 1930	13 Apr 1933	14 June 1960
2 Samuel Putnam	M	13 June 1741	"	"	"		1786 Lydia Putnam	11 June 1935	20 June 1938	14 June 1960
3 Martha Putnam	F	9 Sept 1742	"	"	"	3 Sept 1821	John Endicott	13 June 1935	22 Apr 1936	14 June 1960
4 Tarrant Putnam	M	8 Feb 1744	"	"	"	14 Apr 1776	16 Nov 1768 Sarah Page	11 June 1935	15 Mar 1937	14 June 1960
5 Rufus Putnam	M	31 Mar 1746	"	"	"	21 Nov 1749		child	child	14 June 1960
6 Solomon Putnam	M	13 Nov 1748	"	"	"	12 Nov 1749		child	child	14 June 1960
7 Rufus Putnam	M	18 Oct 1750	"	"	"	1 Sept 1757		child	child	14 June 1960
8 Hannah Putnam	F	19 Mar 1753	"	"	"	20 Aug 1757		child	child	14 June 1960
9 Mary Putnam	F	24 Oct 1755	"	"	"	26 Aug 1757		child	child	14 June 1960
10 Eleazer Putnam	M	4 May 1759	"	"	"	30 May 1836	1) Sarah Fuller *	11 June 1935	18 Mar 1937	14 June 1960
11 Hannah Putnam	F	1 Feb 1762	"	"	"	23 Aug 1796	Elijah Flint	13 June 1935	6 Feb 1936	14 June 1960

ARCHIVE RECORD

Figure 318. Family group record from the Main Records Section.

The symbol *
indicates the individual appears on another family group record in the Main Records Section. (An asterisk behind the name of the spouse of a child indicates additional information on the back of the family group record.)

- -

The symbol @
indicates additional information on the back of the family group record, generally an additional marriage.

- -

The stamped information CHILDREN NOS. _____
HAVE BEEN ADDED TO THIS SHEET BY
NAME _____
ADDRESS _____

indicates additional children have been added to the sheet by an individual other than the person who originally submitted the family group record.

- -

The stamped information THESE CHILDREN WERE SEALED TO
_____ FIRST HUSBAND, AND
TO THEIR MOTHER _____
Date _____
MOTHER SEALED TO FIRST HUSBAND

_____
Approved

_____
President

indicates the children listed on the family group record were sealed to their natural mother and the husband to whom the mother was sealed, which husband is not the natural father.

- -

The stamped information ALL PREVIOUS CHURCH BLESSINGS
RECONFIRMED AND RATIFIED FOR
ABOVE _____ on _____

indicates the individual was rebaptized and previous endowment and sealing ordinances were reconfirmed and considered valid.

- -

The abbreviation SIS
indicates additional information of a confidential nature is available in the Supplementary Information Service file.

- -

The abbreviation GEN SOC
indicates the family group record was submitted as a result of research hired through the Research Department of the Genealogical Society.

- -

Three initials, such as HJR,
indicate the initials of the employee of the Research Department of the Genealogical Society who performed the research.

- -

A serial number, such as 963318,
indicates a processing number of no genealogical significance.

Figure 319.   Special notations, Main Records Section.

records for the same family may vary. The Patrons Section includes the following family group records submitted for filing only:

1. Family group records submitted by genealogists who desired to share the results of their research with others.

2. Family group records submitted by members of The Church of Jesus Christ of Latter-day Saints for the three-and four-generation program.

3. Family group records submitted from 1956 to 1969 for sealings only, where baptisms and endowments had been performed previously (formerly filed in orange-labeled binders).

4. Family group records for previously married couples who went to the temple for sealing (formerly filed in orange-labeled binders).

Miscellaneous Family Group Records

Miscellaneous family group record collections submitted by family researchers and professional researchers are available at the Genealogical Society on microfilm.

PEDIGREE CHARTS

Between 1924 and 1962 pedigree charts were accepted by the Library of the Genealogical Society for filing.

Card-Indexed Pedigree Charts, 1924 - 1942

These pedigree charts were the earliest ones received by the Genealogical Society and were filed in binders; they are now available only on microfilm. The binders were assigned a letter of the alphabet with a "7" prefix ranging from "7" to "7R," and each pedigree chart was then assigned a page number. An index card was made for each person on each pedigree chart, giving the number of the binder, page number of the pedigree chart, and number of the individual. (See Figure 320.)

The number "7B-453-6" at the bottom of the card indicates that in binder 7B on chart (page) 453, individual #6 is Homer Duncan.

The number "7E-750-4" at the bottom of the card indicates that in binder 7E on chart (page) 750, individual #4 is Homer Duncan. The entire reference number prefixed by "7" must be copied from the index card as an aid in locating the correct microfilm for the binder.

```
┌─────────────────────────────────────────────────────────────┐
│        INDEX CARD  TO              TEMPLE  RECORDS            │
│   No.                  No.         Book       Page            │
│   ───────────────────────────────────────────────────────    │
│   Name in full   Duncan, Homer                               │
│   When born          19 Jan. 1815                            │
│   Where born           Barnett, Vermont                      │
│   When died            23 Mar. 1906                          │
│   Father      John Duncan                                    │
│   Mother      Betsy Taylor Putnam            /Banker*        │
│   When married  7 Nov 1841         to  Asenath Melvina/      │
│   Instance of                      Rel.                      │
│   When baptized              When Endowed                    │
│   Sealed Husband             To                              │
│          Wife                Parents                         │
│   References     7B-453-6        2aa-6                        │
│                  7E-750-4                                     │
│                                                              │
└─────────────────────────────────────────────────────────────┘
```

Figure 320.   Index card to the Card-Indexed Pedigree Charts.

The number "2aa-6" refers to an out-dated filing system and need not be copied.

Alphabetized Pedigree Charts, 1942 - 1962

When it became impossible to make an index card for each individual on each pedigree chart, the pedigree charts were arranged alphabetically by individual # 1 on the pedigree. These have been microfilmed in two sections; one section was microfilmed in 1950 and the other in 1962.

Miscellaneous Pedigree Charts

Miscellaneous pedigree chart collections submitted by family researchers and professional researchers are available at the Genealogical Society on microfilm.

AVAILABILITY

Figure 321 illustrates the availability of the family group records and pedigree charts.

After the researcher determines the most logical availability for the family group records and pedigree charts (see Figure 321), he should make surname note cards on which to indicate the results of the search. (See Figures 323, 324, 325, 326, 327, 328, and 329.)

Archive Section	Date Submitted	Purpose Submitted	Binders at Genealogical Society	Microfilm at Genealogical Society	Gen. Soc. Corres. Request Forms*	Branch Libraries	Accredited Researchers****
Main Records Section** Family Group Records	1942-1969	Temple Pro-cessing	Yes (pink labels)	Yes	Yes	Yes	Yes
Sec. #1, Patrons Family Group Records	1924-1962	Filing	No	Yes (1962) (1950)***	No	Yes (1962) (1950)***	Yes
Sec. #2, Patrons Family Group Records	1962-present	Filing	Yes (yellow labels)	Yes	No	Yes	Yes
Miscellaneous Family Group Records	1924-present	Filing	No	Yes	No	Yes	Yes
Card-Indexed Pedigree Charts	1924-1942	Filing	No	Yes	No	Yes	Yes
Sec. #1, Alphabetized Pedigree Charts	1942-1962	Filing	No	Yes	No	Yes	Yes
Sec. #2, Alphabetized Pedigree Charts	1962-1965	Filing	No	Yes	No	Yes	Yes
Miscellaneous Pedigree Charts	1924-present	Filing	No	Yes	No	Yes	Yes

*Family Group Record request forms are available for a small fee at the Church Distribution Center, 1999 West 1700 South, Salt Lake City, Utah 84104. There is a charge for family group record searches made by the Genealogical Society.

**Referenced through TIB.

***Reproduction of poor quality; search when omission is suspected in 1962 film.

****See sample letter, Figure 322.

Figure 321. Availability of family group records and pedigree charts.

Your Name
Your Address
Current Date

Name of Accredited Researcher
Address of Accredited Researcher

Dear Sir:

Enclosed is a family group record with photocopies of
some Temple Records Index Bureau (TIB) cards and some
extracts from the Computer File Index (CFI). Please search
the family group record sections at the Genealogical Society
for copies of the enclosed family group record and send me
a photocopy of each one found:

Main Records Section Family Group Records
Section #1, Patrons Family Group Records
Section #2, Patrons Family Group Records

Please search the pedigree chart sections at the Genealogical Society for the name of the husband listed on the
enclosed family group record and send me a photocopy of
each pedigree chart found:

Card Indexed Pedigree Charts
Section #1, Alphabetized Pedigree Charts
Section #2, Alphabetized Pedigree Charts

Enclosed is an American Express Money Order for
$5.00 as a deposit for this research.

Thank you.

Sincerely yours,

Your Name (signed)

Encls: 1 family group record
TIB cards
CFI extracts
$5.00

Figure 322.   Letter to an accredited researcher.

```
┌────────────────────────────────────────────────────────────┐
│  AUSTIN,  Henry (abt.  1825)          Main Records Section   │
│                                      Family Group Records    │
│                                            1942-1969         │
│                                                              │
│     Copy of family group record filed in research folder.    │
│                                                              │
│                                                              │
│                                                              │
│                                                              │
│                                                              │
│                                                              │
│  GS  F  1,060,129                                            │
└────────────────────────────────────────────────────────────┘
```

Figure 323.   White surname note card for the Main Records Section.

```
┌────────────────────────────────────────────────────────────┐
│  BAUM,  George (1872)                 Main Records Section   │
│                                      Family Group Records    │
│                                            1942-1969         │
│                                                              │
│  No reference in TIB; do not search.                         │
│                                                              │
│                                                              │
│                                                              │
│                                                              │
│                                                              │
│                                                              │
└────────────────────────────────────────────────────────────┘
```

Figure 324.   White surname note card for the Main Records Section.

```
┌────────────────────────────────────────────────────────────┐
│  AUSTIN,  Henry (abt.  1825)              Section #1 Patrons │
│                                      Family Group Records    │
│                                            1924-1962         │
│                                                              │
│     Copy of family group record filed in research folder.    │
│                                                              │
│                                                              │
│                                                              │
│                                                              │
│                                                              │
│                                                              │
│  GS  F  412,108                                              │
└────────────────────────────────────────────────────────────┘
```

Figure 325.   White surname note card for the Patrons Section 1924-1962.

```
AUSTIN, Henry (abt. 1825)            Section #2 Patrons
                                    Family Group Records
                                        1962-present

Did not find.


Submitted 1962-1965--GS F 428,078
Submitted 1966--GS F 510,743
Submitted 1967--GS F 547,604
Submitted 1968--GS F 498,960
Submitted 1969--GS F 828,477
Submitted 1970--GS F 542,476
Submitted 1971--GS F 541,668
Submitted 1972--GS F 822,927
Submitted 1973-1974--GS F 935,003
```

Figure 326.   White surname note card for the Patrons Section 1962-present.

```
DUNCAN, Homer (1815)                    Card-Indexed
                                       Pedigree Charts

Card Index call number:  GS F 820,094

Card Index Reference:  7B-453-6    GS F 271,432
                       7E-750-4    GS F 271,438




GS F 820,094
```

Figure 327.   White surname note card for the Card-Indexed Pedigree Charts.

```
DUNCAN, Homer (1815)            Section #1 Alphabetized
                                    Pedigree Charts
                                      filmed 1962

Did not find.





GS F 281,756
```

Figure 328.   White surname note card for Alphabetized Pedigree Charts.

DUNCAN, Homer (1815)   Section #2 Alphabetized
                                        Pedigree Charts
                                          filmed 1965

Copy of pedigree chart filed in research folder.

GS F 319,918

Figure 329.   White surname note card for Alphabetized Pedigree Charts.

22
Temple Recorders Records

Various ordinances and ceremonies are performed for both the living and the dead in temples of The Church of Jesus Christ of Latter-day Saints. For genealogical purposes one is concerned with the ordinances listed on the family group record:

1. Baptisms
2. Endowments
3. Sealings of couples (wife to husband)
4. Sealings of families (children to parents)

Records of these ordinances are kept in the temple by the temple recorder and are known as temple recorders records. Prior to 1970, each temple recorder generally kept a separate record book for each ordinance, which could result in as many as eight different records being kept concurrently in each temple (see Figure 330):

1. Baptisms for the living
2. Rebaptisms for the living (Logan only)
3. Baptisms for the dead
4. Endowments for the living
5. Endowments for the dead
6. Sealings of living couples
7. Sealings of deceased couples (includes one deceased spouse)
8. Sealings of children to parents (includes living and deceased)

Prior to 1970, record books include the name of the temple, name of the ordinance, date of the ordinance, names of the officiators, names of the witnesses, and names of the recorders. The content and format of each record and each entry varies, as does the genealogical information. After 1970, temple recorders records are microfilmed copies of the computer ordinance lists prepared through the NameTabulation Program.

When an ordinance is performed on behalf of a deceased individual, the deceased person is represented by a living proxy, thus the term "proxy baptism," "proxy endowment," and "proxy sealing." This is the same as "baptism for the dead," "endowment for the dead," and "sealing for the dead."

Time Period or Temple Dedicated	Baptisms Living	Baptisms Dead	Endowments Living
Kirtland 27 Mar 1836	None	None	None
Pre-Nauvoo Period	None	Sep 1840- 3 Oct 1841	4 May 1842
Nauvoo Temple 1 May 1846	None	21 Nov 1841- 9 Jan 1845	10 Dec 1845- 7 Feb 1846
Pre-Endowment House Period	None	None	20 Feb 1851- 24 Apr 1854
Endowment House 5 May 1855	None	5 May 1855- 26 Oct 1876	5 May 1855- 16 Oct 1884
St. George 6 Apr 1877	5 Sep 1882-	9 Jan 1877-	11 Jan 1877-
Logan 17 May 1884	21 May 1884-	21 May 1884-	21 May 1884-
Manti 21 May 1888	4 Sep 1888-	29 May 1888-	30 May 1888-
Salt Lake 6 Apr 1893	None	23 May 1893-	24 May 1893-
Hawaiian 27 Nov 1919	None	2 Dec 1919-	3 Dec 1919-
Alberta 26 Aug 1923	None	6 Nov 1923-	29 Aug 1923-
Arizona 23 Oct 1927	31 Mar 1928-	26 Oct 1927-	27 Oct 1927-
Idaho Falls 23 Sep 1945	None	3 Dec 1945-	5 Dec 1945-
Swiss 11 Sep 1955	None	1 Oct 1955-	16 Sep 1955-
Los Angeles 11 Mar 1956	None	24 Mar 1956-	16 Apr 1956-
New Zealand 20 Apr 1958	None	22 Apr 1958-	24 Apr 1958-
London 7 Sep 1958	None	10 Sep 1958-	10 Sep 1958-
Oakland 16 Nov 1964	None	1 Dec 1964-	5 Jan 1965-

Figure 330.   Chronology of temple ordinances to 1970. (Continued on next page)

Endowments Dead	Sealings Couples Living	Sealings Couples Liv/Dead	Sealings Couples Dead	Sealings Children Liv/Dead
None	None	None	None	None
None	5 Apr 1841	None	None	None
None	9 Jan 1846- 22 Feb 1846	9 Jan 1846- 22 Feb 1846	None	11 Jan 1846- 6 Feb 1846
None	8 Nov 1846- 5 May 1855	8 Nov 1846- 5 May 1855	None	None
None	5 May 1855- 22 Sep 1889	5 May 1855- 22 Sep 1889	5 May 1855- 22 Sep 1889	None
11 Jan 1877-	11 Jan 1877-	11 Jan 1877-	11 Jan 1877-	22 Mar 1877-
21 May 1884-	21 May 1884-	21 May 1884-	21 May 1884-	21 May 1884-
30 May 1888-	30 May 1888-	30 May 1888-	30 May 1888-	6 June 1888-
24 May 1893-	24 May 1893-	23 Apr 1893-	23 Apr 1893-	8 Apr 1893-
3 Dec 1919-	3 Dec 1919-	3 Dec 1919-	3 Dec 1919-	3 Dec 1919-
29 Aug 1923-	29 Aug 1923-	7 Nov 1923-	7 Nov 1923-	29 Aug 1923-
27 Oct 1927-	27 Oct 1927-	27 Oct 1927-	27 Oct 1927-	27 Oct 1927-
5 Dec 1945-	5 Dec 1945-	5 Dec 1945-	5 Dec 1945-	5 Dec 1945-
16 Sep 1955- 14 Apr 1956-	16 Sep 1955- 30 Mar 1956-	16 Sep 1955- 30 Mar 1956-	16 Sep 1955- 30 Mar 1956-	16 Sep 1955- 16 Apr 1956-
24 Apr 1958-	24 Apr 1958-	24 Apr 1958-	24 Apr 1958-	24 Apr 1958-
10 Sep 1958-	10 Sep 1958-	10 Sep 1958-	10 Sep 1958-	10 Sep 1958-
19 Dec 1964-	21 Dec 1964-	5 Jan 1965-	14 Jan 1975-	5 Jan 1965-

Figure 330.   Chronology of temple ordinances to 1970. (Concluded)

Prior to the Name Tabulation Program in 1970, there was not a Churchwide index to all temple ordinance records; therefore, many ordinances have been repeated. The method of indexing temple ordinance records prior to 1970 varies with each temple, each time period, and each type of record; sometimes several indexes are combined to form indexes for larger periods of time. Temple ordinances performed after 1970 are indexed and available through the Computer File Index. (See Chapter 20.)

Records of temple ordinances performed by living individuals for themselves are indexed by the name of the individual. Records of temple ordinances performed for deceased individuals generally are indexed under the name of the heir; the proxy was often the heir in early temple records. The term "instance of" is used in early records for the term "heir." Therefore, in order to use the index to proxy temple records, one must know the name of the heir or at whose "instance" the temple work was performed. The name of the heir can be determined from the following sources:

1. Temple records in possession of the family
2. TIB cards
3. Family group records
4. Pedigree charts
5. Card Index to Heirs

The Card Index to Heirs prepared by the Genealogical Society and available on microfilm is a card file listing the names of heirs in the Church to 1941. (See Figure 331.) The card file is arranged in alphabetical order by surname, and each card contains the following information:

1. The name of the heir
2. Whether or not the heir is deceased
3. Names and address of individuals who submitted names to the Genealogical Society for processing under the name of that particular heir (These persons often hired research through the Research Department of the Genealogical Society, See Chapter 9)
4. Initials indicating the temple(s) where the ordinances were performed

GENEALOGICAL APPLICATION

1. Temple ordinance records are used to verify temple ordinance dates.

```
┌─────────────────────────────────────────────────────────────┐
│  Thomas, William (d)                        SL  AL           │
│ ─────────────────────────────────────────────────           │
│    Mary A. Kirkham                                           │
│    424 N.  2nd E.                                            │
│    Provo, Utah                                              │
│                                                             │
│    Genealogical Society of Utah                             │
│                                                             │
│    Thos. W. Jones                                           │
│    669-3rd Ave.                                             │
│    Salt Lake City, Utah                                     │
│                                                             │
│    Mrs. Emma Asher Hales                                    │
│    242 No. Kellogg St.                                      │
│    Elsinore, California                                     │
│                                                             │
│                                                             │
│  Card Index to Heirs    GS F 026,898                        │
└─────────────────────────────────────────────────────────────┘
```

Figure 331.   Card from the Card Index to Heirs.

2. Names of additional relatives may be found, since an individual usually performed proxy ordinances for more than one relative on a given day.

3. The information may be from a primary source. Temple ordinance records often contain information an individual gave about himself or close relatives: brothers, sisters, aunts, uncles, cousins, parents, and grandparents.

4. General information is given on names, places, dates, and relationships that may verify, or add to presently known information and provide clues to vital records and additional temple records to be searched.

GENEALOGICAL LIMITATIONS

1. Information is often inaccurate and incomplete.

2. The informant or source of information is often unidentifiable.

3. The stated relationships are often inaccurate, particularly for the terms "cousin" and "friend."

4. Some records are missing.

5. There is no Churchwide index to all baptisms and sealings. Records for each ordinance and for each temple are indexed separately. One must determine the name of the heir, the specific temple, the time period, and the condition (living or deceased) in order to use the indexes.

6. Temple ordinances for the dead are indexed by the name of the heir rather than by the name of the individual.

7. Baptisms and endowments are not performed for individuals who died under the age of eight years.

BAPTISMS

Baptisms for the dead have been performed since 15 August 1840 to the present time. A few baptisms for living individuals have been performed in some temples; however, verifications of living baptisms should be obtained from LDS Membership Records. (See *Genealogical Records of Utah.*)

For a history of baptisms in each of the temples with the dates of available records, see Figure 330. The content and format of proxy baptism records vary for each time period and each temple, but may include the following (see Figure 332):

1. Name of individual
2. Birth date
3. Birthplace
4. Death date
5. Death place
6. Name of proxy
7. Name of heir
8. Relationship of heir to deceased

```
SUNDMAN, Catharina Ulrika (1801)            baptism

  #31878  Catharina Ulrika Sunman, born 19 Sep 1801
          Sundsvall, Vestnorrland, Sweden

  Heir:  Albert F. Elg
  Proxy: Lois Lavoile Farrer
  Baptized:  6 May 1939




S. L. Temple Recs of Baptism for the Dead
GS F 183,579, p. 912
```

Figure 332.   Orange surname note card for a baptism record.

There is no Churchwide index to baptisms for the dead; however, the majority of proxy baptism dates after 1877 are included on TIB cards. Records of each temple are indexed by the name of the heir; therefore, it is necessary to know the name of the temple and the name of the heir.

The genealogical researcher should verify each proxy baptism date on the objective family group record. Verification of proxy (temple) baptism dates is obtained by searching the temple ordinance records of baptisms for the dead.

1. Obtain copies of the TIB cards for each individual on the objective family group record, which will provide a proxy baptism date, the name of the temple, and the name of the heir.

2. Obtain the baptism dates from the Computer File Index for each individual listed on the objective family group record.

3. Verify the baptism date by searching the records of the appropriate temple.

4. Copy all information on individuals for whom temple work was performed by the heir on the same day.

5. If family information indicates that individuals on the objective family group record could have performed baptisms for the dead in the Nauvoo Temple or the Endowment House, search the indexes to these temples and copy information on all individuals for whom proxy baptisms were performed.

6. If the specific date cannot be verified, search the temple indexes of the appropriate temple for the name of the heir. (See Figure 330.)

ENDOWMENTS

Endowments for the living have been performed since 1842 to the present time. There were no endowments for the dead performed until the dedication of the St. George Temple in 1877, resulting in a 37-year lapse between the first baptisms for the dead and the first endowments for the dead. For a history of endowments in each of the temples with the dates of available records, see Figure 330.

The content and format of endowment records vary for each time period and each temple, but may include the following (see Figure 333):

1. Name
2. Birth date
3. Birthplace
4. Father's name
5. Mother's maiden name
6. Marriage date
7. Name of spouse
8. Baptism date

```
┌─────────────────────────────────────────────────────────┐
│ SUNDMAN, Catharina Ulrika (1801)          endowment     │
│                                                         │
│   #14450 Catharina Sunman                               │
│     Born 19 Sep 1801, Sundsvall, Vesternorrland,        │
│     Sweden                                              │
│                                                         │
│   Father:  Erik Sundman                                 │
│   Mother:  Anna Bohn [Bolin]                            │
│                                                         │
│   Baptized:  6 May 1939                                 │
│   Heir:  Albert Elg, (d) 2 gg son                       │
│                                                         │
│   Endowed:  31 May 1940                                 │
│   Died:  5 Nov 1868                                     │
│                                                         │
│                                                         │
│   S. L. Temple Recs of Endowment for the Dead           │
│   GS F 184, 237  Bk 6S, p. 652                          │
└─────────────────────────────────────────────────────────┘
```

Figure 333.   Orange surname note card for an endowment record.

If deceased—
9. Death date
10. Death place
11. Name of heir
12. Name of proxy
13. Relationship of heir to deceased

The Temple Records Index Bureau (see Chapter 18) is a Churchwide index to temple endowments for both the living and the deceased. The genealogical researcher should verify each endowment date on the objective family group record.

1. Obtain the TIB card for each individual on the objective family group record, which will provide the endowment date prior to 1970 and the name of the temple. Accept the endowment date unless a copying error is suspected.

2. Obtain endowment date for each endowment after 1970 from the Computer File Index.

3. If no TIB card is available, and the family group record indicates an endowment has been performed, determine the temple where the endowment could have been performed and search the records on the specific date. (See Figure 330.)

4. If the specific date cannot be verified, search the temple indexes for the name of the individual (living endowment) or the name of the heir (proxy endowment).

SEALING OF COUPLES

Sealings of couples (wife to husband) have been performed since 5 April 1841 until the present time. At various times in the history of the Church, sealings of living couples and sealings of couples where one spouse was deceased were performed in places other than a temple. This practice was continued until the early 1900s. These sealings are considered valid if there is a properly signed certificate or if a record is available in a temple sealing book. The practice of sealing couples in places other than a temple has resulted in many couples' being sealed prior to the endowment.

For a history of sealings of couples in each of the temples with the dates of available records, see Figure 330.

The content and format of sealing of couple records vary for each time period and each temple, but may include the following (see Figure 334):

1. Name of husband
2. Name of wife
3. Birth date of husband
4. Birthplace of husband
5. Birth date of wife
6. Birthplace of wife
7. Civil marriage date
8. Civil marriage place
9. Endowment date

If deceased—

10. Death date of husband
11. Death date of wife
12. Name of proxy
13. Name of heir
14. Relationship of heir to deceased

```
JANSSON, Nils (1786)                        sealing
                                            to spouse

  Nils Jansson
     Born:  23 Dec 1786, Stenbacken, Örebrö, Sweden
     Died:  29 Sep 1864
     Endowed:  27 Oct 1897

  Sealed 28 Oct 1897  #6435

     to Anna Kajsa Olson
        Born:  18 June 1789, Ljungstorp, Örebrö, Sweden
        Died:   5 July 1864
        Endowed 20 July 1893

  Heir or proxy:  Gustave Johnson
                  Christina M. N. Bengtson

S. L. Temple Sealings of Couples
GS F 184,589  Bk C, p. 363
```

Figure 334.   Orange surname note card for a sealing to spouse record prior to 1942.

Between 1942 and 1970 the temple record of sealings of couples is a microfilmed copy of the family group records on file in the Main Records Section, arranged chronologically by date of sealing. (See Fig. 318, Chapter 21.)

There is no Churchwide index to sealings of couples prior to 1942; therefore, many sealings of couples have been repeated. The alphabetically arranged family group records in the Main Records Section are an index for sealings of couples performed between 1942 and 1970; however, many of the sealings are repeats of earlier sealings.

Information from the original temple records of sealings of couples from 1841 to 1969 that meets minimum identification standards has been entered in the Name Tabulation Program (see Chapter 19), and is available through the Computer File Index (see Chapter 20).

The genealogical researcher should verify each date of sealing of wife to husband on the objective family group record.

1. Request a search of the Temple Records Index Bureau and obtain copies of the TIB cards for each individual on the objective family group record, which will provide a clue to the name of the temple and the name of the heir, information that is necessary in order to search original temple records of sealings.

2. Search the Computer File Index for the sealing of wife to husband listed on the objective family group record.

3. If the TIB card indicates a reference to the Main Records Section ("P" and/or "C"), refer to the appropriate family group record for a stamped date of sealing of the couple. Dates prior to 1942 and dates that are not stamped should be verified in the original record.

4. If the proxy baptism and the proxy endowment for the couple were performed prior to 1942, and the sealing of the couple after 1942, an earlier sealing may have been performed near the time of the endowment and then repeated after 1942. When this is suspected, one should search the indexes of the records of the appropriate temple(s) for the name of the husband (living sealing) or the name of the heir (proxy sealing). (All St. George Temple Records, 1877-1913, for deceased couples are indexed by the name of the deceased.)

SEALING OF FAMILIES

Sealings of families (children to parents) have been performed continuously in all temples from 1877 to the present. A few sealings of children to parents were performed in Nauvoo, but after the Nauvoo period there were no sealings of children (living or dead) to parents until the dedication of the St. George Temple in 1877.

For a history of sealings of children to parents in each of the temples with the dates of available records, see Figure 330. Records of sealings of parents include adoptions, and in some records all sealings of children to parents are termed "adoptions." Living and deceased individuals are recorded together in the same record book. The content and format of sealing of children to parents records vary for each time period and each temple, but may include the following (see Figure 335):

1. Name of father
2. Birth date of father
3. Birthplace of father
4. Name of mother
5. Birth date of mother
6. Birthplace of mother
7. Names of children
8. Birth dates of children
9. Birthplaces of children
10. Baptism dates (rarely)
11. Endowment dates (rarely)
12. Sealing to spouse date

```
NILSSON, Anna Lotta (1822)              sealing
                                        to parents

Sealed to parents Nils Janson and Anna Kajsa Olson Janson
   27 Sep 1900

#8804 Olof Nilson b. abt. 1819, d. abt. 1821
#8805 Anna Lotta Nilson b. 1822, d. 5 Dec 1896
#8806 Christina Maria Nilson Bengtson b. 24 July 1824
   living
#8807 Erik Johan Nilson b. 1829

   All born in Baggatorp, Örebrö, Sweden
   Proxies: John F. Johnason, Eliza Fletcher, Lars E.
      Anderson, Carl E. Cederstrom, Emma S. B.
      Cederstrom

S. L. Temple Records of Sealings of Families
GS F 184,655   Bk D  p. 338
```

Figure 335. Orange surname note card for a sealing of children to parents record prior to 1942.

If deceased—
13. Name of proxy
14. Name of heir
15. Relationship of heir to deceased (rarely)
16. Death dates of parents
17. Death dates of children

Between 1942 and 1970, the temple record of sealings of children to parents is a microfilmed copy of the family group records on file in the Main Records Section (see Figure 318, Chapter 21), arranged chronologically by date of sealing.

There is no Churchwide index to sealings of children to parents prior to 1942; therefore, many sealings of children to parents have been repeated. The alphabetically arranged family group records in the Main Records Section are an index for sealings of children to parents performed between 1942 and 1970.

The genealogical researcher should verify each date of sealing of children to parents on the objective family group record.

1. Request a search of the Temple Records Index Bureau, and obtain copies of the TIB card for each individual on the objective family group record. These will provide a clue to the name of the temple and the name of the heir, which is necessary in order to search original temple records.

2. Search the Computer File Index for the sealing to parents of each child listed on the objective family group record.

3. If the TIB card indicates a reference to the Main Records Section ("P" and/or "C"), refer to the appropriate family group record for the date of sealing of the child(ren) to the parents. Sealing dates prior to 1942 should be verified in the original record.

4. If the proxy baptism and proxy endowment for the children were performed prior to 1942, and the sealing of the children after 1942, an earlier sealing may have been performed near the time of the endowment and then repeated after 1942. When this is suspected, one should search the indexes of the records of the appropriate temple(s) for the name of the individual (living sealing) or the name of the heir (proxy sealing).

AVAILABILITY

Figure 336 illustrates the availability of temple recorders records.

Temple Recorders Records	Microfilm at Genealogical Soc. General Reference	Microfilm at Genealogical Soc. Special Collections	Genealogical Soc. Correspondence Request Form	Branch Libraries	Temple Recorder at Temple**	Accredited Researcher***
Baptisms: Living*	Yes	No	No	Yes	No	Yes
Deceased	Yes	No	No	Yes	Yes	Yes
Endowments: Living	Prior 1901	After 1901	No	Prior 1901	Yes	Prior 1901**
Deceased	Yes	No	No	Yes	Yes	After 1901
Sealing Couples Living	No	Yes	No	No	Yes	Yes**
Deceased	No	Yes	No	No	Yes	Yes**
Sealing Families (Children to Parents)	No	Yes	No	No	Yes	Yes**

*LDS Church Membership, see Laureen R. Jaussi and Gloria D. Chaston, *Genealogical Records of Utah* (Salt Lake City, Utah: Deseret Book Co., 1974).

**Records and call numbers restricted to LDS Church members with recommend.

***See sample letter, Figure 337.

Figure 336.   Availability of temple recorders records.

Your Name
Your Address
Current Date

Name of Accredited Researcher
Address of Accredited Researcher

Dear Sir:

    Enclosed is a family group record with photocopies
of some Temple Records Index Bureau (TIB) cards and
some extracts from the Computer File Index (CFI). Please
search the following restricted sealing record for me:

        The Manti Temple, sealings of living couples,
    1892 to 1900, for the sealing of Andrew Phillips
    and Barbara Martin.

    I am a direct descendant of this couple, and I would
appreciate receiving an exact copy of the entry. Enclosed
is an American Express Money Order for $5.00 as a
deposit for this research.

    Thank you.

                Sincerely yours,

                Your Name (signed)

Encl: 1 family group record
       TIB cards
       CFI extracts
       $5.00

Figure 337.   Letter to an accredited researcher.

SECTION IV

LESSON ASSIGNMENTS

Lesson Assignments

These lessons are written for the individual who desires to learn how to do his own genealogical research and for teachers of basic genealogical classes. They are adaptable to home study, continuing workshops, and conventional lectures. As an individual completes the lessons eight times, once for each marriage in the first four generations on the pedigree chart, he becomes skilled in basic genealogical research. Individuals who complete these lessons will find that *Fundamentals of Genealogical Research* has the following advantages:

1. Individuals quickly become independent of the teacher.

2. Individuals work on their own genealogy.

3. The lesson assignments are adaptable to youth and adults; separate youth programs are not necessary.

4. Lesson assignments emphasize the first four-generation family group records and are applicable to all geographic areas.

5. The lesson assignments fill LDS genealogy requirements.

6. The lesson assignments fill the requirements for a Boy Scout merit badge.

7. Completion of each lesson assignment provides information necessary for the next lesson assignment.

8. Note keeping, correspondence, and library usage are introduced gradually in relation to each record.

9. All assignments can be completed by correspondence, and it is not necessary to do library research in person.

10. Individuals with access to a genealogical library are prepared to do library research without a teacher.

11. Individuals are qualified to teach a lesson as soon as they have completed the corresponding lesson assignments.

12. Individuals search productive records.

13. Teachers need no previous genealogical experience.

14. Teachers are being trained continuously.

HOME STUDY

Home study is most appealing to individuals who are the only ones in their community interested in genealogical research or individuals who have been asked to teach a genealogy class and feel unprepared to teach. These individuals can train themselves to do genealogical research by following the lesson assignments as outlined, and they will experience the following advantages:

1. Individuals can begin the lessons at any time and do not have to wait for someone to organize a genealogy class.

2. Individuals can progress at their own speed.

3. Individuals can work on their own genealogy at their own convenience.

4. Individuals do not have to take time to listen to questions and lectures that do not apply to their own genealogical research.

A CONTINUING WORKSHOP

Those who are asked to organize and teach genealogical research classes will find a continuing workshop to be the most efficient method for teaching groups of students. A continuing workshop is a teaching method in which all twelve lessons are available at the same time with emphasis on reading the textbook and completing the assignments rather than listening to a lecture. The workshop should meet on a regular weekly or biweekly basis. Each lesson is presented by one or more teachers at a different table and students move from table to table as they complete the assignments. If the group is small, one teacher can be assigned to several lessons, or students can be assigned to teach each other.

The continuing workshop includes all the advantages of home study and, in addition, provides these opportunities not available through conventional lecture classes:

1. Individuals can join the workshop at any time.

2. Individuals can miss meetings and, when they return to the workshop, continue where they left off.

3. Individuals can ask questions without disturbing the entire class.

4. Individuals of all ages can participate together.

5. When an individual completes a lesson, he can be assigned to teach that lesson.

6. Individuals gain confidence when they teach each other.

7. Teachers can specialize in a particular lesson.

8. Visual aids and formal lectures may be eliminated.

9. A continuing workshop is adaptable to any size group: church groups, lineage societies, genealogical associations, historical societies, etc.

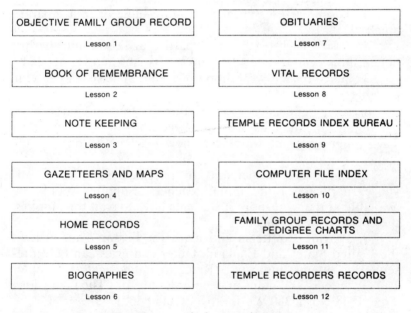

OBJECTIVE FAMILY GROUP RECORD	OBITUARIES
Lesson 1	Lesson 7
BOOK OF REMEMBRANCE	VITAL RECORDS
Lesson 2	Lesson 8
NOTE KEEPING	TEMPLE RECORDS INDEX BUREAU
Lesson 3	Lesson 9
GAZETTEERS AND MAPS	COMPUTER FILE INDEX
Lesson 4	Lesson 10
HOME RECORDS	FAMILY GROUP RECORDS AND PEDIGREE CHARTS
Lesson 5	Lesson 11
BIOGRAPHIES	TEMPLE RECORDERS RECORDS
Lesson 6	Lesson 12

Teaching areas for lesson assignments.

HOW TO ESTABLISH A CONTINUING WORKSHOP

The following are suggestions for establishing a continuing workshop:

1. Select one individual or several individuals to begin the lesson series and to serve as the initial teacher(s). The initial teacher(s) can complete the *Fundamentals* course through the home study method or through attendance at an established continuing workshop. (It is best to select individuals who are interested in learning genealogy but who have had little previous experience. Experienced genealogists have difficulty in adapting to an organized step-by-step approach and in limiting instructions to beginning research.)

2. Arrange for physical facilities, including tables.

3. Teach each lesson at a separate table or in a separate area.

4. Assign each teacher to a particular lesson until he has taught three or four times; later he can assist wherever needed.

5. Schedule the workshop on a regular basis—weekly, if possible.

6. Assign one teacher to each three or four students.

7. Assign students who have completed a lesson(s) to teach others, and the training of new teachers becomes automatic.

8. Encourage participants to purchase supplies in advance, particularly the initial teachers. Supplies should be available at the workshop; if students have to wait for supplies, they become discouraged.

9. Provide gazetteers and maps for Lesson 4 for at least the United States and England. Other countries can be represented as interest indicates. (Refer to *Fundamentals,* Chapter 10.) Gazetteers and maps may be ordered from The Genealogy Tree, 1348 North 380 West, Provo, Utah 84601.

10. Award certificates of merit upon completion of lesson assignments.

11. When students complete the twelve-week *Fundamentals* course, lessons for other geographic areas may be added: Utah, United States, England, Ireland, Scotland, Denmark, Sweden, Germany, etc.

SUGGESTIONS TO STUDENTS

1. Read each lesson in the lesson assignments before doing the assignments.

2. Complete the reading assignments in *Fundamentals.*

3. Begin the assignments with the first-generation family group record, and repeat the course with each succeeding family group record.

4. Do not expect to become an expert in genealogical research the first time through the course; this requires practice.

5. When possible, obtain answers to questions from the textbook without asking the teacher.

6. Do not expect to memorize everything in the textbook; use it as a reference in finding answers to questions.

7. Refer to the illustrations in *Fundamentals* to complete the assignments.

8. Complete each lesson assignment exactly as instructed.

9. Complete the assignments in order, and do not skip any research assignments on the first four-generation family group records; it is not necessary to repeat assignments that have previously been completed.

10. When note cards are made for anticipated searches, file the note cards in the appropriate search section until the search is completed.

11. Note cards for Lessons 5 to 12 may be made in advance and the research completed during one library visit.

12. When the search is completed, record negative results as well as positive results on the note cards.

13. Whether or not other family members have searched the suggested record, repeat the search so as to learn about the record and the proper research procedure.

14. As new names, places, and time periods are determined, repeat the lesson assignments that could not be made or that were unsuccessful because of incomplete or incorrect information.

15. Do all correspondence in the assigned order using the sample letters in *Fundamentals* as a guide.

16. Do not be disappointed if some records produce negative results for some family group records; you are learning about the records.

SUPPLIES

1. *Fundamentals of Genealogical Research,* 3rd edition (includes lesson assignments, which are also available as a separate publication).

2. *Lesson Assignments for Fundamentals of Genealogical Research* (also included in textbook)

3. *Note Keeping Kit:*
   - 100 colored 3″ x 5″ note cards
   - 50 white 3″ x 5″ note cards
   - 12 plain 3″ x 5″ guide cards
   - 1 expando card file
   - 17 pedigree charts
   - 8 family group records
   - 1 personal record
   - 1 manila folder
   - 10 Genealogical Society request forms

4. *Book of Remembrance Index Kit:*
   - 50 white bond guide sheets
   - 1 alphabet/number set
   - 2 clear plastic index strips
   - 2 yellow plastic index strips
   - 1 personal record tab

5. *A Certificate of Merit:*

GENEALOGICAL MAIL ORDER SERVICE

The Genealogy Tree
Dept. A
1348 North 380 West
Provo, Utah 84601

GENEALOGICAL SEMINAR INFORMATION

The Genealogy Tree
(801) 225-7384 Laureen R. Jaussi
(801) 377-2874 Gloria D. Chaston

BASIC GENEALOGICAL RECORDS RESEARCH LIST

The following is an itemized list of basic records to be searched in *Fundamentals of Genealogical Research.* The color of the note card is indicated for each record. Space is provided for the student to indicate the record repository and the most efficient method of search:

Record Repository	*Method of Search*
1. Relatives	1. Personal visit
2. Local library	2. Correspondence
3. Branch library	
4. Genealogical Society	
5. Vital statistics office	
6. Church minister	

Basic Genealogical Records	Color of Card	Record Repository	Method of Search
1. Gazetteer of locality	white		
2. Map of locality	white		
3. Biographies	white		
4. Family histories	white		
5. Locality histories	white		
6. Obituaries	blue		
7. Government birth certificate	yellow		
8. Government marriage certificate	pink		
9. Government death certificate	blue		
10. Church christening	yellow		
11. Church marriage	pink		
12. Church burial	blue		
13. Temple Records Index Bureau (TIB)	orange		
14. Computer File Index (CFI)	orange		
15. Main Records Section Family Groups	white		
16. Patrons Family Groups (1924-1962)	white		
17. Patrons Family Groups (1962-present)	white		
18. Card-Indexed Pedigree Charts	white		
19. Alphabetized Pedigree Charts (1962)	white		
20. Alphabetized Pedigree Charts (1965)	white		
21. Card Index to Heirs	white		
22. Temple Baptisms	orange		
23. Temple Endowments	orange		
24. Temple Sealing Wife to Husband	orange		
25. Temple Sealing Children to Parents	orange		

Lesson One

OBJECTIVE

Begin a pedigree chart and a corresponding first four-generation family group record.

READING ASSIGNMENT

Fundamentals of Genealogical Research, 3rd edition
  Chapter 1. Introduction
  Chapter 2. Elements of Identity
  Chapter 3. The Origin and Classification of Records
  Chapter 4. Analyzing and Evaluating Genealogical Information

NOTE KEEPING KIT

  1 pedigree chart
  1 family group record
  1 manila folder

____1. On a blank pedigree chart, write your name on line # 1. With information in your possession, continue the pedigree chart with names of male ancestors on even-numbered lines and names of female ancestors on odd-numbered lines; add identifying information as indicated. (See *Fundamentals,* page 7, Figure 1.)

____2. Select an ancestral couple that corresponds with one of the first four generations on the pedigree chart (see *Fundamentals,* page 14, Figure 4).
  1st time through the course—the first-generation family group record
  2nd time through the course—the second-generation family group record
  3rd and 4th times through the course—a third-generation family group record
  5th, 6th, 7th, and 8th times through the course—a fourth-generation family group record

_____3. Begin a family group record for the selected couple and consolidate onto the selected family group record all information in your possession concerning the particular family. Use the selected family group record as the objective family group record to complete the assignments in the course.

_____4. Analyze the objective family group record by answering the questions in *Fundamentals,* Chapter 4, pages 41, 42, and 43.

_____5. Place the objective family group record in the research folder (manila folder).

_____6. Place the pedigree chart in the research folder behind the objective family group record.

Lesson Two

OBJECTIVE

Organize a Book of Remembrance.

READING ASSIGNMENT

Fundamentals of Genealogical Research, 3rd edition
Chapter 5. Book of Remembrance

NOTE KEEPING KIT

16 pedigree charts
1 personal record
white 3" x 5" note cards

BOOK OF REMEMBRANCE KIT:

49 white bond index guide sheets
1 alphabet/number set
2 clear plastic index strips
2 yellow plastic index strips
1 personal record index tab

____1. On the pedigree chart in the research folder, write a number 1 in the upper right-hand corner to indicate that this is chart no. 1. (See *Fundamentals,* page 53, Figure 40.)

____2. Number 16 additional pedigree charts in the upper right-hand corner beginning with no. 2 and proceeding to no. 17. (See *Fundamentals,* page 53, Figure 40.)

____3. Begin the extension of pedigree chart no. 1 by writing numbers 2 through 17 in the right-hand column. (See *Fundamentals* page 54, Figure 41.)

____4. Cross-reference pedigree charts nos. 2 through 17 to chart no. 1. (See *Fundamentals,* page 54, Figure 41; page 55, Figure 42; and page 56, Figure 43.)

____5. Assemble the index for the pedigree section of your Book of Remembrance. (See *Fundamentals,* page 50, Figure 38):

   a. Cut each numerical section, fold on the dotted lines (do not sharply crease), place each section of the numerical inserts in the yellow plastic index tabs, and cut each number.

   b. Glue each yellow numerical index tab to one white bond guide sheet.

   c. Place the guide sheets in numerical order in the front of the Book of Remembrance.

   d. Place each pedigree chart behind the appropriate guide sheet, except for pedigree chart no. 1 in the research folder.

____6. Assemble the index for the family group section of your Book of Remembrance (see *Fundamentals,* page 50, Figure 38).

   a. Cut each alphabetical section, fold on the dotted lines (do not sharply crease), place each section of the alphabetical inserts in the clear plastic index tabs, and cut each letter.

   b. Glue each clear index tab to a white bond guide sheet.

   c. Place the guide sheets in alphabetical order behind the pedigree chart section in the Book of Remembrance.

   d. Alphabetize by surname of the husband all of the family group records in your possession, except the objective family group record in the research folder.

  e. Place the alphabetized family group records behind the appropriate guide sheet.

_____7. Complete the personal information requested on the left-hand side of the personal record. (Non-LDS may choose to omit this assignment.) (See *Fundamentals,* page 58, Figure 45.)

_____8. Record information concerning each important event of your life on a separate 3″ x 5″ white note card; arrange the cards chronologically. Continue to add cards as important events are recalled. (See *Fundamentals,* page 59, Figure 46.) Place the note cards in the research folder until the note keeping file is assembled (Lesson #3).

_____9. When all important dates have been recalled and recorded on 3″ x 5″ white note cards, transfer the information from the note cards to the important events side of the personal record, one event to each line. (Non-LDS may prefer a plain bond sheet.) (See *Fundamentals,* page 58, Figure 45.)

___10. When the outline of personal events is complete, write a more detailed life story.

___11. Organize the personal record section of your Book of Remembrance (see *Fundamentals,* page 50, Figure 38).

  a. Glue the personal record index tab to 1 white bond index guide sheet.

  b. Place the personal record guide sheet behind the family group section of the Book of Remembrance.

  c. Place the personal record behind the personal record guide sheet.

  d. Place the life story behind the personal record.

Lesson Three

OBJECTIVE

Assemble a card file for note keeping.

READING ASSIGNMENT

Fundamentals of Genealogical Research, 3rd edition
   Chapter 6. Note Keeping
   Chapter 7. Correspondence

NOTE KEEPING KIT

   1 expando card file
   12 plain 3″ x 5″ guide cards
   2 white 3″ x 5″ note cards

_____ 1. On one plain 3″ x 5″ guide card write the surname of the husband, and on another guide card, the maiden surname of the wife, from the objective family group record (see *Fundamentals,* page 62, Figure 48), and file these surname guide cards alphabetically in the file box (see *Fundamentals,* page 61, Figure 47).

_____ 2. On a plain 3″ x 5″ guide card, write the title "LO-CALITIES" (see *Fundamentals,* page 62, Figure 49), and file the locality guide card behind the surname section in the file box (see *Fundamentals,* page 61, Figure 47).

_____ 3. On a plain 3″ x 5″ guide card, write the title "AD-DRESSES" (see *Fundamentals,* page 63, Figure 50), and file the address guide card behind the locality section of the file box (see *Fundamentals,* page 61, Figure 47).

_____ 4. On six plain 3″ x 5″ guide cards write the titles for the search section (see *Fundamentals,* page 63, Figure 51):

"CORRESPONDENCE," "VISIT RELATIVES," "VISIT LOCAL LIBRARY," "VISIT BRANCH LIBRARY," "VISIT GENEALOGICAL SOCIETY," and "NEED MORE INFORMATION." File these guide cards behind the address section of the file box. (See *Fundamentals,* page 61, Figure 47.)

___5. On a plain 3″ x 5″ guide card, write the title "PERSONAL EVENTS" (see *Fundamentals,* page 64, Figure 52), and file the personal event guide card behind the search section in the file box (see *Fundamentals,* page 61, Figure 47).

___6. File the white 3″ x 5″ important event note cards from Lesson #2 behind the personal record guide card in the file box.

___7. Make a separate white 3″ x 5″ spelling variation note card for the surname of the husband and the surname of the wife from the objective family group record. Record the standard spelling of the surname in the upper left-hand corner; list all known variations, and continue to add variations as they are discovered. (See *Fundamentals,* pages 20 and 21, Figures 7, 8, and/or 9.) File the surname variation cards in the file box behind the appropriate surname guide card.

Lesson Four

OBJECTIVE

Use gazetteers and maps to establish correct place names.

READING ASSIGNMENT

Fundamentals of Genealogical Research, 3rd edition
    Chapter 8. Libraries
    Chapter 9. The Genealogical Society
    Chapter 10. Reference Books

NOTE KEEPING KIT

white 3" x 5" note cards

_____ 1. For each different country listed on the objective family group record, refer to the example note card(s) for the recommended gazetteer, "Bibliography—Gazetteers and Maps," *Fundamentals:*

Country	Page Number	Example Locality Note Card	Jurisdiction Headings For Locality Note Cards
Belgium	160	Fig. 146	Country, province, city (town/village)
Canada	162	Fig. 148	Province, county,* City (town/village)
Denmark	164	Fig. 150	Country, county, parish, town, (village/farm)
England	167	Fig. 152	Country, county, parish, city (town/village)
France	171	Fig. 157	Country, department, city (town/village)
Germany	172	Fig. 158	Country, state, province, city (town/village)
Ireland	175	Fig. 160	Country, county, parish, city, (town/village)
Italy	179	Fig. 164	Country, province, municipality, (town/village)
Netherlands	180	Fig. 166	Country, province, city (town/village)
Norway	181	Fig. 167	Country, old county, parish, town (village/farm)
Scotland	184	Fig. 170	Country, county, parish, city (town/village)
Sweden	187	Fig. 174	Country, county, parish, town (village/farm)
Switzerland**	189	Fig. 176	Surname (determine localities for surname)
	190	Fig. 178	Country, canton, parish, city (town/village)
United States**	192	Fig. 181	State, county, city (town/village)
	198	Fig. 190	State, county (determine history of county)

| Wales | 201 | Fig. 192 | Country, county, parish, city (town/village) |
| Other countries | 203 | Fig. 194 | See also pages 153 to 155, Figure 141 and example note cards, page 156, Figures 142 and 143 or write to the Genealogical Society, page 158, Figure 145. |

* If province has counties.
** Make two locality note cards.

_____2. Make a white 3″ x 5″ locality note card for each different place name listed on the objective family group record by writing the name of the place in the upper left-hand corner of the card, largest division to the smallest, with the appropriate jurisdiction in parentheses under the name of the place as illustrated in the example note card for the particular country. If some jurisdictions are not known, leave space in the heading as illustrated in *Fundamentals,* page 156, Figures 142 and 143.

_____3. Group the locality note cards by country and alphabetize the cards within each country.

_____4. Obtain the first recommended gazetteer for each country. If the first gazetteer is not available and there is more than one gazetteer listed, obtain the next recommended gazetteer, etc. Record the name of the gazetteer and the Genealogical Society call number of the gazetteer in the lower left-hand corner of the locality note card as illustrated in the example note cards.

_____5. Search the gazetteer for the place names listed on the locality note cards. Record the genealogical information on the appropriate locality note cards as illustrated in the example note cards. (If the particular place name cannot be found in the gazetteer, write to the Genealogical Society for assistance. See sample letter, *Fundamentals,* page 158, Figure 145.)

_____6. Make necessary corrections on the objective family group record and on the headings of the locality note cards, and file the completed locality note cards alphabetically by country in the file box behind the locality guide card.

_____7. If unfamiliar with the locality, refer to the particular country, "Bibliography—Gazetteers and Maps," page 160 through 204. Obtain a copy of the appropriate map; locate each place name on the map.

_____8. As additional place names are obtained for events on the objective family group record, repeat the above steps.

Lesson Five

OBJECTIVE

Obtain the names and addresses of unknown relatives, and begin an address file.

READING ASSIGNMENT

Fundamentals of Genealogical Research, 3rd edition
    Chapter 11. Family Organizations
    Chapter 12. Tax-Exempt Organizations
    Chapter 13. Research Services
    Chapter 14. Home Records

NOTE KEEPING KIT

white 3″ x 5″ note cards

_____1. If you have in your possession names and addresses of relatives who may have information that pertains to the objective family group record, make address note cards (see *Fundamentals,* page 241, Figure 214), and file them behind the address guide card in the file box.

_____2. If little is known about the individuals on the objective family group record, make a white 3″ x 5″ surname note card for each of the above relatives, and indicate on each surname note card the address of the relative and the type of genealogical information they could possibly provide by correspondence. (See *Fundamentals,* page 241, Figure 215.) Write to each relative and request the genealogical information. File each note card behind the correspondence guide card in the file box until a reply is received.

_____3. If little is known about the individuals on the objective family group record, make a white 3″ x 5″ surname note card to write to the newspaper offices in each of the localities listed on the objective family group record to obtain names and addresses of unknown relatives. (See *Fundamentals*, page 243, Figure 217.) File the surname note cards behind the correspondence guide card in the file box.

_____4. If little is known about the individuals on the objective family group record, make a white 3″ x 5″ surname note card to write to the postmaster(s) in each of the localities listed on the objective family group record to obtain names and addresses of unknown relatives. (See *Fundamentals*, page 243, Figure 218.) File the surname note cards behind the correspondence guide card in the file box.

_____5. Write to the local newspapers and postmasters. (See sample letters, *Fundamentals*, pages 245 and 246, Figures 220 and 221.) When a reply is received, note the results on the appropriate surname note card and file each surname note card behind the appropriate surname guide card in the file box.

_____6. If little is known about the individuals on the objective family group record, make a white 3″ x 5″ surname note card to call your local telephone company and request a copy of a telephone directory for each of the localities listed on the objective family group record. (See *Fundamentals*, page 244, Figure 219.) After the telephone call is made, file the note card behind the appropriate surname guide card in the file box.

_____7. If additional addresses of relatives are obtained through the local newspaper offices, postmasters, and/or telephone directories, make white 3″ x 5″ address note cards (see *Fundamentals*, page 241, Figure 214), and file them behind the address guide card in the file box. If no additional names and addresses are obtained, record the negative results on the appropriate surname note card.

——8. If information is obtained from the above relatives on individuals listed on the objective family group record, extract the family information for each individual on a separate white 3″ x 5″ surname note card. (See *Fundamentals,* pages 236 to 240, Figures 207 to 213.)

——9. Compare the information on the surname note cards with the information on the objective family group record, and add new information to the family group record.

——10. File the completed surname note cards behind the appropriate surname guide card in the file box; place any additional information from relatives in the research folder for future reference.

Lesson Six

OBJECTIVE

Obtain genealogical information from biographies, family histories, and locality histories.

READING ASSIGNMENT

Fundamentals of Genealogical Research, 3rd edition
Chapter 15. Biographical Records

NOTE KEEPING KIT
white 3″ x 5″ note cards

——1. Make a separate white 3″ x 5″ surname note card for a biography for the husband and the wife listed on the objective family group record; list on the note cards the possible availability of a biography. (See *Fundamentals,* page 249, Figure 224.)

——2. Determine the most logical availability of the biographies (relatives, local library, branch library, or the Genealogical Society), and determine the most logical method of obtaining the biographies (correspondence or personal visit); file the surname note cards for biographies behind the appropriate search guide card (correspondence, visit relatives, visit local library, visit branch library, or visit Genealogical Society).

___3. Make a separate white 3″ x 5″ surname note card for a family history for the husband and the wife listed on the objective family group record; list on the surname note cards the possible availability of a family history. (See *Fundamentals*, page 251, Figure 227.)

___4. Determine the most logical availability of the family histories (relatives, local library, branch library, or Genealogical Society), and determine the most logical method for obtaining the family histories (correspondence or personal visit); file the surname note cards for family histories behind the appropriate search guide card in the file box (correspondence, visit relatives, visit local library, visit branch library, or visit Genealogical Society).

___5. Make a separate white 3″ x 5″ surname note card for a locality history for the husband and the wife listed on the objective family group record for each locality listed on the objective family group record; list on the note cards the possible availability of each locality history. (See *Fundamentals*, page 252, Figure 229.)

___6. Determine the most logical availability of the locality histories (relatives, local library, branch library, or Genealogical Society), and determine the most logical method for obtaining the locality histories (correspondence or personal visit); file the note cards for locality histories behind the appropriate search guide card in the file box (correspondence, visit relatives, visit local library, visit branch library, or visit Genealogical Society).

___7. Obtain information from biographies, family histories, and locality histories (for correspondence, see sample letter, *Fundamentals*, page 250, Figure 225); photocopy and/or extract the biographical information which pertains to the husband and the wife listed on the objective family group record using a separate white 3″ x 5″ surname note card for each biographical sketch (see *Fundamentals*, page 248, Figures 222 and 223; page 251, Figure 226; and page 252, Figure 228).

____8. When information is obtained, compare the genea-
logical information with the information on the objective family group record, and add new information to
the family group record. If biographical information is
not obtained, record the negative results on the appropriate surname note card.

____9. File the completed surname note cards for biographies
behind the appropriate surname guide card in the file
box; place photocopies in the research folder for future
reference.

Lesson Seven

OBJECTIVE

Obtain genealogical information from newspaper obituaries.

READING ASSIGNMENT

Fundamentals of Genealogical Research, 3rd edition
    Chapter 15. Biographical Records

NOTE KEEPING KIT
    blue 3" x 5" note cards

____1. Make a blue 3" x 5" surname note card for an obituary
for each deceased individual listed on the objective
family group record; list on the note cards the possible
availability of an obituary. (See *Fundamentals,* page
253, Figure 231.)

____2. Determine the most logical availability of each obituary
(relatives, local library, or newspaper office) and determine the most logical method for obtaining each
obituary (correspondence or personal visit). File the
surname note cards for obituaries behind the appropriate search guide card (correspondence, visit relatives,
or visit local library).

____3. Obtain copies of the obituaries (for correspondence, see
sample letters, *Fundamentals,* page 250, Figure 225; and
page 254, Figure 232).

____ 4. When an obituary is obtained, copy or paste the information onto the appropriate surname note card for an obituary. Compare the genealogical information in the obituary with the information on the objective family group record, and add new information to the family group record.

____ 5. If an obituary is not obtained, record the negative results on the appropriate surname note card for an obituary.

____ 6. File the completed surname note cards for obituaries behind the appropriate surname guide card in the file box.

Lesson Eight

OBJECTIVE

Obtain government and church vital records.

READING ASSIGNMENT

Fundamentals of Genealogical Research, 3rd edition
Chapter 16. Vital Records

NOTE KEEPING KIT

yellow 3" x 5" note cards
pink 3" x 5" note cards
blue 3" x 5" note cards

____ 1. Make an appropriately colored surname note card for each birth (yellow card), marriage (pink card), and death (blue card) for each individual listed on the objective family group record. (See *Fundamentals,* page 257, Figure 233; page 258, Figure 235; and page 259, Figure 237.)

____ 2. Refer to the availability of government vital statistics, *Fundamentals,* pages 263 to 267, Figure 241, and pages 269 to 276, Figure 242, and determine which vital events occurred after government vital registration. If there was government registration at the time of the event, record the address of the government vital record on the surname note card.

____3. If the event occurred in the United States prior to the availability of state vital records, write the address of the county clerk on the surname note card, and if a large city, write the address of the city clerk. (See *Fundamentals*, page 261, Figure 239.)

____4. If the event occurred in a foreign country prior to the availability of government vital records, record on the surname note card, "Too early for government registration;" file behind the appropriate surname guide card in the file box.

____5. Determine which government vital records can be obtained from relatives and which must be obtained by correspondence with the government vital record office. File the surname note cards behind the appropriate search guide card in the file box (correspondence or visit relatives).

____6. Obtain copies of the government vital records. (See sample letters, *Fundamentals*, page 262, Figure 240, and page 277, Figure 243.)

____7. Compare the genealogical information in the government vital records with the information on the objective family group record, and add new information to the family group record.

____8. Extract the information from each government vital record onto the corresponding surname note card, using the back of the card if necessary. If no government vital record is available, indicate on the note card.

____9. Place the government vital records in the research folder, and file the surname note cards for vital records behind the appropriate surname guide card in the file box.

____10. If the religious denomination is known for the individuals listed on the objective family group record, make appropriately colored surname note cards for each christening (yellow card), marriage (pink card), and burial (blue card). (See *Fundamentals*, page 257, Figure 234; page 258, Figure 236; and page 260, Figure 238.)

____11. Determine which church vital records can be obtained from relatives and which must be obtained by correspondence with the minister. File the surname note cards for church vital records behind the appropriate search guide card in the file box (correspondence or visit relatives).

____12. Obtain copies of the church vital records. (See sample letter, *Fundamentals,* page 280, Figure 245.)

____13. When church vital records are obtained, compare with the genealogical information on the objective family group record, and add new information to the family group record.

____14. Extract the information from the church vital record onto the appropriate surname note card, using the back of the card if necessary. If no church vital record is available, indicate on the surname note card.

____15. Place the church vital records in the research folder, and file the surname note cards for church vital records behind the appropriate surname guide card in the file box.

Lesson Nine

OBJECTIVE

Search the Temple Records Index Bureau.

READING ASSIGNMENT

Fundamentals of Genealogical Research, 3rd edition
Chapter 17. Genealogical Society Temple Processing Records
Chapter 18. The Temple Records Index Bureau

NOTE KEEPING KIT

orange 3″ x 5″ note cards
Genealogical Society request forms (Temple Ordinance Indexes Request)

_____1. Make an orange surname note card for the TIB for each individual listed on the objective family group record who lived beyond eight years of age. (See *Fundamentals,* page 287, Figure 248.)

_____2. Refer to the chart, "Availability of the Temple Records Index Bureau," (*Fundamentals,* page 307, Figure 276), and determine the most logical availability of the TIB (correspondence with the Genealogical Society or correspondence with an accredited researcher); file the surname note cards for TIB records behind the correspondence guide card.

_____3. Complete and mail a Genealogical Society request form for each individual on the above surname note cards for whom a country of birth is known, or hire an accredited researcher to search the TIB. (See sample letter, *Fundamentals,* page 308, Figure 277.)

_____4. When the photocopies of the TIB cards are obtained, trim the photocopies, and paste onto the appropriate orange surname note cards.

_____5. Record in the endowment column of the objective family group record, the ordinance date and the abbreviation for the temple where each endowment was performed. (For abbreviations, see *Fundamentals,* page 327, Figure 291.)

_____6. If no information is found, mark in pencil "CF" (can't find) in the endowment column of the objective family group record and also on the appropriate orange surname note card.

_____7. Compare the genealogical information on the TIB card with the information on the family group record; add new information to the family group record; and file the note cards behind the appropriate surname guide card in the file box.

Lesson Ten

OBJECTIVE

Search the Computer File Index.

READING ASSIGNMENT

Fundamentals of Genealogical Research, 3rd edition
   Chapter 19. The Name Tabulation Program
   Chapter 20. The Computer File Index

NOTE KEEPING KIT

   orange 3″ x 5″ note cards
   Genealogical Society request forms (Temple Ordinance
      Indexes Request)

____1. Make orange surname note cards for individuals on the
   objective family group record:
   a. Individual ordinances—each individual on the ob-
      jective family group record for each birth/christen-
      ing. (See *Fundamentals,* page 355, Figure 316.)
   b. Marriage ordinance—the husband and the wife.
      (See *Fundamentals,* page 355, Figure 317.)

____2. Refer to the chart, "Availability of the Computer File
   Index," (*Fundamentals,* page 352, Figure 313), and determine the most logical availability of the CFI (branch
   library or Genealogical Society) and determine the
   most logical method of obtaining the information (correspondence or personal visit); file the surname note
   cards behind the appropriate search guide card in the
   file box (correspondence, visit branch library, or visit
   Genealogical Society).

____3. Search the Computer File Index and record the results
   of the search on the appropriate surname note cards;
   record new information on the family group record,
   and file the note cards behind the appropriate surname
   guide card.

Lesson Eleven

OBJECTIVE
Search Genealogical Society family group records and pedigree charts.

READING ASSIGNMENT

Fundamentals of Genealogical Research, 3rd edition
    Chapter 21. Family Group Records and Pedigree Charts

NOTE KEEPING KIT

white 3″ x 5″ note cards
Genealogical Society request forms (Temple Ordinance
    Indexes Request)

_____ 1. Refer to the chart, "Availability of Family Group
Records and Pedigree Charts" (*Fundamentals,* page 362,
Figure 321), and determine the most logical availability
of the family group records and pedigree charts (branch
library or Genealogical Society) and the most logical
method of obtaining the information (correspondence
or personal visit).

_____ 2. Make white surname note cards for the husband on the
objective family group record:
    a. Main Records Section Family Group Records (see
Fundamentals, page 364, Figures 323 and 324)
    b. Patrons Section # 1 Family Group Records, 1924-
1962 (see *Fundamentals,* page 364, Figure 325)
    c. Patrons Section # 2 Family Group Records, 1962-
present (see *Fundamentals,* page 365, Figure 326)
    d. Card-Indexed Pedigree Charts (see *Fundamentals,*
page 365, Figure 327)
    e. Section # 1 Alphabetized Pedigree Charts, 1962 (see
Fundamentals, page 365, Figure 326)
    f. Section # 2 Alphabetized Pedigree Charts, 1965 (see
Fundamentals, page 366, Figure 329)

_____ 3. Obtain the applicable call numbers, and record them in the lower left-hand corner of the appropriate surname note card.

_____4. File the surname note cards behind the appropriate search guide cards in the file box (correspondence, visit branch library, or visit Genealogical Society).

_____ 5. Obtain photocopies of the available family group records and pedigree charts. Record only the results of the search on the appropriate surname note cards; do not transfer the information from the family group record and pedigree chart onto the note cards. Compare the photocopies obtained with the information on the objective family group record, and add new information to the objective family group record; file the note cards behind the appropriate surname guide card in the file box.

_____ 6. Place the photocopies of family group records and pedigree charts in the research folder.

Lesson Twelve

OBJECTIVE

Search Temple Recorders Records.

READING ASSIGNMENT
Fundamentals of Genealogical Research, 3rd edition
Chapter 22. Temple Recorders Records

NOTE KEEPING KIT

orange 3″ x 5″ note cards

_____1. Make orange surname note cards for baptisms, endowments, and sealings for each individual listed on the objective family group record:
a. Baptism—each individual who lived beyond the age of eight (see *Fundamentals,* page 372, Figure 332)
b. Endowment—each individual who lived beyond the age of eight for whom there is evidence an endow-

ment has been performed, but no TIB card was
available (see *Fundamentals,* page 374, Figure 333)
   c. Sealing to spouse—wife to husband (see *Fundamentals,* page 375, Figure 334)
   d. Sealing of children to parents—Each child on the
family group record (see *Fundamentals,* page 377,
Figure 335)

_____2. Refer to the chart, "Research Steps to Verify Ordinance
Dates," *Fundamentals,* page 286, Figure 247. Review
the research steps, and remove the appropriate records
from the file box and the research folder:
   a. Surname note cards for the TIB
   b. Surname note cards for the CFI
   c. Copies of family group records from the Main
Records Section (Archive Record)
   d. Copies of family group records from the Patrons
Section
   e. The objective family group record

_____3. Determine which baptisms were performed in life, and
file the surname note cards for living baptisms in the
file box under "Need More Information."

_____4. On each surname note card for a proxy ordinance,
record each different ordinance date and name of the
temple for the particular ordinance with a notation of
the source.

If the name of the temple is unknown, refer to the
chart, "Chronology of Temple Ordinances to 1970,"
and determine a possible temple where the ordinance(s)
could have been performed.

AUSTIN, Henry   baptism
                                                      (proxy)

   9 Apr 1912 SG TIB
   26 Aug 1911 Patrons Section #1 Family Group Record

```
┌─────────────────────────────────────────────────────────────────┐
│                                                                   │
│   AUSTIN, Henry                        sealing to spouse          │
│                                                                   │
│     19 July 1952  SL  Main Records Section Family Group           │
│                       Record                                      │
│     28 Jan 1932   SG  Patrons Section #1 Family Group             │
│                       Record                                      │
│      6 June 1927      Patrons Section #1 Family Group             │
│                       Record                                      │
│                                                                   │
│                                                                   │
│                                                                   │
│                                                                   │
│                                                                   │
│                                                                   │
└─────────────────────────────────────────────────────────────────┘
```

____ 5. If there is no evidence that a particular ordinance has been performed, file the surname note card for the particular ordinance in the file box under "Need More Information" until the ordinance is completed.

____ 6. Refer to the chart, "Availability of Temple Recorders Records" (*Fundamentals,* page 379, Figure 336), and determine the most logical availability of each temple recorders record (branch library or Genealogical Society) and the most logical method of obtaining the information (correspondence or personal visit).

____ 7. Obtain the Genealogical Society call numbers for the records that are not restricted. Record each call number in the lower left-hand corner of the appropriate surname note card.

____ 8. File the surname note cards behind the appropriate search guide cards in the file box (correspondence, visit branch library, or visit Genealogical Society).

____ 9. Search the records, and record the results on the appropriate surname note cards. Compare the information obtained with the information on the objective family group record, and add new information to the objective family group record. If there is more than one date for a particular ordinance, record each date on the family group record.

____ 10. File the surname note cards behind the appropriate surname guide card in the file box.

Index